CORONAVIRUS NEWS, MARKETS AND AI

Coronavirus News, Markets and AI explores the analysis of unstructured data from coronavirus-related news and the underlying sentiment during its real-time impact on the world and particularly on global financial markets. In an age where information – both real and fake – travels in the blink of an eye and significantly alters the market sentiment daily, this book will be a blow by blow account of the economic impact of the COVID-19 pandemic.

The volume:

—Details how AI-driven machines capture, analyse and score relevant on-ground news sentiment to analyse the dynamics of market sentiment and the markets' reaction to good or bad news across the 'short term' and the 'long term';

—Investigates what have been the most prevalent news sentiment during the pandemic and its linkages to crude oil prices, high profile cases, the impact of local news and even the impact of Trump's policies;

—Discusses the impact on what people think and discuss, how the COVID-19 crisis differs from the Global Financial Crisis of 2008, the what unprecedented disruptions exist in supply chains and our daily lives; and

—Showcases how easy accessibility to Big Data methods, cloud computing, computational methods and the universal applicability of these tools to any topic can help analyse and extract the related news sentiment in allied fields.

Accessible, nuanced and insightful, this book will be invaluable for business professionals, bankers, media professionals, traders, investors and investment consultants. It will also be of great interest to scholars and researchers of economics, commerce, science and technology studies, computer science, media and culture studies, public policy and digital humanities.

Pankaj Sharma is a partner at EMAlpha, a data analytics and investment management firm focused on making emerging markets (EMs) accessible to global investors and unlocking EM investing using machines. EMAlpha's focus is on Unstructured Data as the EMs are particularly susceptible to swings in news flow driven investor sentiment. Pankaj has 20 years of diverse work experience in various leadership roles with global investment banks, Indian equity brokerages, state–owned enterprises and startups. Earlier, he was a ranked equity analyst and tracked multiple sectors at UBS, Citi and JP Morgan. Pankaj has also been a regular contributor to print and electronic media. For Routledge, he has so far co-authored the following titles – *Artificial Intelligence: Evolution, Ethics and Public Policy* and *Big Data: A Beginner's Introduction*. Pankaj published his first two books in 2017 and these were the following – *Demonetisation: Modi's Political Masterstroke* and *2019: Will Modi Win?* This was followed by *Rafale, Raga, Reuniting Forces for 2019* and *The Anatomy of an Indian General Election*. Pankaj is an engineer from IIT Kharagpur, India, with an MBA from the Faculty of Management Studies, University of Delhi, India.

CORONAVIRUS NEWS, MARKETS AND AI

The COVID-19 Diaries

Pankaj Sharma

Routledge
Taylor & Francis Group

LONDON AND NEW YORK

First published 2021
by Routledge
2 Park Square, Milton Park, Abingdon, Oxon OX14 4RN

and by Routledge
52 Vanderbilt Avenue, New York, NY 10017

Routledge is an imprint of the Taylor & Francis Group, an informa business

British Library Cataloguing-in-Publication Data
A catalogue record for this book is available from the British Library

Library of Congress Cataloging-in-Publication Data
A catalog record has been requested for this book

ISBN: 978-0-367-63413-1 (hbk)
ISBN: 978-0-367-68772-4 (pbk)
ISBN: 978-1-003-13897-6 (ebk)

Typeset in Sabon
by MPS Limited, Dehradun

CONTENTS

CONTENTS

LIST OF FIGURES

LIST OF TABLES

ACKNOWLEDGEMENTS

First and foremost, I am immensely grateful to all of the teachers, colleagues, professional associates, friends and family members who have not only influenced my thought process knowingly or unknowingly, but also helped in moulding who we are – as people and as professionals. There are so many of them that it would be virtually impossible to remember each and every one but, still, none of them would have a contribution which is insignificant. I have a deep sense of gratitude towards each and every one of them. The background research during the course of writing earlier books *Artificial Intelligence: Evolution, Ethics and Public Policy*[1] and *Big Data: A Beginner's Introduction*[2] also made me aware of some of these interesting developments and stories on companies and the investment approaches.

I would be keen to acknowledge the contribution and encouragement received from so many people that it would be impossible to name all of them. However, my friends – Sandip Bansal, Sunil Teluja, Saurav Sanyal and Rupal Mehrotra – have made valuable contributions to this book. I am also grateful to Pradip Seth of S-Ancial Technologies for his kind support. The consent to proceed and cooperation from immediate family is never a sufficient condition for an endeavour like this, but these are almost an absolute necessity. I am deeply thankful to my wife, Shikha, and son, Pulin, for their patience. This book would not have been possible without support from them. I am also thankful to my parents, Shri Kamlesh Kumar Sharma and Mrs Veena Sharma for their support in continuous learning. For me, their support and motivation have been a strong driving force behind experiential learning since childhood.

My expression of gratitude will not be complete without us mentioning EMAlpha. I have done a few years of research for EMAlpha Investment Managers and Advisors (www.emalpha.com), and a large part of this text is owed to our work at EMAlpha. EMAlpha use a systematic 'unstructured data analysis' approach for public investments and employ thoroughly researched Machine Learning tools to track evolving news flow on various emerging markets. We do this by paying special attention to factors like the timely measurement of news sentiment for investors as the markets can be finicky, and sentiment can be capricious. In the context of coronavirus news analysis, this is very important, because unstructured data analysis will give one of the earliest warning signs if it is followed regularly and with objectivity.

The EMAlpha team have deep expertise in capital markets research and trading. EMAlpha's collaborative approach to combining Machine Learning tools with a fundamental investment management approach helped us understand these financial markets and the importance of unstructured data much better. While EMAlpha primarily focus on emerging countries, the basic principles of AI and Machine Learning are the same across markets and across several different asset classes. The EMAlpha team consist of members with diverse backgrounds and experience covering emerging markets, portfolio management and trading, quantitative analysis and Machine Learning and regulatory expertise. The team consist of domain experts in emerging markets with significant experience in fundamental and quantitative analysis. It was a great learning experience to work on this book at EMAlpha.

I also want to thank Deeksha Garg, Shambhashib Narayan Roy and Gopi Krishna Sriram for their valuable contribution to this book. All three of them are students of IILM and as a part of their project work, they assisted us in this book. They have not just diligently worked on different aspects of this text, but the entire sentiment analysis inferences section has been heavily influenced by the work they have done. The speed at which we have been able to finish this book is owed a great deal to the tireless efforts they made. It is always a pleasure to work with the younger generation, and the energy they bring is infectious. Thank you so much, Deeksha, Shambhashib and Sriram!

I wish to acknowledge our sincere gratitude for Mr Aakash Chakrabarty of Taylor & Francis, whose continuous support and encouragement made this book possible. We have been working with Aakash for more than four years now, and it is rare to come across a person who is as warm, as understanding, as helpful and as knowledgeable about his craft as him. Right from the time we discussed the idea with him, he has been a source of great strength for us. To be very honest, we were never very good at making a realistic and fair assessment of the key areas of development for this book since the time we had submitted the first version of our manuscript, but it was Aakash and his team who helped us at each step. We are also grateful to Brinda Sen and all other team members at Taylor & Francis for their unwavering patience during the entire time that this book took shape.

Notes

1 Artificial Intelligence: Evolution, Ethics and Public Policy (ISBN: 9781138625389, Routledge). This book deals with the impact of Artificial Intelligence on humankind's future. What will the future be? A dystopian

landscape controlled by machines or a brave new world full of possibilities? Perhaps the answer lies with Artificial Intelligence (AI) – a phenomenon much beyond technology that continues to and will shape lives in ways we do not understand yet. This book further explores the dystopian prospect of mass unemployment and takes up ethical aspects. https://www.routledge.com/ Artificial-Intelligence-Evolution-Ethics-and-Public-Policy-1st-Edition/Sarangi-Sharma/p/book/9781138625389 (Accessed on 19th March 2020).

2 Big Data: A Beginner's Introduction (ISBN: 9780367148904, Routledge). Big Data is everywhere. It shapes our lives in more ways than we know and understand. This comprehensive introduction unravels the complex terabytes that will continue to shape our lives in ways imagined and unimagined. Drawing on case studies like Amazon, Facebook, the FIFA World Cup and the Aadhaar scheme, this book looks at how Big Data is changing the way we behave, consume and respond to situations in the digital age. It looks at how Big Data has the potential to transform disaster management and healthcare, as well as prove to be authoritarian and exploitative in the wrong hands. This accessibly written volume is essential for the researcher in science and technology studies, media and culture studies, public policy and digital humanities as well as being a beacon for the general reader to make sense of the digital age. https://www.routledge.com/Big-Data-A-Beginners-Introduction-1st-Edition/Sarangi-Sharma/p/book/9781138598577 (Accessed on 19th March 2020).

ABOUT THE BOOK

Some of the most commonly used words and phrases in the first half of the year 2020 are:

Infection, Virus, Lockdown, Exponential growth, Contagion, Hubei, Flattening the Curve, Containment, Vaccine, Ventilator, Wuhan and many more. Most are related with Coronavirus or COVID-19 pandemic.

The last few months across the world have only been about the coronavirus pandemic. There is politics; there are conspiracy theories; there is debate on lockdowns and strategies to fight the spread of infection. There are depressing statistics on rising fatalities, job losses, the severe economic impact and rising frustration among people but, at the same time, there are also stories of exemplary courage and of the shining stars of humanity. There also efforts to find a cure, to develop a vaccine and to find some remedy that will work. There are no sports events. Movie theatres are closed, and normal life has been disrupted for millions of people worldwide. Effectively for the past many months, all the good, the bad and the ugly is just about the coronavirus pandemic.

The infection caused by COVID-19 – the way it spreads and the consequences in serious cases – has disrupted normal lives as we knew it, bringing the global economy to a grinding halt. Our idea behind this book is to focus on the role of coronavirus news coverage: the machine-generated sentiment analysis[1] on this news, the methodology for how it is conducted and the important inferences. To give you a better idea, the book's title is *Coronavirus News, Markets and AI*, but it includes several other themes such as (a) AI-ML-driven approach to analyse unstructured data, (b) how AI machines saw the coronavirus pandemic, (c) AI, Big Data and ML for news analysis for the pandemic, (d) AI as a window to the world during the pandemic, (e) how AI saw the coronavirus pandemic, (f) the pandemic through the eyes of AI, (g) coronavirus news, market sentiment and data science coronavirus news, and, (h) unstructured data analysis using machines: method, results, inferences and utility.

However, before that, the most important question is why should you care at all about this and why does unstructured data analysis matter? The significance of unstructured data analysis lies in two important aspects: (a) the first is that the developments over the last decade or two have opened new vistas in technology (Big Data, Machine Learning, artificial Iintelligence and several others) so that unstructured data analysis can be carried out effectively and efficiently, and (b) unstructured data analysis can offer clues about important future developments that conventional analytics methods fail to offer. An edge in understanding the contours of tomorrow's world is of significant, practical value and, simply speaking, unstructured data analysis magnifies the 'signal' and makes the 'noise' feebler. There is another important reason why this is important, and it is the immense potential that unstructured data analysis offers in interpreting what the news tell on the surface and what it is trying to tell you in reality and in greater depth.

This has emerged from our daily diary

This is not really a book. It essentially emerged from a daily diary that we maintained at EMAlpha, a data analytics firm that is focused on understanding the impact of unstructured data analysis on financial markets and its use for better quality decision-making. There are multiple aspects of Unstructured Data analysis at EMAlpha. Out of many topics, one thing that EMAlpha also specialise in is news flow analysis on the basis of a proprietary dictionary to arrive at sentiment scores for countries for important keywords such as 'Fed' or 'US economy' or 'oil'. EMAlpha machines also do unstructured data analysis individually or collectively for specific topics like 'coronavirus' or generic aggregate market sentiment for countries. However, how did we arrive at tracking coronavirus news?

As a part of our unstructured data analysis exercise that we do for more than 1,200 stocks in more than 30 emerging markets across the globe, we collect news on a daily basis. Since the end of January 2020 when, for the first time, the coronavirus started spreading beyond China, we started noticing interesting news items on coronavirus, and this pushed us to probe further. Some of the initial items that attracted our attention are that, despite China being the origin of this infection, a few other countries were suffering a lot more, because the perception of them was worse, and it was playing a more important role. As the rest of the world started getting concerned about the spread of this deadly virus, we started noticing a few peculiar things while tracking the news sentiment on the coronavirus and the movement of markets.

- The coronavirus news followed a pattern from the detection of the virus and then the cases of infection initially being ignored, to more serious phases such as a rise in serious illness and fatalities. As a result, the volatility induced by this change in sentiment started impacting the financial markets. This was a classic case of 'underestimating your enemy' until it was too late. This has also played a role in how we have structured this book, which we will talk about a bit later. The life cycle has been similar to other challenges and threats which occur regularly – starting at denial and closing at lamenting because of unpreparedness.

- In the initial phases of the coronavirus spread in the world, the fear induced by this virus led to a more general impact on markets, but as things evolved, the daily ups and downs in news started playing a bigger role. We have done a country-by-country analysis on coronavirus news, and this was the clear message from this unstructured data analysis. There are several things that matter in forming the sentiment and the actual on-ground situation is only one of the factors.

- The swing in the markets was always much bigger than the swing in coronavirus news. The reason is very simple: the market always overreacts, and the investors and speculators become irrationally pessimistic or exuberant. The 'signal'[2] from sentiment analysis always gets magnified when projected on stock markets. This is an important point. There is no real scientific method to prove how much an event will tangibly impact a company or an economy and, hence, the initial panic always leads to an overreaction. For example, oil price turning negative a few months ago because there was no storage space combined with demand slowdown due to the coronavirus pandemic was an overreaction.

- There is a difference in Coronavirus News Sentiment and Market Sentiment. Even in the worst of the times, there are people who would 'buy' because they understand the extent of market swing – which is usually more than what fundamentals would warrant. However, since the coronavirus pandemic was an economic crisis as well and the central banks and governments have been proactive in their response at an unprecedented scale too. In fact, there is also an arguement that they have done more than they actually should have. This led to a dichotomy between Coronavirus News Sentiment and Market Sentiment.

The underlying theme of this book is that, in the age when information travels so fast, sentiment plays a far bigger role in determining the direction of markets. If you can understand sentiment correctly and without the filters of your known or unknown biases, then you can use it.

The Structure of the Book

Let us admit that this was not an easy book to write. Therefore, as a corollary, it might also not be an easy book to read, though we have made all of the efforts to make it so that the reader does not find it too hard to follow. While we were regularly maintaining the diary on how the coronavirus crisis was unfolding, the text also needed background and context to make it clear why unstructured data analysis and sentiment matters. In addition, it was also important to add the inferences to summarise what we have observed and how the coronavirus crisis was reflecting in multiple themes. To make it easier to read, this book is divided into four parts;

Part I – Method: This part provides the background and context. For most people, this is important to understand Part II and Part IV. However, if you are an expert in Machine Learning and understand unstructured data analysis well, then you can skip this part. Here we talk about the basics of unstructured data analysis, but not from a technical knowledge enhancement perspective but rather, to understand the method behind it. This part has four chapters.

Chapter 1 – How to Read this Book?

Chapter 2 – Reading Coronavirus News

Chapter 3 – Sentiment Analysis, Big Data and AI

Chapter 4 – Unstructured Data: How to Tame the Beast?

Part II – Results: These writings were the original diary we were writing at EMAlpha on the coronavirus pandemic and how it was engulfing the entire world. These are raw and the purest parts of the book. This is also our favourite section, because when we were writing them, we had no clue how future events would unfold. Accordingly, for us, it was more like reading a detective novel which was full of mystery. This part has four chapters.

Chapter 5 – The Ebbing May: 'Are We Celebrating Too Early?'

Chapter 6 – The Deadly April: 'Blame Game and Vaccine'

Chapter 7 – The Intense March: 'Coronavirus Goes Global'

Chapter 8 – The Build-up in February: 'Come on, Don't Worry Too Much'

In Part II, we would mention that we did not write this diary daily because we did not get the chance to do it every day. The markets were far more exciting than documenting our thoughts, and, we regret this. However, this does not really make whatever we were able to write less useful or meaningful.

Part III – Sample: This part is where we have put some of the news items which were captured by our machines for more than 30 countries including the United States of America, South Africa, India, the United Kingdom, Singapore, China, Canada, Brazil, Malaysia, the Philippines and many others. There are two parts: (a) some of the news items were in English, and (b) most of the others were in local languages, and then these were translated by the machines to English. We want to add a disclaimer that though we have taken all possible precautions to maintain accuracy, any mistakes or errors are totally unintentional and caused only by our oversight. For simplicity, we have put the news items from the beginning of March to early May. This is because those two months had the most rapidly evolving situations across countries and the most interesting developments related to the coronavirus pandemic. This part has five chapters.

Chapter 9 – Politics, Conspiracy Theories and Religious Mass Gatherings

Chapter 10 – The Coronavirus Pandemic's Economic Impact

Chapter 11 – Disease, Devastation and Hope

Chapter 12 – Human Nature and the Impact on Normal Life

Chapter 13 – Bizarre, Funny, Scams and Fake News

Part IV – Inferences: This part is more about the inferences one draws when one looks at the news and sentiment analysis in a consolidated way. It is comparable to the edited 15-minute version of a 90-minute football match that only covers the highlights and important developments. For the people with whom we shared the manuscript for feedback and review, this was the most important part, because it deals with the major conclusions. This part has four chapters.

Chapter 14 – Country Sentiment

Chapter 15 – COVID-19 has Turned the World Upside Down

Chapter 16 – What Do We See More in this Coronavirus News?

Chapter 17 – How Do We Use Sentiment Analysis – A Case Study

Chapter 18 – Conclusion

Hope you like it, but as long as you learn something from it, then that will be more important. All the best and thank you very much!

Notes

1 Sentiment Analysis is the process of determining whether a piece of writing is positive, negative or neutral. A sentiment analysis system for text analysis combines natural language processing (NLP) and Machine Learning techniques to assign weighted sentiment scores to the entities, topics, themes and categories within a sentence or phrase. Sentiment analysis helps data analysts within large enterprises gauge public opinion, conduct nuanced market research, monitor brand and product reputation, and understand customer experiences. https://www.lexalytics.com/technology/sentiment-analysis (Accessed on 21st June 2020).

2 In electronics, noise is an unwanted disturbance in an electrical signal. Electronic noise is an unwanted signal characteristic of all electronic circuits that comes from many different electronic effects and is measured in watts of power. https://www.sciencedirect.com/topics/engineering/electronic-noise (Accessed on 21st June 2020).

INTRODUCTION

In the 21st century, in particular, the pace of technological change has been overwhelming, and there are very few areas where it is more visible in than 'data'. Especially over the last decade, there have been two important developments in the area of 'information' or 'data'. The first of these developments is a massive increase in the quantum of news. For some people, it is general news. For others, it is their social media feed. For several people, it is the information on specific areas such as key political developments, stock markets or sports. It does not matter which category of information consumption you belong to, but you would have noticed that the quantum of news has increased to unimaginable quantities.

In other words, there has been an explosion of data.

'Unstructured data' and the huge quantities of information

The storage, processing and communication of data have become so easy and so cheap that we have surely come a long way from daily newspapers or weekly magazines satiating our thirst for information on the latest developments. Pankaj still remembers the days of the First Gulf War (1991) when the first thing to be done in the morning was to tune in the radio and listen to the 6 AM news from Aakashvaani (All India Radio). No wonder the newspapers are going through a tough time in most of the world. However, let us forget about newspapers! Today, we are not exclusively dependent on radio or television as the case was when electronic media came into prominence and started complementing print media. The internet has truly revolutionised this for many younger people and, especially for the millennials, the internet has become 'the only' source of information.

There is a massive quantum of this kind of news and information, but it can be very clearly defined under certain categories. For a human being, it is easy to see a certain news item and immediately figure out what it pertains to. News or commonly available data are just some examples, but this form of classification and categorisation is easily possible for many other types of information. When the number is in the tens or even in the hundreds, then it

1

is humanly possible. However, imagine a situation when the number of news items is in the thousands, or the data is not very clearly defined under categories. Also, think about the level of subjectivity involved. How one person would see a data point could be entirely different versus another person, and the output may not be really consistent. This will often make the final output less comparable with other results.

'Structured data' versus 'unstructured data'

What most people do realise is that there has been a data explosion in the last few years and that the amount of information that is being generated has increased and continues to increase further and further. However, what is often missed is an important or defining characteristic that this huge quantum of data is mostly 'unstructured'. While there are clear-cut technical definitions available on what 'structured data'[1] is and what 'unstructured data' is,[2] it suffices to say here that 'structured data' is neat information which can be readily used by a user for a defined purpose, while 'unstructured data' is rough and dirty. In other words, the 'unstructured data' will require some processing such as sorting, keyword search or some other method to convert it into 'structured data'.

While this is the first development as we have mentioned above (i.e. the amount of data has increased so much that it is not possible to do analysis about this without help from machines), the second development is that, thankfully, there are efficient and cost-effective tools which have now become available. If you know the basic fundamentals of methods you want to apply and have clarity on what you are trying to achieve with this analysis, then there are machines available that can help you, and this is happening at a rapid pace. Several aspects of data analytics today were simply not possible a decade ago. In fact, the entire discipline of 'data analytics' was not in the mainstream a decade ago. However, that is not the case anymore. If you look at any job board today, data analytics, AI, ML, data sciences and other similar job postings form the bulk of jobs available.

As the quantum of data is increasing, data analytics is keeping pace. Accordingly, while almost all of us are aware that there is a huge amount of data being generated now, and we do understand the impact of Facebook, Instagram, WhatsApp and others, most of us do not get to see how much data analytics has advanced and what new dimensions are being added continuously. What most people may not have noticed is that 'analysis' and 'quantity' are two sides of the same coin called 'data'. However, as we said earlier, the challenge is that most of this data is in an unstructured form. If the unstructured data is to be used, then you have to work on it first, and it has to be processed. The processing will depend on what the end-use is and what it is that you want to do with this data, but it cannot be used in its raw form.

Significance of 'unstructured data'

The next question is why is 'unstructured data' so important? The short answer is that 'unstructured data' can help you in 'connecting the dots'. There are four core ingredients to make use of 'unstructured data': (a) the authenticity and genuineness of data sources, (b) the relevant algorithms which can help you in choosing what is useful for you and in understanding this data reliably and accurately, (c) the tools to perform analytics which can generate output efficiently and optimally, and (d) the human input which can draw the important and correct inferences from this output. These are the basic building blocks and when these are in place, the 'structured data' could become extremely useful in decision-making. The analysis of 'unstructured data' is not just helpful in decision support, but it can also act as the main contributing factor in this aspect.

Which are the applications? There are several, but the more important thing is that we are still just scratching the surface only. Very regularly, consistently and almost every day, there are new vistas opening up, and there are more and more areas finding this useful. If these four ingredients are balanced well, then the 'unstructured data' can help in arriving at actionable conclusions and, therefore, results including (a) key business insights, (b) an increase in 'web traffic', (c) sentiment analysis for the political and the financial worlds, (d) aggregate data for further analysis, (e) web-crawled data for specific needs, (f) consumer insights for focused marketing and sales effort leading to higher sales, (g) summaries and trends in data from consumer transactions, (h) geolocation data and associated analysis, (i) pricing decisions on the basis of user data, (j) the analysis of the news for early warning systems, and, (k) the analysis of government data for performance assessment and acquiring a better handle on the 'cause and effect' analysis.

What is 'unstructured data' analysis and how are we doing it?

'Unstructured data' analysis is the mining of large amounts of text for meaningful words and expressions that evaluates the unstructured data and subjective information for the underlying theme. With the latest advances in Machine Learning, the algorithms can now analyse the text significantly better. For example, a rudimentary analysis of news results can yield a conclusion whether the underlying sentiment is positive, negative or neutral. It might not be that easy when the words are more difficult to classify in either of these categories or when we are dealing with opinions or deliberate attempts to misguide the machines. Therefore, there has to be continuous improvement required (i.e. machines need to become smart about the process, and these have to continuously learn to make the process better).

In some ways, this is similar to the process improvement in manufacturing where efficiency and optimisation are regular exercises.

There are different aspects of the broader picture, and there are different interpretations possible when we answer questions such as news sentiment versus the real impact of the coronavirus or perception versus the reality of the coronavirus. This book is more about the discussion on the different ways we can think about the news on the coronavirus pandemic as well as the underlying sentiment in the news. Examples are how we can use this to make our decision-making better and how we interpret the inferences from this 'unstructured data' analysis on information available on the coronavirus pandemic as the crisis unfolded and evolved. To collect the most comprehensive unstructured data, we have tried to cast a net wide by looking at several countries and also at the news in local language apart from the news delivered in English. In the later chapters, we will spend more time explaining why it is important to do that.

The importance of 'multiple sources', 'local language news' and 'translation'

We need information from multiple countries to get a balanced view of an issue. Let us understand this with an example: the controversy around the origin of the coronavirus. We have discussed this in the other places of the book and in the news collection as well. While the United States of America and a few other countries have accused China that (a) they were not transparent in sharing information about the virus;[3] (b) they did not react on time and delayed sharing information a ta bit too long and by then, the virus had already spread to other countries; (c) had China reacted proactively and seriously, then it would have been possible to stop the spread of the virus to other geographies; (d) the coronavirus was not a natural virus but rather, it was manufactured in Wuhan, and it was a part of a grand design to test biological warfare. We cannot understand the picture in totality unless we look at three independent sources: (a) what the media is reporting in the United States of America, (b) how the Chinese are responding with their own propaganda and (c) how the other countries are reacting to and taking sides in this matter.

While it is important to look at what politicians are saying and what official line governments are maintaining, there will also be a need to look at what the investigative agencies and independent voices are saying. For example, while United States President Donald Trump has been regularly blaming China with statements like 'this is a very bad gift from China'[4] and 'China did not share the information',[5] some of the United States agencies have contradicted the line of thinking that the virus originated from a lab.[6] There are other angles as well: (a) some of the Chinse reports also launched a counter-attack that the virus was actually exported from the United States to China;[7] (b) China has also acted with vengeance against some other countries like Australia when they did not agree with the Chinese view;[8] (c) there is a business angle too, as countries like Japan wanted to reduce their dependence on Chinese facilities for manufacturing at Japanese companies.[9]

In all of this, an essential piece is still missing: the ability to translate local language news into English and see the issues that are being discussed there. This makes a critical difference. To make a holistic and objective assessment, the machines need to capture the local language news in their respective countries and then see what they contain. This is relevant for two main reasons: (a) often, the amount of news on a particular subject in the English language is very small, while it is abundant in the local languages; and (b) the issues being discussed in the local language are often different. It is like comparing English news with a 'filtered version' and the local language news as 'unfiltered sources'. Of course, one understands the issue better and more deeply when accessing the 'unfiltered source'. This is what the machines do. They look at local language news and then translate it into English. It makes the analysis richer.

Coronavirus pandemic: The key global event for 2020

With the background on 'unstructured data', it is fair to claim that it is important for new age analysis. However, it is an extremely wide area. While there are several possibilities with 'unstructured data', as highlighted above, this book is about a specific subject. In the year 2020, the most important global event has been the 'coronavirus pandemic' and its devastating effects. The coronavirus crisis has affected individuals through serious health issues, loss of loved ones, job losses and untold miseries in even their normal, day-to-day activities. However, the cumulative and collective impact on economies and businesses is no less severe. For several countries, it is a fact that the dip in economic growth rates will be serious enough for CY20 (1 January 2020 to 31 December 2020) or FY21 (1 April 2020 to 31 March 2021), as the case may be. By exploring the collection and analysis of 'unstructured data', we have tried to explore a few interesting questions;

- How did the data or news flow on the coronavirus change from February to May 2020?
- What are the important and recurring themes in the news flow, and how did these change over time?
- How did the unstructured data or the news flow from different countries look?
- What are the methods that can be used to analyse this huge amount of information on the coronavirus?
- What are the important inferences that can be drawn from the analysis?
- How can this 'analysis' be used for forecasting, such as the development of an 'early warning system'?

These are broad contours, but there are other subjects as well which are taken up in this book, and they will be explained in more detail as we move forward. However, the fact remains that, as more unstructured data becomes available on a subject, there is more analysis possible. This happened with news flow on the coronavirus too. Initially, we had noticed that the news flow was relatively light but, with time, we started to see more than 20 to 25 very relevant news items on the coronavirus pandemic from a single country. There are wide-ranging topics. Apart from news items covering the huge impact of increased infections and the spread of the coronavirus reflected on a COVID-19 dashboard, there were other usual subplots such as (a) how the government is handling the pandemic in their respective countries, (b) how people were looking at the political angle and how it influenced decision-making and (c) how the conspiracy theories got stronger.

Overreaction and the coronavirus pandemic

These COVID-19 diary entries had begun with commentaries on markets, because that is what we were initially tracking. It still remains the major theme in how the financial markets reacted to the coronavirus pandemic and what were the major driving factors on commodities like crude oil. There are several important aspects of how markets have reacted to the spread of the coronavirus and other COVID-19 related key developments. The virus attacks are very much like terrorist attacks. These generate more coverage than the events with similar or an even higher impact. Naturally, financial markets also react more to these events. The fundamental characteristic of the markets is that there will always be some participants who will overreact to new developments, and there will be others who will barely flinch.

Things may look very easy to explain after the event, but, as proven, it is difficult to tell *a priori* who is right and who is not – only time will tell. However, the point remains that sentiment plays a much important role than the tangible impact of material developments. Whether the impact of the coronavirus is 'noise', 'signal' or a little bit of both, the reaction of financial markets proves the age-old dictum 'News may be the same, but the impact could be vastly different because of the varied nature of sentiment'. The tangible impact and news flow matter for the markets, but does sentiment matter much more? Would it not be interesting to explore the connection of news with a tangible impact on public policy, government response and also on stock markets?

All of these are interesting angles that need to be explored and taken into consideration when we are analysing the linkage between financial markets and the spread of the coronavirus pandemic. When we began, we only had a hunch about the connection between the news on the coronavirus and its actual impact. Then, why did we focus on financial markets more? There is one simple reason: the time lag between news sentiment and the impact on stock price is the shortest. The coronavirus is an unprecedented crisis, but we had an intuition that it was different from the regular market turmoil. Why? The intuition was based on data as the EMAlpha sentiment signal started reflecting unusual and above-average volatility, just like what the Richter Scale does immediately before and during earthquakes.

The conversations did not begin with a realisation on our part that something big is in the offing, but there was a variance in how different countries were reacting and how their perceptions were different, and that is why we started paying more attention. When the coronavirus started spreading beyond China for the first time and since the beginning of January and despite different physical locations, we broadly started to discuss these five things almost on a daily basis;

- How is country news getting swamped from the coverage of the coronavirus across the world?
- How is this impacting the global financial markets and leading to a panic?
- How was EMAlpha very effectively capturing the sentiment in the news?
- How were the volatility signals reflecting the unprecedented situation?
- How quickly are the central banks reacting and what is the impact that this is making on the markets?

How do we calculate the coronavirus sentiment?

We are presenting *Coronavirus News, Markets and AI: The COVID-19 Diaries* as our findings from the analysis of sentiment and its impact on markets. However, this is not a book in a conventional sense. It is more like a daily diary which we maintained. The underlying theme of this book is that, in the age when information travels so fast, sentiment plays a far bigger role in determining the direction of markets. If you can understand sentiment correctly and without the filters of your known or unknown biases, then you can use it. Here are a few words on our methodology:

- To calculate the sentiment scores for the coronavirus, we collect coronavirus-related targeted news flow in a number of languages.
- For a number of emerging market countries, most of the news flow is in the local language and, hence, we focus on news collection in both the local language and in English.
- After the collection of news, we then use natural language processing tools to extract the sentiment for each country and capture the important issues.
- We have used our proprietary sentiment measure to first find the raw sentiment for each country for news related to the coronavirus. The raw scores where then Z-scored for standardisation.

- While we focused on the coronavirus pandemic, the same tool can be applied to any topic in extracting related news sentiment. This analysis has universal applicability.

Big data and AI (Artificial Intelligence) texts are the foundation for this book

This book on Coronavirus-Related News Sentiment and its impact on markets has close linkage with our previous works on Big Data and artificial intelligence (AI). The collection of news on a regular and almost real-time basis and the analysis of inherent sentiment is not possible without Big Data and AI tools. After we worked on these texts and explored Big Data and AI applications across diverse fields, we were even more convinced that the implications for financial markets are important not just because markets react to good or bad news, but also because sentiment would be dynamic and can also be seen differently across different time frames such as 'short term' versus 'long term'.

The higher prevalence of technology and major developments in Big Data and AI have contributed immensely to this endeavour of finding sentiment and the linkage with market movement. There are several important contributing factors: (a) many scientific developments have come together in the new millennium to give technological development a major boost in the field of data, and it has become easier to store an ever-increasing amount of data easily and cheaply; (b) the computational resources have become powerful enough to allow easy access and analysis of this data and, as result, over last 20 years, our ability to store, analyse and manipulate tremendous amounts of data has increased by leaps and bounds. This has played a critical role in the advancement of Big Data, and it was instrumental in our efforts.

Another interesting area is a rather steep decline in associated costs. The need to own and pay for expensive infrastructure to benefit from Big Data and analytics have declined considerably with the advent of cloud computing. Moreover, a number of mathematical and statistical tools in Machine Learning have become widely tested and freely available. Access to Big Data, cloud computing and AI-ML (Artificial Intelligence-Machine Leaning) has also become democratised, with researchers and companies willing to share information. The easy accessibility to Big Data methods, cloud computing and computational methods can potentially make the progress even faster in the future for projects similar to what we are doing.

Big Data, computing power and cloud computing, have all been important in making huge amounts of data and enormous computing power available for anyone who is interested. All these developments may seem unconnected at first, but these were not only just happening simultaneously, but were also feeding into one another in some ways. For example, unless there is storage available for large data, computing capability may not progress as fast or vice versa. Unless one can use and process these large volumes of data with the help of faster and more efficient computing, the large volumes of data storage may not help. More information also requires a more proactive effort to store, analyse and understand the available data.

EMAlpha sentiment technology

Sentiment Classifier: We use a standard sentiment classifier. The classifier can use both static dictionaries supplied by the user, as well as create custom dictionaries. The underlying method is similar to what one might read in a standard textbook – where the sentiment classifier is typically based on support vector machines. The sentiment classifier can automatically develop a sentiment dictionary as it gets feedback from the end-user.

Filtering: The above step gives us sentiment scores. The calculation of the score is done as follows: the sentiment classifier classifies the words as positive, negative or neutral based on the dictionary. Next, the final sentiment score for the text/document is simply given by sentiment score = $(p - n)/t$, where p is the number of positive words; n is the number of negative words; and t is the total number of words in the text/document. After this, we apply any required filters based on the application.

News Collection and Translation: We collect news using our automated scripts and use machine translation to translate local news into English. In other words, we collect news in Chinese, Polish, Spanish, Korean, etc. and use machine translation to translate. This is something considered as cutting edge, because mass-scale machine translation technology is new. Also, based on our experience, sentiment analysis done on translated news text maintains its integrity quite well. This also opens up some very interesting questions – such as, should sentiment score be 'normalised' to take into account a natural 'sentiment bias' in each country and in each language? For example, in Brazil, the news flow was not relatively negative for a rather long time despite a huge increase in coronavirus cases. On the contrary, the panic was at a peak in Iran.

Data Collection: News data for each country is collected every morning before the market opens. We currently have a 24-hour look back on news collection, which means that we look at the news flow over last 24 hours. We are working on collecting hourly intraday sentiment data – which would be very exciting.

Crude oil price and its linkage with coronavirus sentiment

We analysed the extraordinary price movements in the crude oil market. The massive demand destruction because of the coronavirus has created a deep and unprecedented crisis in the crude oil market. On Monday,

20 April 2020, the May United States oil futures contract went into negative territory for the first time in history. This is visible on the EMAlpha Oil News Sentiment tracker as well. While the market movements like futures' are related to specific reasons like storage issues, the general sentiment on the demand side is extremely negative. The oil news sentiment is at the lowest level after the impact during the dip in March because of supply glut expected as a result of the price war between Russia and Saudi Arabia.[10] There have been many interesting events in the crude oil market, but it is fair to say that sentiment has a strong linkage with price movement.

News sentiment on the president of the United States, Donald Trump

How did sentiment from news flow about the United States President Donald Trump quickly worsen, and why may that be important for the direction of markets? The perception that Trump has handled the 'corona crisis' poorly has been fairly strong in the media and logically, this could hurt the markets. On the contrary, while Trump may be doing badly on news flow sentiment, the markets have been doing rather well. After the market hit the bottom on 23 March, S&P 500 has gained 25% and during this time, (a) the coronavirus crisis has worsened significantly in the United States, and (b) the common perception is that the handling of this major health and economic challenge by the United States President has not been optimal. How do we explain that, and why do we say that Trump matters for the market?

Why local news-based sentiment analysis matters

On news flow sentiment analysis, a question is often being asked: In this day and age of global interconnection, does local news matter anymore? Our experience with news collection for different countries in different languages confirms this. English news and translated (from the local language to English) news can be quite different. It is probable that analysis becomes necessary to check what is the more important driver of sentiment: is it the English news sentiment or the local news sentiment? We think this debate is redundant. Ultimately, the news collection in English and news collection in the local language have to complement each other. To effectively capture sentiment and the important issues currently being discussed, it is not a matter of 'either' 'or', rather, it is an 'and' that will work better.

How base rate changes everything

Why are 'Aggregate Market Sentiment for India' and 'News Sentiment on Coronavirus Sentiment for Several Countries Including India' showing very different patterns, and how should these be read to take a call on the market? The 'base rate' can explain this. the coronavirus pandemic in itself is a negative event, but the change in news flow sentiment would be at a continuous spectrum that is sometimes good and sometimes bad. Things will start to look worse in some situations, and in some other situations, these will start to look better. While the sentiment in the news about the coronavirus would keep changing, the overall impact on the market is going to remain negative. Sometimes, the negative impact is less, and sometimes it is more. The Coronavirus News Sentiment Chart only talks about this sentiment which is in a narrow range.

High-Profile cases and the impact on coronavirus sentiment

On a time-series for individual countries, huge fluctuations in the coronavirus sentiment can be noticed. In some cases, in which the United States of America is the most prominent, the news flow sentiment has deteriorated rapidly. The same is the case with Canada in which the coronavirus news flow sentiment has deteriorated sharply. However, the reasons are perhaps different than the United States' reasons. In Canada, this could be because of a high-profile case of infection (i.e. the Prime Minister's wife).[11] The variance between countries on a day-to-day basis continues; for example, Japan is the country with the most 'negative' sentiment on the basis of news flow for 14 March, while things look much better for Korea, Chile and Brazil. Changes like these are visible when one looks at day-to-day comparisons and country-by-country comparisons.

The country-by-country sentiment on the coronavirus

We have also divided the two-month period into three distinct phases to assess if there are differences in sentiment scores.

- Phase 1–6 March 2020 to 26 March 2020
- Phase 2–27 March 2020 to 14 April 2020
- Phase 3–15 April 2020 to 2 May 2020

There are other interesting results in different countries, but it is clear that machines did a great job of capturing relevant news and calculating sentiment scores. Here is what we learned from the sentiment analysis;

- The sentiment scores capture the on-ground sentiment fairly well (e.g. observe where Iran is and where New Zealand stands).
- The sentiment scores are reflecting not just the impact of the coronavirus pandemic, but also the efforts to contain it (e.g. look at Italy).

- The sentiment in local news and English language news is different but not by much. For example, pay attention to Turkey (English versus local news) and Japan (English versus local news).
- Base rates matter and the absolute value of sentiment scores are higher for countries where the base rate is high – in other words, where the usual news sentiment is highly positive (e.g. look at Italy).
- The severity of the coronavirus crisis is influencing the sentiment scores, but another key factor is what is being discussed by global media in that country.
- There are other factors. For example, China is blamed that they did not disclose vital information at the right time, and there are also theories that the coronavirus was born in a lab in Wuhan. All of this impacts China's score.
- The smaller countries that are at extreme ends usually indicate that, when the quantum of news is smaller, the sentiment scores will become too influenced by a news item.

COVID-19 has turned the world upside down

Based on what we have noticed in the news and the sentiment analysis on the news collection, it is easy to see why this coronavirus crisis has turned the whole world upside down, and it has hit conventional thinking hard. The people from this generation have seen wars. They have seen the collapse of the Union of Soviet Socialist Republics (USSR). They have seen terrorist attacks. They have seen financial bubbles, and they have seen climate change. However, they had not seen anything like the coronavirus. A similar case has not existed for more than a hundred years. They were not prepared for it, and they also did not know how to respond to it. Since it was something that no one really had any prior experience with, the coronavirus pandemic has also led to rethinking over some of the things which were always considered either right or wrong.

- The best countries in the world are not always prepared.
- Supply chain efficiency was not all that good.
- Globalisation is not a one-way street.
- Leadership is not just about power and money alone.
- There are stars other than those from sports and movies.
- Rhetoric does not always work in crunch time situations.
- Nature can strike back whenever it wants.
- The coronavirus pandemic has been a great equaliser.
- Growth is a treadmill that is turning faster and faster.
- The choice between democracy versus one-party rule is situational on which works better.
- Conventional thinking changes with new data points.
- There has been reverse migration from cities to villages.

What are the factors that influence the pandemic news?

We have regularly been collecting news on the coronavirus across more than 30 countries to analyse the underlying sentiment, and this has offered us interesting insights on how sentiment has evolved on the coronavirus pandemic as well as insights on its disastrous impact. While doing the sentiment analysis, we have also noticed that, when we analyse the news collection on the coronavirus from the end of January onwards, we find that there are some recurring themes in this news flow. While one would expect that the regular tracking of the spread of the coronavirus pandemic will be covered by the media – and this includes statistics on new cases, the rate of spread and COVID-19 cases of death – there are some other topics which are covered frequently. This leads to some important conclusions about how the news selection and the focus of media on what is important and in relative importance get influenced by several extraneous factors.

- **The national agenda reflects in the news often** – The origin of the news determines the tone, but the sign of free media in a country is often found in the diversity of the news reports and the versions of news which are against the official one.
- **Media will look for interesting subplots** – The plain statistics are boring, and numbers are dry. To make the coverage interesting, the media will look for subplots that make the news interesting for the masses.
- **Celebrity figures get more attention, and this is not always good** – being a known figure does not always help. There will always be media stories about how a particular politician did not follow the social distancing norms or how a movie star has not donated much.
- **Everyone loves conspiracy theories** – This is an age-old truth, but, even in the most serious circumstances, there is absolutely no dearth of news reports which prominently cover conspiracy theories. These may be difficult to justify or believe but that does not stop the media from picking them.
- **Speculation continues even in the most straightforward situation** – Media coverage is often focused on the future, as in how an event will have implications in the years to come and how the events today could shape the world in the future. Most of this is pure speculation though.
- **The quantum of news impacts the sentiment scores** – exceptionally low or high sentiment represents days when there were few or relatively few news. The sentiment score is less volatile when the number of news items becomes fairly large. This has how news flow has evolved on the coronavirus.

What do we see more in this coronavirus news?

The more common recurring themes are as follows. Please note that we have listed these recurring themes in alphabetical order and this does not reflect relative importance or frequency of occurrence.

- Blame Game between Countries and even Non-Government Organisations
- Brazil's Response to the Coronavirus Threat
- Celebrity Connections with the Coronavirus
- Conspiracy Theories behind the Origin and Spread of the Coronavirus
- Employment Opportunities and the Impact of the Coronavirus on Unemployment
- Fake News and Scams Related to the Coronavirus
- Geopolitical and Business Shifts in the Future
- Globalisation Paused or Even Reversed
- Government Response Across countries
- Hoarding of Essential Commodities, such as Food Items
- Impact on Airlines, Travel, Tourism, Prepared Food and Hospitality Industries
- Oil Demand Slump and Volatility in Crude Oil Prices
- Religion and the Role of Congregations in Spreading the Coronavirus
- Sports Events Cancellation and How the Coronavirus May Change Some Sports Forever
- Technology can Help in Fighting the Coronavirus Pandemic
- The Rush for Toilet Paper and Other Essential Items
- Traditional Medicines and the Efficacy of Treatment for the Coronavirus
- Trump and His Handling of the Coronavirus Crisis

How do we use the inferences drawn from 'unstructured data'?

The coronavirus impact is disastrous, both for health and economic reasons. However, it is interesting to note that the media coverage on the coronavirus pandemic – the news and the messages on the crisis – has been made more interesting despite it being one of the biggest and most impactful pandemics that we have seen in almost a century. This is not to say that the coverage is being more positive than negative on average. Rather, it only means that news reports have given enough space to other related developments which have impacted the sentiment on the coronavirus pandemic. This is important because then, the reporting becomes more nuanced and layered – a prerequisite for a balanced analysis.

Once we are reasonably sure about the quality of our news sources, and we have the confidence that we are not excluding any major sources, the next thing is to explore is if there is a link between market news, sentiment signals and market timing. Is it possible to position for market volatility in a timely manner using sentiment signal as a guide? For example, we closely looked at two major emerging equity markets: Brazil and India. We use our sentiment-based signals, constructed using machine translation and sentiment analysis on news flow in Portuguese, Hindi and English, to trade the broad equity indices in these two countries.

We construct our Brazil and India sentiment signals every morning at 8 AM local time in both the countries respectively, and we use this to predict the day's market movements. More specifically, if the sentiment improved from the previous day, then we go long in the market. If it deteriorated from the previous day, we go short in the market. The result, in terms of the cumulative return in excess of the equity benchmarks, shows that sentiment signals for Brazil and India seem to have navigated the recent unprecedented market volatility quite well. This is an important conclusion, because the entire premise that the unstructured data analysis is useful is based on its practical utility and if it can be used for better decisions.

As reflected in the performance of the MSCI World Equity Index during this period, the negative sentiment directly fed the market capitulation. Both emerging and developed markets fell as the coronavirus spread in multiple regions beyond Asia – from Italy and the Middle East to Brazil. It started to look more and more likely that the virus-related sentiment will drive the markets for some time. Market volatility spiked and a number of investment fund strategies started performing poorly against this backdrop. However, as EMAlpha monitored the market sentiment and used it as an input of its EM India strategy, the EMAlpha long/short model systematic equity strategy delivered better return versus BSE Sensex's performance.

Therefore, all of this leads to the question: Can sentiment analysis be used to navigate market volatility? In our opinion, the answer is in the affirmative. The EMAlpha model portfolio incorporating the coronavirus sentiment has done significantly better versus its benchmark, the BSE Sensex Index. There are other important inferences, such as how the oil prices have moved and how they are linked with Oil News Sentiment. The sentiment, by nature, will remain volatile, but broad trends can be ascertained, and they prove to be helpful. This is often the case with the coronavirus pandemic news and market movement. However, the story does not really end there, because there are other possible implications.

The unstructured data analysis can be used in multiple ways, such as, (a) 'national security agencies' need to keep an eye on the prominent issues covered by the local language news coverage across neighbouring countries, and that analysis will be useful for them; (b) there are also opportunities for REGULATORS – for example, the market regulators should be aware of what people are talking about in Indian companies in other countries to keep track of any manipulation attempts from overseas; (c) the businesses will benefit from unstructured data analysis on competitors and clients to save them from unpleasant shocks. These are only a few possibilities, but there are thousands of applications possible, and, more importantly, the list will be growing continuously and consistently.

Notes

1 Structured data versus unstructured data: structured data is comprised of clearly defined data types whose pattern makes them easily searchable; while unstructured data – 'everything else' – is comprised of data that is usually not as easily searchable, including formats like audio, video, and social media postings. Unstructured data versus structured data does not denote any real conflict between the two. Customers select one or the other not based on their data structure, but rather on the applications that use them: relational databases for structured, and most any other type of application for unstructured data. https://www.datamation.com/big-data/structured-vs-unstructured-data.html (Accessed on 21st June 2020).

2 Unstructured data is information, in many different forms, that does not hew to conventional data models and, thus, typically is not a good fit for a mainstream relational database. Thanks to the emergence of alternative platforms for storing and managing such data, it is increasingly prevalent in IT systems and is used by organisations in a variety of business intelligence and analytics applications. https://searchbusinessanalytics.techtarget.com/definition/unstructured-data (Accessed on 21st June 2020).

3 https://www.voanews.com/science-health/coronavirus-outbreak/china-still-not-sharing-coronavirus-information-experts-say (Accessed on 21st June 2020).

4 https://economictimes.indiatimes.com/news/international/world-news/donald-trump-says-coronavirus-a-very-bad-gift-from-china/articleshow/76075469.cms?from=mdr (Accessed on 21st June 2020).

5 https://www.nytimes.com/2020/05/29/health/virus-who.html (Accessed on 21st June 2020).

6 https://www.outlookindia.com/newsscroll/contradicting-us-intel-trump-says-covid19-developed-in-lab-ld/1820295 (Accessed on 21st June 2020).

7 https://www.theguardian.com/world/2020/mar/12/conspiracy-theory-that-coronavirus-originated-in-us-gaining-traction-in-china (Accessed on 21st June 2020).

8 https://www.aljazeera.com/ajimpact/china-considers-penalising-australian-goods-virus-dispute-200520064912380.html (Accessed on 21st June 2020).

9 https://www.businesstoday.in/current/world/coronavirus-impact-japan-to-offer-22-billion-to-firms-shifting-production-out-of-china/story/400721.html (Accessed on 21st June 2020).

10 https://www.worldoil.com/news/2020/4/9/saudi-arabia-and-russia-end-their-oil-price-war-with-output-cut-agreement (Accessed on 21st June 2020)

11 https://www.thehindu.com/news/international/canadian-pms-wife-has-recovered-from-coronavirus-illness/article31196932.ece (Accessed on 21st June 2020).

Part I

THE METHOD

1

HOW TO READ THIS BOOK?

A few suggestions before you begin

To get the best out of it, here are a few suggestions:

- This book is divided into four parts. Read Part I first, as it gives vital details that will help you understand what are we trying to do and how we are doing it. Parts II and III are not mutually exclusive, but Part II is better suited for people who have some basic understanding of financial markets or those who are interested in it. Similarly, Part III is more suitable for readers with a general interest. Part IV is the gist of the key themes in this book. As such, Parts II, III and IV can be read in any order.
- Read it slowly, preferably one chapter in one sitting. Try to recall how you personally would be thinking about the markets and the world on that day and how others would be thinking on that day according to your opinion – for example, would your thinking be influenced by which part of the world you were in and so on. Think about these scenarios, and think hard. That way, you will get more out of it.
- Refer to the charts and try to understand them first without referring to the accompanying text. Make your own assessment and try to infer what these pictures are conveying. If you draw your inferences and find them different in comparison to the text we have put, then it is better because there are multiple dimensions a reader needs to really think about.
- Think about the Coronavirus Sentiment and the Market Sentiment differently and understand that these are measures of two very different things. Similarly, the sentiment on keywords will be different from either Coronavirus or Market Sentiment. Why is it important? Because it matters to understand the cause and effect. That is different from correlation.
- No subjective thing can ever be perfect because of possibilities for improvement nor can anything ever be completely right or completely wrong. Think about the linkage of sentiment with markets on those lines. The Coronavirus News Sentiment or Market Sentiment will never

have a perfect mathematical relationship with actual market movement, but as long as you get it mostly right, then you will be doing fine.

A sample of our machine-aided observations

1 **Oil, Again (27 April 2020), Oil's Historic Fall: Precipitated by Quickly Worsened Sentiment? (22 April 2020), Crude and Coronavirus: Oil Futures in Negative for the First Time in History and Its Implications (21 April 2020)** – We analyse the extraordinary price movements in the crude oil market. The massive destruction of demand because of the coronavirus has created a deep and unprecedented crisis in the crude oil market. On Monday, 20 April, the May United States oil futures contract went into negative territory for the first time in history. This is visible on the EMAlpha Oil News Sentiment tracker as well. While the market movements like on April 20 are related to specific reasons like storage issues, the general sentiment on the demand side is extremely negative. The oil news sentiment is at the lowest levels after the impact experienced during the dip in March because of supply glut expected as a result of the price war between Russia and Saudi Arabia.

2 **Markets and Coronavirus Sentiment: Battle between Optimism and Pessimism (20 April 2020)** – We are struggling to figure out until when the divergence between sentiment on coronavirus-related parametres and market performance may continue. Most markets are up by at least 15 to 20%, and we are now far away from the lows of March. However, this is only half the story. The on-ground situation on the coronavirus seems to be telling something very different. On the Global Coronavirus News Sentiment and Country-By-Country Coronavirus Sentiment, things continue to deteriorate. Except for a few exceptions like the United States of America and China, most countries are struggling to contain infections, and the statistics are plummeting. Similarly, the Global Coronavirus Sentiment has deteriorated sharply this week.

3 **News Sentiment on Donald Trump and Markets (17 April 2020), Trump Losing 'Perception Battle' on the Coronavirus, and Why It Matters? (15 April 2020)** – How did sentiment from news flow on the United States President Donald Trump quickly worsen, and why may that be important for the direction of markets? The perception that Trump has handled the 'corona crisis' poorly has been fairly strong in the media and logically, this could hurt the markets. On the contrary, while Trump may be doing badly on news flow sentiment, the markets have been doing rather well. After the market hit the bottom on 23 March, S&P 500 has gained 25% and during this time, (a) the coronavirus crisis has worsened significantly in the United States, and (b) the common perception is that the handling of this major health and

economic challenge by the United States President has not been optimal. How do we explain this, and why do we say that Trump matters for the market?

4 **Timing the Virus: Market Timing Possible with Sentiment Analysis?** (13 April 2020) – Is it possible to position for market volatility in a timely manner? As our focus tends to be EM, we consider two major emerging equity markets: Brazil and India. We use our sentiment-based signals, constructed using machine translation and sentiment analysis on news flow in Portuguese, Hindi and English to trade the broad equity indices in these two countries. We construct our Brazil and India Sentiment Signals every morning at 8 AM local time, and we use it to predict the day's market movements. More specifically, if the sentiment improved from the previous day, we go long in the market. If it deteriorated from the previous day, we go short in the market. The result, in terms of the cumulative return in excess of the equity benchmark, suggests that sentiment signals for Brazil and India seem to have navigated the recent unprecedented market volatility quite well.

5 **Fed Making Data on Fundamentals Irrelevant for Markets?** (9 April 2020) – The coronavirus pandemic has clearly made the United States Central Bank extremely active, and it began with an announcement of an emergency interest rate cut in the first week of March. Now, interest rates have become almost zero and the Federal Reserve is also doing big-scale asset purchases. Since 2008 when Quantitative Easing (QE) proved effective in averting a huge disaster during Global Financial Crisis (GFC), QE has become a 'tool of choice' for the Fed. This leads to a dichotomy in this respect. How the signals from fundamentals of the economy (such as jobless claims) will be interpreted and how markets will react to what the Fed is doing will pull the markets in opposite directions.

6 **Why Local News-Based Sentiment Analysis Matters?** (8 April 2020) – On news flow sentiment analysis, this question is being asked often: In this day and age of global interconnection, does local news matter anymore? Our experience with news collection for different countries in different languages confirms this. English news and translated (from local language to English) news can be quite different. It might be that analysis becomes necessary to check what is the more important driver of sentiment: is it the English news sentiment or the local news sentiment?

7 **Coronavirus: Darkest Before the Dawn or No Light at End of the Tunnel?** (6 April 2020) – The coronavirus news sentiment has deteriorated in 11 out of the 12 countries in our main panel (the United States of America, China, Germany, Brazil, Italy, India, Mexico, Malaysia, Norway, Colombia, Australia and Poland). This does not inspire much confidence that we are anywhere close to recovery. Also,

21

when we do sentiment analysis for some keywords such as 'Donald Trump', 'Fed Rate', 'Nasdaq Composite', 'Chinese Economy' and 'US Economy', we find that, after his proactive steps over the last week or so, there has been a big turnaround in news sentiment for the United States President Donald Trump. This matters for its linkage with how quickly and efficiently the biggest economy of the world will respond to the coronavirus threat. The bad news here is that things do not look that great for S&P 500 and the United States economy sentiment.

8 **How Base Rate Changes Everything (1 April 2020)** – Why 'Aggregate Market Sentiment for India' and 'News Sentiment on Coronavirus Sentiment for Several Countries Including India' are showing very different patterns and how to read them to take a call on the market. The 'base rate' can explain this. The coronavirus in itself is a negative event, but the change in news flow sentiment would be continuous – sometimes good and sometimes bad. While the sentiment in the news about the coronavirus would keep changing, the overall impact on the market is going to remain negative. Sometimes, the negative impact is less, and sometimes it is more. The Coronavirus News Sentiment Chart only talks about this sentiment, which is in a narrow range.

9 **The Dichotomy of Worse Coronavirus Situations and the Better Markets (30 March 2020)** – There have been some key developments and inferences that can be drawn on the Coronavirus News Sentiment and its impact on the global, as well as country-specific, themes. While there is unprecedented coverage of the market impact of the Coronavirus COVID-19, the massive volume of this coverage makes it difficult to draw any conclusions. Related market analysis has focused on specific countries or specific asset classes or government and central banks' responses. How do we simplify the event analysis and what are the inferences we can draw?

10 **Better News Sentiment on the United States Help Emerging Markets (25 March 2020)** – Over the last ten days, there have been interesting takeaways from sentiment analysis for news flow around some very important and immensely popular keywords, which matter for the United States of America. First, we discuss the key positive from this analysis. We find a little bit of improvement in the overall news sentiment on words such as 'Donald Trump', 'Dow Jones Index', 'Fed Rate', 'Nasdaq Composite', 'Chinese Economy' and 'US Economy'. On a cumulative basis, the news sentiment for keywords which matter for the United States of America has improved in the last few days but only by a little. Overall, the improvement in news sentiment over the United States economy is reflecting in the United States markets as well. However, what is needed now is more confidence in Trump and the Fed on their ability to pull this off.

11 **Coronavirus News Sentiment and Indian Markets (24 March 2020)** – If we map the Aggregate Market Sentiment for India (not just the

Coronavirus News Sentiment for the country, which will be a part of overall sentiment anyway) with the market indices, there is a clear message. The market volatility is not likely to go away until the time there is some stability in the news sentiment. The smart recovery in market performance on Friday, 20 March, when the market was up about 6%, was followed by an even deeper fall on Monday, 23 March when there was a 13% decline, gels very well with the India Coronavirus News Sentiment. The worst possible news for the global markets is that United States markets continue to remain in deep turmoil. From the behaviour of markets so far, it is likely that any turnaround will not happen until news sentiment on the coronavirus starts to get better.

12 **Coronavirus, News Sentiment and Investor Behaviour (23 March 2020)** – From the recent coronavirus-driven reaction of global markets, it has become quite clear that sentiment is a dominant driver of investor behaviour. In an age when the speed of news dissemination is at its peak, market sentiment requires careful consideration by investors. The initial reaction of the markets to global shocks tends to be somewhat broad-based, as all markets react to the same overall shock. However, as events evolve, local news flow sentiment also starts playing a significant role. High-profile cases lead to further deterioration in sentiment and a more negative market reaction. It is possible to use a systematic approach and use quantitative measures of sentiment to make investment decisions, and this can lead to outperformance versus the broader market.

13 **Coronavirus Sentiment Deteriorating Further and What We Learn (18 March 2020)** – The latest country-by-country 'Coronavirus Sentiment' based on news flow continues to show further deterioration in many countries including the United States of America. However, things have started to look up in China. Considering this was the origin country for COVID-19, this is a good sign. India is seeing a further fall in coronavirus sentiment and that is bearish. The bigger worry is that the cumulative sentiment, or the sum of total of news flow across all countries which we track, continues to plunge and it is very likely that, unless there is an improvement here, the global markets may not stabilise. The Indian markets continue to swing wildly, and the other important takeaway is that the cumulative market sentiment is still bearish which may not help in an immediate market recovery.

14 **High Profile Cases and the Impact on Coronavirus Sentiment (15 March 2020)** – On a time-series for individual countries, one notices huge fluctuations in coronavirus sentiment. In some cases in which the United States is the most prominent, the news flow sentiment has deteriorated rapidly. The same is the case with Canada in which the coronavirus news flow sentiment has deteriorated sharply. However, the reasons are perhaps different than the United States' reasons. In

Canada, this could be because of a high-profile case of infection (i.e. the Prime Minister's wife). The variance between countries on a day-to-day basis continues; for example, Japan is the country with the most 'negative' sentiment on the basis of news flow for 14 March, while things look much better for Korea, Chile and Brazil.

15 **Spike in Volatility and Coronavirus Sentiment (10 March 2020)** – The global markets see an unprecedented spike in volatility. On 9 March in the VIX Index, the widely monitored gauge of market volatility shot up to levels that have not been seen since the Great Financial Crisis almost ten years ago. While the immediate reason was the breakdown of oil production cut negotiations between Russia and Saudi Arabia, the stage was already set for such a big market movement by the recent developments in the spread of the coronavirus. We monitor daily news sentiments in a range of emerging and developed markets. As it has become clear that Coronavirus-Related News Sentiment could continue to be a driver of market sentiment, we will continue to monitor coronavirus news and sentiment.

16 **Coronavirus, Human Irrationality and Daniel Kahneman (7 March 2020)** – As reflected in the reaction of global markets to the coronavirus' threat to the global economy, it is easy to see why sentiment is often much more powerful than facts alone. This is not just limited to markets, however. Events that appeal to human emotions and our primitive instincts always have a disproportionate impact than what objective assessment would warrant. This is true for terrorist threats, fears of recession and how broad-based the impact of negative events will be, in general. In many of these areas, one of the most elegant explanations and lucid examples backed by years of research and experiments with a large sample size have come from Daniel Kahneman. In his book *Thinking, Fast and Slow*, Nobel Laureate Kahneman has spoken at length about 'human irrationality' and the way the process of thinking gets influenced by rather unexpected factors.

17 **Coronavirus Sentiment Watch (3 March 2020)** – The markets have reacted strongly to Coronavirus-Related News Sentiment. While it remains topical, we will try to regularly post a heat map of our country-level sentiment score for the coronavirus. China, Thailand and Iran saw the most negative sentiments, while England saw the least negative sentiment. As the daily sentiment changes for a number of countries, we believe that the sentiment score-which is an input into our systematic trading model – can be valuable in risk managing or creating new signals for any international portfolio.

18 **Coronavirus and Markets: Is Local Sentiment More Important? (2 March 2020)** – The sharp downward market movements across the world in the previous week has removed any doubts about the kind of impact the

coronavirus would have on the investor sentiment. In the initial response, most markets globally reacted in a predictably negative fashion, but this is slowly changing now. Just like the sharp fall in the United States markets on Thursday, 27 February followed by a significant decline in major Asian markets on Friday, 28 February, the major Index of Indian markets fell. The decline in NIFTY 50 was among the 'Top 5 Steepest' in the last more than ten years with a fall of more than 3.5%, but the trend reversed on Monday, 2 March morning. However, all of this changed towards the end of the session. In the last one and a half hours, the NIFTY 50 not only gave all its gains for the day but also closed 0.6% down. Thus, the intraday fall of 3% was only marginally better than Friday's, 28 February Indian market performance – completely unexpected and very quick. However, how did this happen? The news came that two fresh cases of the coronavirus were detected in India.

19 **Coronavirus and Markets (27 February 2020)** – Markets have seen a sharp negative reaction to coronavirus news. The news sentiment has evolved daily leading to the market gyrations. We have tracked the overall market sentiment, specifically in regard to the coronavirus, on a daily basis. After a bit of relaxation last week, the sentiment soured again over the weekend. As the markets opened on Monday, this negative sentiment stocked market nervousness. As reflected in the MSCI World Equity Index over the last few days, the negative sentiment has directly fed the market capitulation. How has the EMAlpha long/short equity strategy done? The chart below shows the benchmark Sensex Index and the EMAlpha year-to-date returns. The EMAlpha long/short strategy has delivered 3% YTD return versus Sensex's –4% YTD return.

20 **Coronavirus and How Sentiment Impacts the Market (9 February 2020)** – Over the last few weeks, The coronavirus has led to a worldwide scare. As expected, this is affecting the global markets too. Though it is believed that there is a serious clampdown by Chinese authorities on the type of news flow leaving its borders, but with each piece of good or bad news, the fortunes are fluctuating. For example, global markets heaved a sigh of relief when it was reported that Gilead Sciences has offered an experimental drug for coronavirus treatments and are testing and that the biotech firm has formalised an agreement with. After we have spoken about the recent developments related to coronavirus and related news flow, it is important to mention that the impact on the markets seems to have a local component, as Asian markets close to China have suffered more than others.

2

READING CORONAVIRUS NEWS

Coronavirus: neither the first nor the last pandemic

There is no doubt that most of the people currently living on this planet have not seen anything like the coronavirus pandemic. They will have no memory to fall back upon to understand what COVID-19 has done to this world. Words like 'pandemic', which belonged to the dark ages when humankind was completely at the mercy of nature, became mainstream all of a sudden. Life, as more than half of the people in the world knew it, changed completely. The global powers – wealthy and powerful countries – had to surrender to a virus so tiny that it cannot be even seen yet so powerful that it was enough to shake the entire humanity. There were threats of viruses previously such as SARS, NIPAH and H1N1, but the coronavirus has surpassed all of them, and the only thing it is being compared with today is the Spanish Flu[1] which happened around a hundred years ago or the London Plague of the 17th century.[2]

However, is the coronavirus the worst disease we have ever seen? No, it is not, not yet at least. The world has seen far deadlier diseases. Malaria, tuberculosis and HIV-AIDS have killed far more people and, even in the worst-case scenario, the coronavirus could only be responsible for a fraction of the damage these diseases have caused and still continue to cause. Mental health issues and even 'depression' are responsible for a bigger human toll. Then why did the coronavirus become so powerful in public perception? Was coronavirus news more damaging and more powerful than the virus itself? This is not to say that the coronavirus was not a difficult healthcare challenge. The moot point is how deadly it was and how was the perception towards it. Was it more serious than the collective impact that all the news coverage made on the people's psyche or was it less? Or in other words, did it get more attention than it deserved?

What is sentiment analysis?

Take a simple everyday example: when you are asked for a suggestion, how do you recommend a book to your friend? If you do not know what kind of books your friend likes, then you may ask him what type of books they like to read. However, in general, you describe a book as 'comic', 'interesting', 'depressing', 'feel-good' or with some other similar expression. Basically, you are describing the underlying sentiment in the book with just one word. This is a simple analogy, but, in other words, sentiment analysis is a process by which you look at loads of qualitative information and then try to come up with a description for it in such a way that it can be used quantitatively. It is like shortening the length of the decision-making process by glancing through the material and then looking for words that will help you decide on the tone of the material.

The understanding of sentiment analysis has evolved through various phases and at several different places and, hence, there is no consensus on a standard definition for the term. However, broadly and technically speaking, sentiment analysis is the mining of large amounts of text for meaningful words and expressions which evaluates the unstructured data and subjective information for the underlying theme. With the latest advances in Machine Learning, the algorithms can now analyse the text significantly better. For example, a rudimentary analysis of news results can yield a conclusion whether the underlying sentiment is positive, negative or neutral. It might not be that easy when the words are more difficult to classify in either of these categories or when we are dealing with opinions or deliberate attempts to misguide the machines. However, that discussion is for another day and is not relevant at this point.

News sentiment versus real impact

Let us come back to the coronavirus pandemic and its effects once again. There are different aspects of the broader picture and there are different interpretations possible when we answer the questions on news sentiment versus the real impact of the coronavirus or perception versus the reality of the coronavirus. However, as such, we are in no rush to reach the answers. If we have done our job well, then that is what you will be able to decide for yourself by the time you finish reading this book. This book is more about the discussion on what are the different ways that we can think about the news on the coronavirus pandemic and the underlying sentiment in the news. How we can use this to make our decision-making better, and how do we interpret the inferences from this sentiment analysis?

While we do not want to immediately jump to conclusions, we can surely look at the spread of the coronavirus across countries and the associated news sentiment from these geographies. We can also look at the prevailing sentiment in the news on specific topics with the help of keywords and then what it did to the markets individually and collectively from the perspective of separating the role of the coronavirus' real impact and the role played by sentiment on the financial markets. It is often said that markets always overreact, irrespective of whether the news is good or bad. This is just another way of saying that sentiment is driven by the news, and we are making an attempt to measure it quantitatively.

The media coverage on the coronavirus and the impact on financial markets

There are several important aspects of how markets have reacted to the spread of the coronavirus and other COVID-19-related major developments. Of course, this is a global health emergency, and there is no proven cure yet in sight. Media coverage is still disproportionate in considering the tangible impact estimated as of now. The virus attacks are very much like terrorist attacks in the sense that they generate more coverage than the events with a similar or an even higher impact. In the age of rapid information dissemination and the huge role played by social media, this skew is even more prominent. Naturally, financial markets also react more to these events.

The fundamental characteristic of the markets is that there will always be some participants who will overreact to new development, and there will be others who will barely flinch. It is difficult to tell *a priori* who is right and who is not, and only time will tell. However, the point is reiterated that the sentiment plays a rather important role than the tangible impact of material developments. Whether the impact of the coronavirus is 'noise', 'signal' or a little bit of both, the reaction of financial markets proves the age-old dictum 'News may be the same, but the impact could be vastly different because of the varied nature of sentiment'. The tangible impact and news flow matter for the markets, but the sentiment matters much more. Moreover, the analysis of sentiment helps one position better with respect to market developments.

Would it not be interesting to explore the connection of news with a tangible impact on public policy, government response and also on stock markets? When we began, we only had a hunch about the connection between news on the coronavirus and its actual impact. The coronavirus pandemic is a global health emergency and, because of long lockdowns that were required to contain the spread of the virus, it rapidly evolved into a major economic crisis. In creating the most important challenge for the economy, in the league of the Global Financial Crisis of 2008[3] and even The Great Depression of 1929 onwards,[4] there were other factors as well, such as the disruption in global supply chains, unavailability of workers as a result of reverse migration and across-the-board demand destruction as incomes fell. Then, why have we focused on financial markets more? This is because of one simple reason: the time lag between news sentiment and the impact on stock price is the shortest.

The coronavirus pandemic crisis versus the global financial crisis of 2008

There is no consensus on this but, arguably, how global financial markets were impacted because of the coronavirus is a far bigger event than what we have ever seen. This includes the Global Financial Crisis (GFC) of 2008. Why? During the GFC, it was clear what had caused it and how it could be controlled and, except for a very brief initial period, there was sufficient visibility on the effectiveness of methods that were used to fight the crisis. In the case of the coronavirus and even in the best-case scenario, we are still at least a few weeks away from understanding the damage that the coronavirus has caused to the global economy. A 'top-down' crisis is a little easier to manage than a 'bottom-up' crisis – which is what the COVID-19 crisis is. Just take one example of how general movement and traffic got restricted as a result of the coronavirus. This itself is enough to disrupt several industries, as it breaks their flow of goods and services.

The GFC spread from the United States real estate sector, and the stress in the United States of America's financial system started affecting other countries. There were big failures like the bankruptcy of the Lehman Brothers at the beginning of the GFC, and the panic swept over the next few months. Due to this, confidence plummeted. It was like a 'big bang' towards the beginning of the GFC, and then things started to normalise. The coronavirus crisis is very different versus the GFC, because we can easily forget expecting any massive Big Bang explosion, as there was hardly any noise outside Wuhan at Hubei in China during the beginning of this crisis. Not only for weeks, but for a couple of months, the virus hardly did anything significant outside China. While the beginning was lacklustre for the coronavirus, the crisis continued to aggravate with each passing day. For several months, the numbers kept on increasing, and the impact kept getting multiplied.

There is another important difference between the GFC and the coronavirus crisis. The GFC did not involve much physical production and demand-related impact. There were bankruptcies and job losses in the GFC, but the impact was still largely localised. The demand for products and goods, to a large extent, remained intact. Supply chains remained connected on both ends with production and customer respectively, and several sectors – we could even say that majority of them – escaped any significant disruption. For example, think of airlines, hotels and restaurants. As a result of the coronavirus pandemic, business vanished for them overnight. For that matter, any sector that was directly or indirectly related to the tourism and travel industry has been very badly affected because of the pandemic. The effects are immediate and severe, and the statistics such as GDP growth numbers and people enroling for unemployment benefits confirm it. The coronavirus pandemic is different and, in a sense in some ways, a more 'real' crisis. As a result of lockdown which affected more than 60% of the global population, the disruption is widespread, and there is virtually nothing that has not been negatively impacted.

Real physical crises just like the Great Depression and the challenge of rebuilding war-ravaged countries are more difficult to overcome. The impact lingers longer and even accurate assessments on the true extent of damage take a while. In the overall scheme of things, there are several unanswered questions: (a) no one can safely forecast how long the 'road to recovery' will be; (b) will the changes in normal life affect some industries forever; (c) what will the 'new normal' entail and how we will deal with it. There are several known 'unknowns', but more worrisome is the fact that there are several 'unknowns' in which we have not much idea. As we know, the last serious pandemic was more than a hundred years ago, and the world has significantly changed in this timeframe. There are several important aspects of how governments, central banks, financial markets, companies and ordinary people have reacted to the spread of the coronavirus and related developments.

This book is a diary of market analysts watching sentiment on the coronavirus

In Part II of this book, another very important thing that the readers will notice is that there is a discontinuity in the dates that we have the text for and the topics we discuss. While we were discussing the idea on how to bring these writings to a wider audience, Aakash – Aakash Chakrabarty, Senior Commissioning Editor at Routledge Taylor & Francis Group and the most important reason why this book has reached you – mentioned that our approach and treatment of the subject is more like *The Diary* of Samuel Pepys, which covered the decade of the 1660s and includes horrors of the Plague in the city of London and The Great Fire. Samuel Pepys (3 February 1633 to 26 May 1703) was an administrator of the Navy of England and a Member of Parliament in the United Kingdom.

On 1 January 1660, Pepys began to keep a diary and recorded his daily life for almost ten years. This record of a decade of Pepys' life is more than a million words long and is often regarded as Britain's most celebrated diary. Pepys has been called the greatest diarist of all time due to his frankness in writing concerning his own weaknesses and the accuracy in which he records events of daily British life and major events in the 17th century. He covered major political and social occurrences in great detail, and his diary is still used to gain greater insight and understanding of life in London in the 17th century. Pepys commented on the significant and turbulent events of his nation, and his assessment was mostly objective.

As authors, we do not know how far this comparison is valid and if it even makes sense to see the link of the coronavirus sentiment with markets as the most important area of concern in this pandemic. However, just like Pepys, we have tried to remain as objective as possible. We are not trying to inference on the basis of what we want to see and what, in our opinion, is happening in the markets because of the coronavirus sentiment. Rather, we work the other way round. We get the data and then we try to see what the data is telling us and, in the process, we do not add our view nor do we subtract anything which is purely our opinion. You may notice that we have kept the text minimal deliberately, because we want the readers to see the data and the charts and draw their own inferences without our writing clouding their judgement.

How do we calculate the coronavirus sentiment?

The goal of EMAlpha is to give the investors a window to some of the main drivers of news and market sentiments followed by the assessment of the impact of this sentiment on market direction. In recent times because of the coronavirus, we have seen an unprecedented spike in volatility in the global markets. For example, on 9 March 2020, the VIX Index – the widely monitored gauge of the market volatility - shot up to levels not seen since the Great Financial Crisis almost ten years ago.

While the immediate reason was the breakdown of oil production that cut negotiations between Russia and Saudi Arabia, the stage was already set for such a big market move by the recent developments in the spread of the coronavirus. In the near term, as it has become clear that the Coronavirus-Related News Sentiment could continue to be a driver of market sentiment, we will continue to monitor coronavirus news and the associated sentiment. However and firstly, here are a few words on our methodology:

- To calculate the sentiment scores for the coronavirus, we collected coronavirus-related targeted news flow in a number of languages.
- For a number of emerging market countries, most of the news flow is in the local language and, hence, we focused on news collection in both the local language and in English.
- After the news collection, we then use natural language processing tools to extract the sentiment for each country.
- We have used our proprietary sentiment measure to first find the raw sentiment for each country for news related to the coronavirus. The raw scores where then Z-scored for standardisation.
- While we focused on the coronavirus, the same tool can be applied to any topic in extracting the related news sentiment.

Notes

1 The 1918 influenza pandemic was the most severe pandemic in recent history. It was caused by an H1N1 virus with genes of avian origin. Although there is no universal consensus regarding where the virus originated, it spread worldwide during 1918–1919. In the United States, it was first identified in military personnel in spring 1918. It is estimated that about 500 million people or one-third of the world's population became infected with this virus. The number of deaths was estimated to be at least 50 million worldwide, with about 675,000 occurring in the United States. https://www.cdc.gov/flu/pandemic-resources/ 1918-pandemic-h1n1.html (Accessed on 21st June 2020).

2 This was the worst outbreak of the Plague in England since the black death of 1348. London lost roughly 15% of its population. While 68,596 deaths were recorded in the city, the true number was probably over 100,000. Other parts of the country also suffered. The earliest cases of the disease occurred in the spring of 1665 in a parish outside the city walls called St Giles-in-the-Fields. The death rate began to rise during the hot summer months and peaked in September when 7,165 Londoners died in one week. Rats carried the fleas that caused the plague. They were attracted by city streets filled with rubbish and waste, especially in the poorest areas. https://www.nationalarchives.gov.uk/education/resources/great-plague/ (Accessed on 21st June 2020).

3 The Global Financial Crisis (GFC) was primarily caused by deregulation in the financial industry. This permitted banks to engage in hedge fund trading with derivatives. Banks then demanded more mortgages to support the profitable sale of these derivatives. They created interest-only loans that became affordable to subprime borrowers. In 2004, the Federal Reserve raised the fed funds rate just as the interest rates on these new mortgages reset. Housing prices started falling in 2007 as supply outpaced demand. That trapped homeowners who could not afford the payments, but could not sell their house. When the values of the derivatives crumbled, banks stopped lending to each other. That created the financial crisis in 2008 and later years. https://www.thebalance.com/what-caused-2008-global-financial-crisis-3306176 (Accessed on 21st June 2020).

4 The Great Depression was the worst economic downturn in the history of the industrialised world, lasting from 1929 to 1939. It began after the stock market crash of October 1929, which sent Wall Street into a panic and wiped out millions of investors. Over the next several years, consumer spending and investment dropped, causing steep declines in industrial output and employment as failing companies laid off workers. By 1933, when the Great Depression reached its lowest point, some 15 million Americans were unemployed and nearly half of the country's banks had failed. https://www.history.com/topics/great-depression/ great-depression-history (Accessed on 21st June 2020).

3

SENTIMENT ANALYSIS, BIG DATA AND AI

Big data and AI (artificial intelligence) texts are the foundation for this book

This book on Coronavirus-Related News Sentiment and its impact on markets has close linkage with our previous works on Big Data and Artificial Intelligence (AI). The collection of news on a regular almost real-time basis and the analysis of inherent sentiment is not possible without Big Data and AI tools. After we worked on these texts and explored Big Data and AI applications across diverse fields, we were even more convinced that the implications for financial markets are important, not just because markets react to good or bad news, but also because sentiment would be dynamic and can also be seen differently across different time frames – such as 'short term' versus 'long term'.

For example, imagine a company which is doing well and is also much liked by investors trades at 60× price to earnings multiple – which is a 200% premium to 20× market multiple - will reflect a very strong underlying long-term 'positive' sentiment, but when there is a 'miss' in earnings or some negative development for business, then short-term market sentiment will turn 'negative'. This may last for a few seconds, for a couple of minutes or even for a couple of hours of a trading session or two, but the effect of a 'negative' short-term sentiment will wear off after a while (i.e. after some correction in the stock or underperformance in the market, in all likelihood). Then, the 'long-term' 'positive' sentiment will take over again.

This is relevant in the context of this book in multiple ways including (a) the daily sentiment on the coronavirus could remain negative, but it might have a lower-level negative than yesterday, and that is what the market will focus more on; (b) the 'base rate' will determine if the sentiment is negative or positive on a relative basis, and absolute levels matter much less, and (c) the country-by-country sentiment on the coronavirus will be seen on two parametres – change and status versus others. All of this is dependent on four key factors: (a) the specific kind of news that one is looking for and its relevance,

(b) the most relevant sources for news, (c) the tools one uses for news collection and (d) the sophistication of one's sentiment analysis methods.

Similarly, there are other important inferences that you draw when you read the book, but you get the gist. The higher prevalence of technology and major developments in Big Data and AI have contributed immensely to this endeavour of finding sentiment and the linkage with market movement. There are several important contributing factors: (a) many scientific developments have come together in the new millennium to give technological development a major boost in the field of data, and it has become easier to store an ever-increasing amount of data easily and cheaply; (b) the computational resources have become powerful enough allowing easy access and analysis of this data and as result, over last 20 years, our ability to store, analyse and manipulate tremendous amounts of data has increased by leaps and bounds. This has played a critical role in advancement in Big Data, and it was instrumental in our effort.

The drivers of sentiment analysis

The discussion is incomplete without a commercial angle. Therefore, another interesting area is a rather steep decline in associated costs. The need to own and pay for expensive infrastructure to benefit from Big Data and Analytics has declined considerably with the advent of cloud computing. Moreover, a number of mathematical and statistical tools in Machine Learning have become widely tested and freely available. Access to Big Data, cloud computing and AI-ML (Artificial Intelligence-Machine Leaning) has also become democratised with researchers and companies willing to share information. The easy accessibility to Big Data methods, cloud computing, and computational methods can potentially make the progress even faster in the future for projects similar to what we are doing.

Big Data, computing power and cloud computing, have all been important in making huge amounts of data and enormous computing power available for anyone who is interested. All of these developments may seem unconnected at the first, but these were not only happening simultaneously, but also feeding into each other in some ways. For example, unless there is storage available for large data, the computing capability may not progress that fast or vice versa (i.e. unless you can use and process these large volumes of data with the help of faster, more efficient computing, then the large volumes of data storage may not help). More information also requires a more proactive effort to store, analyse and understand the available data.

Social media and significantly faster dissemination of data and information are also becoming important catalysts for news and sentiment analysis. In the last few decades, the way people source information and get their news and updates have changed. The speed of information dissemination has increased, but the cost of receiving it has had an exponential decline. Another side of this transformation is that easy and instant availability of information has impacted the attention span of people. This means that any piece of news has to compete fiercely with other similar stimuli and has to evolve continuously to stay relevant to investors and market participants.

As a concept, there is nothing new in this. For centuries, access to information and data has been central for the development and growth of civilisation and at the same time, the evolution of humankind. However, it has reached altogether different dimensions in the 21st century as collection, processing and the use of insights developed from unprecedented volumes of data and is redefining all conventional definitions on the way we live. This transformation is not just changing humans' social habits and impacting economic value creation, but it has also become a significant competitive advantage for companies that are at the forefront of this initiative and have been able to benefit from it. The significantly faster dissemination of data and information has immense importance for businesses too, and this will be crucially linked to how financial markets will access it and use it.

'Efficient market hypothesis' versus 'inefficiencies of markets'

There is another aspect of sentiment in news affecting markets and stock prices – the 'Efficient Market Hypothesis' versus 'Inefficiencies of Markets'. If we believe that financial markets are efficient, then the news will affect markets, and every additional news and underlying 'positive' or 'negative' sentiment will get priced in immediately. We cannot comment on how quickly this happens, because we have no way to substantiate this. However, if we think that news will affect prices, then we are discounting the impact of sentiment as well. Wait for a second, are we supporting the Efficient Market Theory? No, we are not, at least not completely. While we believe in the importance of the news in affecting stock prices, it is not necessarily in conflict with believers of inefficient market and investors who think that, with better research and superior insights, one can get an edge over others in the market. However, how will both of these be true at the same time?

When we talk of sentiment's impact on stock price, we are more worried about the direction of impact and less about the quantum of impact. For example, a piece of negative news should ideally lead to a 5% impact – we can always debate if there is any scientific way to estimate how much exactly the impact should be but, honestly, there is none – but the sentiment analysis will tell you about the correction in stock price. It will not be able to exactly estimate if it is 5% or lower (4%) or higher (6%). However, that is acceptable. If we capture the sentiment well and can assess the direction of impact, then 4%, 5% or 6% is fine; these are all equally good. That is what this book is all about. All of us know that the coronavirus has been a disruptive force, and the market impact should be negative. However, there are undercurrents and differences on the basis of country-by-country impact and 'news keywords' impact. That is what we have tried to capture.

More information = more data, more data = more analytics

As we discussed at the beginning of this chapter, more information also requires a more proactive effort to store, analyse and understand the available data. The large data or 'Big Data' has now reached almost every sector in the society and economy. In the case of the economy, it competes with other essential factors of production – such as capital and labour – and, in the context of society, it has become the 'agent of change' for how we interact with one another in the real world and in the virtual world. Nevertheless, we have just scratched the surface on the possibilities that open up because of Big Data. A growing majority of businesses are now seeking to leverage data as a critical strategic asset, helping to uncover new sources of business value, and 'Big Data' is playing a critical role in business strategy.

However, the use of Big Data and analytics transcends across sectors, and it can help in (a) creating more transparency by making information more easily, (b) understanding the ways and means to improve the efficiency and effectiveness of policies and (c) segmenting specific populations to customise actions in order to meet their precise needs. For Big Data applications to be useful, the data needs to be used effectively. The dramatic increase in data storage capacity combined with much faster and efficient computing capabilities has played a critical role in the advancement of Big Data Analytics. This is not to mean that the advanced algorithm is not the backbone, but, without the supporting hardware, that may not have worked. The parallel developments in several areas have contributed to the evolution and growth of Big Data.

How precise is big data inferences?

There are two broad methods of reasoning which are deductive and inductive approaches. These two methods of reasoning are characteristically different. Inductive reasoning is open-ended and exploratory and leads to possibilities hitherto unexplored. While on the other hand, deductive reasoning is narrow and is only concerned with testing and confirming or disproving hypotheses. Big Data Analytics is not a precise science, because it is not based on deductive reasoning and works mostly on inductive reasoning. This makes Big Data prone to mistakes in inferences drawn and, hence, the actionable insights will also vary.

Big Data works on looking at a large set of data followed by pattern recognition and then offering insights and making recommendations. The process is inductive reasoning, and, hence, Big Data is not yet at a stage where it can deliver a 100% foolproof solution. Even when you are interested in employing the services of Big Data, it is not always conventional that it will work in a desired and expected manner. Secondly, the Analytics tools are only as good as the data that they are using. Moreover, there are times when not everything can be captured in data, and not everything which data is capturing will be important.

There are some famous examples when the data collected was not truly representative for the analysis of the problem at hand, and though there was not anything wrong in the data collection and the algorithms used, the net result was nothing short of a disaster. If the insights really have to be useful, then there is a need to apply serious thought before managers and decision-makers can freeze the variables – including what data will be collected, how it will be collected, for how long it will be collected and how it will be processed. 'more data' will not always mean 'better data' or 'more useful data' and the decision-makers need to be wary of these pitfalls.

The path from unstructured data to actionable insights

The typical process for data analytics is as follows: **Unstructured Data –> Data Capture –> Data Sorting –> Structured Data –> Data Analysis –> Actionable Insights –> Predictive Models –> Future Forecast –> Results Evaluation –> Process Modifications.** One of the important issues with Big Data is that the data is so vast that looking for meaningful and actionable reference points is like looking for a needle in a haystack. Moreover, the data will be in an unstructured format, which means that it is hard to see any patterns in it unless it gets sorted and become more structured. If we want to understand and interpret large data, then the data sets must first be made manageable. This is a cumbersome process, and time is of the essence, because the analysis has to be done on a real-time basis, and the recommendations need to be acted upon quickly.

There is another challenge for managers and decision-makers. Every decision has a consequence, and each consequence has several side effects. These unintended, side effects are called second-order effects. Every decision will have these second-order effects, and the managers have to be careful because the decisions may have the opposite effect of what they had aimed for. Big Data Analytics will not be able to shed much light on many of these second-order effects, and it is the responsibility of decision-makers to consider all aspects before they move forward with a decision. This clearly implies that neither Big Data nor analytics can be trusted blindly.

Big data applications: they are everywhere

Amazon is one of the prime examples of analytics success stories. They were early adopters in analysing personal information from customers and use predictive analytics for targeted marketing to increase customer satisfaction to achieve enhanced profitability. Another example is Facebook. Facebook is one of the most valuable public companies in the world – with a market value of hundreds of billions of dollars, because it has so much data. Facebook is not in the business of connecting the world or facilitating your interactions with your friends, rather, it is in the business of data analytics, so that it can use the information it has on you.

There are several more of Big Data success stories ranging from Germany winning the 2014 FIFA World Cup and Big Data helping Barack Obama in winning the United States Presidential Elections. For all of us, it is vital to understand how much customers matter, and there are several possible data points including location, age, past behaviour, interests, activity time, brand interaction, purchasing power, habits and more. The data will help you in more effective and personalised marketing plans that will contribute to the growth of the business. Big Data offers clues to make segmentation and targeting better and more efficient. There are reasons other than commercial reasons as well to feel excited about the potential utilisation of Big Data.

For example, personalised information about an individual – including his or her genetic analysis and DNA analysis – is already being used to detect the likelihood to contract a disease and risk for specific conditions. With the help of this data, people can take preventive steps to avoid the behaviour which might increase their risk of getting a disease or an undesirable medical condition. There are already molecular diagnostics companies that are doing this to make people more aware of their health. These companies offer personalised recommendations based on genetic tests and diagnosis. This is an important and big enhancement in preventive healthcare.

The authorities and governments which have the right intention and want to be accountable are already – and if not, will be shortly – using data to measure everything. Once they have a good handle on data capture and analysis, they will be able to set goals and compare results and accomplishments against expectations or targets. There are already several governments and administrative bodies using data to devise better policies and more effective responses from the administration. If the processes are streamlined, then more data is captured in an efficient manner, and this data is then used to devise better policies without bias. Some of the developing countries in Asia and Africa can benefit much more than developed countries.

No turning back

Big Data is a technology that is leading to serious disruptions and significant changes in how the governments and organisations function. It is also playing a key role even in the case of individuals, either knowingly or unknowingly and whether consciously or unconsciously in making decisions. Big Data has made an impact across industries – including retail, healthcare, the delivery of public services and politics. It has also been observed that, in most cases, the use of Big Data is not a choice anymore. Either you have to get on the bandwagon, or you will be left behind. In the case of companies, apart from the increased top line and better profitability, Big Data is also responsible for creating a competitive advantage and could also be a source of innovation.

However, as it happens with most of the other technologies, there are challenges as well, and most of them are linked with the understanding and implementation of what Big Data can do and what it cannot. There are also cases when vendors lure organisations by making far-fetched promises and setting unrealistic expectations. It is hardly a surprise that many of the Big Data success stories are either sponsored by vendors, or they are examples of sensationalized reporting where the gains and contribution to the bottom line are magnified and exaggerated, if not completely baseless. Hence, we believe that a regular cost-benefit analysis and a follow-up on progress is an absolutely integral part of Big Data Analytics.

Having said this and after we have identified and discussed the important bottlenecks in realising the true potential of Big Data, we need to make a candid admission. Despite the many perils of modern lifestyle, we cannot go back to the lifestyle of the 'caveman', return to the pre-electricity era or stop using air travel and the internet. Similarly, we cannot and will not turn the clock on Big Data. Big Data is not a fad; it is a transformative technological innovation that has solid foundations and an extremely compelling business case. It will not just be able to sustain its importance, but there is also no doubt at all that Big Data will grow in its influence and importance. If there is anything certain about Big Data, it is the fact that it is here to stay and grow.

4

UNSTRUCTURED DATA: HOW TO TAME THE BEAST?

EMAlpha sentiment technology

Sentiment Classifier: We use a standard sentiment classifier. The classifier can use both static dictionaries supplied by the user, as well as create custom dictionaries. The underlying method is similar to what you might read in a standard textbook where the sentiment classifier is typically based on support vector machines. The sentiment classifier can automatically develop a sentiment dictionary as it gets feedback from the end-user. Our dictionary starting point is a simple one based on Loughran-Mcdonald (https://papers.ssrn.com/sol3/papers.cfm?abstract_id=1331573) and our own India-specific proprietary dictionary developed by the EMAlpha Research Team. As we cover more and more countries, we will let our sentiment classifier create enhanced dictionaries for each country. This type of idea is already successfully done in other domains by a number of AI companies. This point (i.e. the sentiment classifier) is also where there is scope for improvement. For example, it looks like neural nets are being applied more and more to the field of natural language processing (NLP).

Filtering: The step above gives us sentiment scores. The calculation of the score is done as follows: The sentiment classifier classifies the words as positive, negative or neutral based on the dictionary. The final sentiment score for the text/document is simply given by sentiment score $= (p-n)/t$, where p is the number of positive words; n is the number of negative words, and t is the total number of words in the text/document. After this, we apply any required filters based on the application. For example, for our trading strategies, we apply a Z-score based on all of the stocks that are being traded. Therefore, if we have 20 stocks that we want to trade, and the raw sentiment score for each stock is s_i, then the Z-scored sentiment score will be given by $z\_i = . (s\_i - \text{mean}(s))/\text{stdev}(s)$, where both the mean and the standard deviation are taken over the 20 stocks for the same day. In our experience, finance users really do not like filters applied to raw data. Accordingly, we are happy to keep the scores raw and to let the users apply their filters. The attached spreadsheet shows both the raw sentiment scores for the stocks with no Z-scoring or any other filtering.

News Collection and Translation: We collect news using our automated scripts and use machine translation to translate local news into English. In other words, we collect news in Chinese, Polish, Spanish, Korean, etc., and use machine translation to translate. This is something rather cutting edge because mass scale machine translation technology is new. Also, based on all of our experience, sentiment analysis done on translated news text maintains its integrity quite well. This also opens up some very interesting questions – such as should sentiment score be 'normalised' to take into account a natural 'sentiment bias' in each language?

Data Collection: News data is collected every morning for each country before the market opens. We currently have a 24-hour look back on news collection, which means that we look at the news flow over last 24 hours. We are working on collecting hourly intraday sentiment data, which would be very exciting.

Out-of-Sample Behaviour: We have about a year and a half's worth of out-of-sample data for India, and we have used it for our EMAlpha Quantitative Trading Strategy for trading Indian stocks. It has worked well. The contemporaneous correlation between sentiment scores and equity returns is quite high, showing that our measurement of sentiment is correct, and the lagged correlation decays slow enough that it can be used for intraday trading strategies.

How Do We Help in Better Investment Decisions: Instead of just blindly generating stock sentiment scores, which we will still do and can be used by any interested party, we would rather understand the final goal first and then work backwards. Once a user defines their objective, then we can design the news/sentiment data collection and the 'experiment'. This sort of user-specific data collection will be more effective than blindly producing the same sentiment score for all.

The major challenges

There are major problems related to accessing information:

- Unavailability of 'information' quickly and in an efficient and easy-to-use format across all countries,
- 'Diversity' of geography, language and culture – from China to the Czech Republic to Chile, and
- 'Language' as a big hurdle as in many countries, the most relevant news flow is in the local language.

What have we done?

- In terms of breadth and depth, we have tracked more than 30 emerging markets on a daily basis.
- In terms of a proprietary dictionary for each country, our domain expertise gives us a real edge in marrying machine capability and human understanding.

Machine sentiment combined with human expertise

- Sentiment analysis is fairly established in developed countries but quite underexplored in emerging and developing countries.
- Sentiment analysis is likely to become more powerful in emerging and developing countries as data analysis there is still not as sophisticated as in developed markets.
- Emerging markets news data collection and sentiment analysis are our focus. Our studies show that sentiment analysis is effective in developing countries and can give good results.
- Each developing country is different. Human expertise is needed to help navigate the details and idiosyncrasies in each country. However, these domain experts can help train the algorithm underlying sentiment analysis.
- Machine translation and sentiment analysis can be combined with human domain expertise. Our studies show that domain experts can improve the quality of results generated by machines.

Part II

THE RESULTS

We would advise the readers to start reading this part of the book from the end (i.e. the last chapter first and so on until you reach the first chapter in this part. This means that first, you read Chapter 8, 'Build-up in February: Come on, Do Not Worry Too Much' and then Chapter 7, followed by Chapter 6 and in the end, the last and fifth chapter, 'Ebbing in May: Are We Celebrating Too Early?' Why? The reason is that this is how it was written, and reading this part in reverse order will build the context in a much better way. If you follow February –> March –> April –> May order, you will follow how the COVID-19 pandemic crisis has actually unfolded.

Even in a particular chapter, it will be good if you read it starting from the end, following the dates. For your convenience, the dates and topics have been highlighted at the beginning of the chapter. Another reason why the reverse order will help is that Part II of the book was written like a diary. The readers will notice that there is a discontinuity in the dates we have the text for and in the topics we discuss. Usually, that is how a diary is. You do not plan what you will write, and, often, you do not write every day. One reason why we did not write this diary daily is that we did not get the chance to do it every day The markets were far more exciting as compared to documenting our thoughts.

In this part and in most of the chapters, there are six things that we track continuously, which we believe cover the market impact comprehensively. These are:

1   **Coronavirus Country-by-Country Sentiment –** This is one of the most important charts because local market reaction depends much more on how the Coronavirus News Sentiment is evolving in that particular region or country. We track both English and local language news to track this sentiment.
2   **Global Coronavirus Sentiment –** The ebbs and flows of optimism and pessimism in global market sentiment on the influence of the growth of

broad trends. The Global Coronavirus Sentiment helps make an educated assessment of how the global markets' reactions might evolve.

3   **News Topic Sentiment** – Certain search terms can help track news sentiments that can potentially evolve into major market themes. Currently, we track the terms 'Donald Trump', 'Dow Jones Index', 'Fed Interest Rate', 'Nasdaq Composite', 'Chinese Economy' and 'US Economy'.

4   **Crude Oil-Related News Sentiment** – Oil sentiment matters for any macro investor. One does not have to look further than how a potential price war between Russia and Saudi Arabia sent shock waves to the global markets. Due to its importance, we track the oil sentiment as a separate stand-alone measure.

5   **Coronavirus Sentiment Heat Map** – Just like most things in life, relative scores matter much more than absolute scores in the case of the Coronavirus News Sentiment. When we do a country-by-country time series analysis for Coronavirus News Sentiment. It is easier to see what is getting better and where the situation is deteriorating. This relative change on two scales – as compared to other countries and versus the immediate past – influences the market direction locally.

6   **Coronavirus Numbers and Statistics** – These statistics help understand the gravity of the situation. Notwithstanding the massive stimulus by the United States Government and the proactive stance of central banks across the world, the fundamental reason behind this crisis has not weakened. In fact, the statistics – as captured by the number of reported cases, the growth rate of cases or the per capita number of COVID-19 reports – keep getting worse. This implies that while the tug-of-war continues between government stimulus and the COVID-19 cases, volatility is here to stay.

5

EBBING IN MAY
'Are We Celebrating Too Early?'

29 **May 2020:** Oil News Sentiment Captures the Firmness in Crude Prices
   16 May 2020: Oil Sentiment: Conflicting Signs from the IEA and Aramco Stock Price
   14 May 2020: Did World Media Underestimate the Coronavirus Crisis in Latin America?
   14 May 2020: Is Oil Sentiment Telling that the Worst of the Coronavirus Is Behind Us?
   10 May 2020: Coronavirus Threat: Who Can Afford a Lockdown and for How Long?
   1 May 2020: Beauty Lies in the Eyes of Beholder, So Does Risk!

29 May 2020: Oil news sentiment captures the firmness in crude prices

We have been closely tracking the oil prices and the EMAlpha Oil Sentiment, and there is something interesting happening there. First, here is a little bit of information on oil prices. The last couple of weeks have been good for crude prices. Around the middle of May, WTI Crude prices started to break out from a US$25 per barrel price range to a higher range. At first, the prices were forming a base at that level. For the last ten days and more, the prices have been consistently above US$30, and they are fairly stable. While upward price movement is important, we think that a fairly consistent and narrow range is equally relevant.

Now comes the more interesting part. The next chart shows the EMAlpha Oil News Sentiment. While the sentiment is volatile, and it should be because it is based on multiple unstructured and varying data points, the sentiment is clearly showing a significant improvement in the last 15 days. As such, the average EMAlpha Oil News Sentiment in May is much more positive than it was in either March or April. In the last two weeks, the volatility also has been on the lower side.

This implies that the news sentiment is doing a good job of making the price forecast. The oil sentiment was having its 'break out' moment at

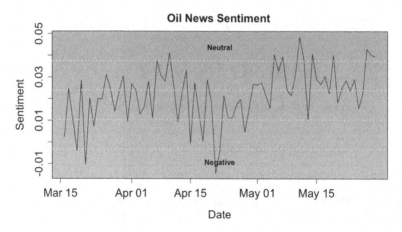

Figure 5.1 EMAlpha Oil News Sentiment (March to May 2020).

around 10 May, and this change in Oil News Sentiment indicated that we are past the worst of the coronavirus crisis, and things will get better from now on. This is exactly how it has turned out. On the basis of the Oil News Sentiment, it is unlikely that oil is going below US$30 in the near term, but we will keep watch.

16 May 2020: Oil sentiment: conflicting signs from the IEA and aramco stock price

One of our most closely tracked sentiments at EMAlpha is on oil news. Over the last few months and as the coronavirus became a global pandemic, concerns on how much crude production the global markets can absorb started rising. However, is the change in Oil News Sentiment telling us that we are past the worst of the coronavirus crisis, and things will get better from now on? We looked at a few other possible signals on what may happen next in the crude oil market. However, the most interesting were two data points that are giving us conflicting signals on the outlook for crude. On 21 April 2020, we had discussed that, despite the turmoil in crude oil prices on Monday, 20 April, the broader outlook was not looking that bad. One of the supporting arguements for this was that the biggest and most profitable oil company's stock price was largely doing fine.

How has the Saudi Aramco stock price done in the last few weeks? If we observe the stock price, it is hardly reflecting any optimism. What could be the reasons for this? The first and most direct explanation is that the investors see that global oil demand is still a concern. The other could be that there is no pricing power with producers, and there is no consensus among major producers on their respective production quotas. Therefore, does the

Saudi Aramco stock price movement tell us that there is a possibility of a pick-up in the demand? No, it does not, at least not really!

The second data point is the International Energy Agency (IEA) was saying a couple of days ago that the outlook for global oil markets has improved.[1] This should be seen as positive, though there are still concerns that while the IEA observes signs of consumption improving, the demand recovery could only be gradual. However, this is a positive data point on oil demand and prices after a disastrous month in April. Effectively, both these data points (i.e. the Saudi Aramco stock price and the IEA demand commentary) are in conflict with each other, and only one can then be a correct indication for what will happen in this market in the coming weeks.

Nevertheless, crude has left the 'negative price' way behind, and, despite uncertainties, the prices have staged a smart recovery. However, have they run ahead of fundamentals now? Only time will tell. While we do not forecast the oil sentiment trajectory, we will keep a close watch on the EMAlpha's Oil Sentiment and keep track of what it indicates on global crude prices. We are entering an exciting territory for sure.

14 May 2020: Did world media underestimate the coronavirus crisis in Latin America?

Joseph Stalin may not have actually said that 'a single death is a tragedy; a million deaths is a statistic'. The case is not very different for the coronavirus crisis, and, while the first few hundred cases were closely monitored by a panicked audience which was hungry for more information, these numbers soon turned into rather impersonal figures appearing on a dashboard. As the number of cases of coronavirus infections swelled from thousands to millions, and the death toll continued to increase beyond hundreds of thousands, the people behind these cases just became numbers.

This is not entirely unexpected often because (a) the effect of stimulus wanes with an increase in frequency and with more regular occurrence; (b) the stories involving real people are more powerful in making a connection rather than dry numbers; (c) there is a built-in defence system in use which, after a while, makes us completely immune to negative news. However, there was still something very disturbing when we looked at our daily news collection on the impact of the coronavirus pandemic. While the tragedy was big and the situation was grim in countries like Italy and Spain in Europe and the United States of America in North America, the news flow on the coronavirus pandemic was only a mild trickle in South America and in countries like Brazil, Peru and others.

While EMAlpha machines were collecting the news and doing sentiment analysis, we were struggling to figure out what was happening here. Is it because the coronavirus was impacting European countries and the United States much more than it was in South America, or was it because there was not much news coming from South America while the tragedy unfolding there was equally serious? After tracking the news from around the world and from more than 30 countries for a considerable period now, the evidence is conclusive that it was the latter, unfortunately. The effect of the coronavirus pandemic on South America was equally bad, if not worse than other parts of the world, and countries like Brazil, Peru and Ecuador were struggling, but there was not much news coming from there.

There could have been multiple reasons: (a) people were not very confident about the state's ability to provide healthcare support and were not reporting cases despite being in a bad shape; (b) the level of testing was very low and not all infected patients with symptoms were being tested for COVID-19 infection; (c) this was creating a false sense of confidence among authorities, and the lockdown norms were not being implemented stringently, thus, making the situation even worse. The net result was that, expectedly, the coronavirus was as fatal in South America as it was in New York, Milan or Madrid, but, still, the channels of news were not reporting the on-ground situation adequately.

When we look at the effectiveness of the 'lockdown strategy' versus a country's ability to afford it and key factors such as the size of the economy and wealth distribution over the population, are there different conclusions from different geographies? How the coronavirus pandemic tragedy has unfolded showcases that threat perception[2] does not follow logic, and the government's response is influenced more by perception and sentiment. Government policies on lockdowns have been determined more by threat perception than the ability to afford it.

There are other cases as well where the lower level of threat perception made the crisis look less serious than it actually was, and the policymakers were casual about it. Brazil is a prime example where the president himself has shown little regard for scientific evidence and the need for social distancing.[3] The response to the coronavirus pandemic from Brazil is an interesting case. While most countries went for 'lockdowns' to contain the spread of the virus, the Brazilian President Jair Bolsonaro continued to downplay the COVID-19 situation with his comments and actions. While the pandemic has not been kind to Brazilians, and there is no indication that the curve for the spread of the coronavirus and new infections is any different for Brazil versus other countries, Bolsonaro has continued to ignore the statistics for a very long time. However, it was reported that, after he himself was tested as COVID-19 positive, he started following the norms on wearing a mask and maintaining social distancing.[4]

The EMAlpha analysis of news and underlying sentiment indicates that, while the coronavirus is not partial, news coverage surely is. This directly impacts sentiment on threat perception and how serious the crisis will appear in the different parts of the world. The contrast between how the world thinks about the impact of the coronavirus pandemic in Europe and the United States versus South America speaks a lot about the supremacy of underlying news sentiment over actual facts. This shapes several factors including the local government's response, foreign aids to deal with the crisis and global sympathy for affected countries – in summary, how effectively countries will fight COVID-19 and how efficiently they will be in their response.

This also has important inferences for financial markets. Sometimes - or rather, more often than not – the news follow is dominated by events in particular geography because of simple reasons like proximity, the ease of access for journalists and the availability of more information from there. This makes the investors' decision-making skewed, because the mindshare that the news command is not always proportional to the ideal relative importance of events. However, if the investors allow machines to capture the news and do the sentiment analysis, then they may pick up the signals early and also differentiate between pure noise from useful signals in the news. For sure, there are several places where understanding the news sentiment can really help.

14 May 2020: Is oil sentiment telling that the worst of the coronavirus is behind Us?

One of the most closely tracked sentiments at EMAlpha is on oil. This is not just important in assessing how the impact of the coronavirus pandemic is playing out, but also how much confidence people have on the recovery of global manufacturing and transportation. All of this is closely linked to global energy demand and the price of crude oil. The short-term price movement in crude depends on the near-term outlook for oil – which is influenced heavily by the news flow sentiment.

Over the last few months, as the coronavirus became a global pandemic and the disease became much more serious than what the present generation has ever seen, concerns started rising on how much crude production the global markets can absorb. If we mostly go by the prevailing sentiment, then the demand is unlikely to pick up anytime soon. That is bad news for crude oil prices too, and that is bad news for the global markets. The only thing we were hoping for is a turnaround in news sentiment, but let us see how long that takes.

The month of April was particularly bad for the global crude oil market, and the volatility was unprecedented with prices falling below zero for the first time in history. In our writings, *Oil's Historic Fall: Precipitated by Quickly Worsened Sentiment?* on 22 April 2020 and *Crude and Coronavirus: Oil Futures in Negative and Key Implications* on 21 April 2020, we had discussed the most bizarre price movement in oil futures. As May WTI futures traded in negative, the event was a big negative for demand revival hopes.

· It was an unprecedented event when the price of a barrel of benchmark United States oil plunged below US$0 a barrel on Monday, 20 April 2020 for the first time in history. The contract for West Texas intermediate (WTI) crude is the benchmark for United States crude oil prices. The price of a barrel of crude varies based on factors such as supply, demand and quality. The supply of fuel was above demand since the coronavirus forced lockdowns across several economies. Because of oversupply, storage tanks for the WTI are becoming so full that it is difficult to find space.[5]

However, the question now is whether things are changing. As you can see in the following chart, the oil sentiment is having its 'break out' moment. While for the last week, the sentiment has been more positive than most days since the beginning of March (i.e. it is in the top ten percentile consistently, with only a couple of exceptions), the Oil News Sentiment has scaled its new peak on 11 May 2020. This is an entirely different picture from what we had seen in the month of April.

Is this change in Oil News Sentiment telling us that we are past the worst of the coronavirus crisis, and things will get better from now on? Conversely, is this just false hope, as people have gotten tired of too much bad news? While we do not forecast the oil sentiment trajectory, we think that it is possible that, at least for this phase of the coronavirus pandemic transmission, things have started to look up. Many countries, and even the worst affected ones, have started to come out of lockdown, and the two largest economies of the world - the United States and China – are certainly at a stage where they are less worried about the coronavirus and more about economic revival. We will keep a close watch on EMAlpha's Oil Sentiment and see if this positive momentum in oil sentiment indicates a solid turnaround or is just giving us false hopes.

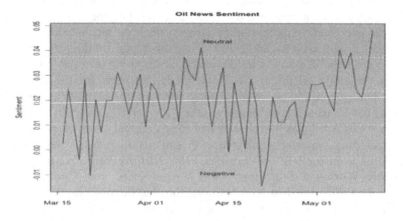

Figure 5.2 Daily Oil-Related News Sentiment (March to mid-May).

10 May 2020: Coronavirus threat: who can afford a lockdown and for how long?

All across the world, countries are dealing with coronavirus pandemic scare differently. However, the most popular and common strategy is the 'lockdown.' Although, is each country's government's proactive stance dependent on threat perception? When we analyse our country-by-country sentiment scores for our news collection, we find that there are significant differences in the tone and frequency of Coronavirus-Related News Flow. Nonetheless, what is even more surprising is that some of the countries that are nowhere close to the disastrous impact that some other countries have seen are still more scared.

We agree that we are using the word 'scared' loosely, but what we are really measuring is the negativity of news flow. While it would be a big surprise that two countries at different levels of threat perception do not have much difference in their coronavirus factual report card, the bigger questions are: (a) Are some countries overconfident and suffer as a result such as the United States of America, Italy or Brazil? (b) Are some other countries worrying unnecessarily – for example, Turkey or Japan? (c) Are there countries that have relaxed the lockdown stipulations too early, such as Germany?

This could be because of multiple reasons such as (a) the countries may worry more when they are relatively less developed and where the healthcare infrastructure is in poor shape. When people know that even a mighty superpower like the United States of America has struggled to meet even the most basic healthcare needs of what the coronavirus pandemic demanded, then the excess worry seems rational. Also, (b) people in some countries respect their authorities a lot more.

Apart from it being a healthcare emergency, the economic cost of the coronavirus pandemic is staggering. What is hurting almost equally and even more is the cost of a lockdown, and the tragedy is that this cost will be

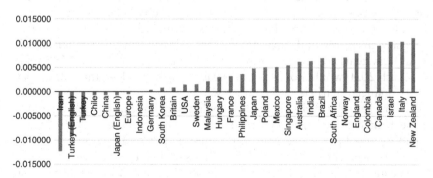

Figure 5.3 Average Sentiment for Coronavirus (EMAlpha Country-by-Country Sentiment).

borne more by the segment which can afford it the least - the poor people like daily wage labourers and workers in unorganised segments. Two questions are still unanswered. The first is that just how much worry is rational? When you worry less than you should, then you become careless and, at the same time, when you worry too much and more than you should, then you lose opportunities.

The second is that does a country's ability to afford a lockdown depends on its economy - both in size as well as in wealth distribution over the population. What does this mean? (a) A rich country can afford a lock-down longer than a poor country can, and (b) a rich country but one with high wealth distribution inequality can afford it less than an equally wealthy, or even less wealthy, country which has more equality. However, threat perception does not follow these rules and neither does government response. The government policy on lockdowns will be determined more by threat perception rather than the ability to afford it, and that is where the problem lies. Unfortunately, there are no easy answers and no easy solutions to this.

1 May 2020: Beauty lies in the eyes of the beholder, so does risk!

This has been an exciting week for markets, and we will do a follow up on our recent writing on 30 April, 'News Sentiment Impact on Markets Back in Business?' which had also mentioned our 9 April write up, 'Is the Fed Making Data On Fundamentals Irrelevant For Markets?' These focused more on the dichotomy between fundamentals and market performance over the last six to eight weeks – more specifically, about how the signals from the fundamentals of economy (e.g. jobless claims) are linked with market movement.

There are important points like (a) what are the options investors have and need to invest somewhere or others, (b) when circumstances change, the perceptions also change and the risk appetite is linked to market cir-cumstances. When central banks are responding globally with powerful monetary measures and governments are releasing massive financial sti-mulus in systems across the world, the 30% plus recovery in S&P 500 since 23 March 2020 would not look that strange.[6] More or less, this is the story across financial markets in the entire world.

The market rally is closely linked to what happened in the bond markets in the United States. The Federal Reserve announced on 9 April that it would include lower-rated debt in its latest asset-purchasing programme.[7] The announcement was followed by billions of dollars of inflow into funds specialising in high-yield debt – this will be low quality, by definition. The Fed was also buying bonds that were downgraded and no longer investment grade. The European Central Bank adopted the same policy and effectively, the associated risk with more risky investments was artificially lowered by central banks.

What does this do? We think that the signalling mechanism by central banks is a very powerful tool on how to change the risk perception by market participants. By these measures, when a central banker is telling investors that it is acceptable to indulge in high-risk investments, then investors would think like this, 'Yes, it makes sense. What I gain is mine and if lose something, there is someone to share these losses, so, let me add a little more of the high yield, low-quality investments'. Effectively, central banks were lowering the risks of low quality globally, or, in other words, financial assets and investments that will be impacted more by the coronavirus pandemic crisis. This, to a large extent, has been a driving force for markets.

How long can this can continue? In a way and theoretically speaking, this can continue forever, or until the time people have faith in the Fed or in their respective central banks, but practically, the momentum will swing again when investors think that the rewards have become lesser compared to risks after the sharp run-up in prices. How far are we from that point, or have we already crossed it? No one knows, but the belief is still strong that there is more firepower available with the Fed, and that perception alone can support the markets.

...

The month of May has been different in the news flow in several ways: (a) Oil News Sentiment continued to recover, and there was more firmness in prices; (b) the world media coverage was very different across geographies on the coronavirus pandemic; (c) the global markets moved forward indicating that the worst of the coronavirus crisis is behind us and is strongly supported by global liquidity; (d) there has also been a debate on who can afford a lockdown and for how long; (e) overall, the preference has globally shifted to more risky assets.

Notes

1 25 May 2020. 'IEA: Oil market outlook improved, major uncertainties remain.' *Oil and Gas Journal*. https://www.ogj.com/general-interest/article/14176921/ iea-oil-market-outlook-improved-major-uncertainties-remain (Accessed on 28th May 2020).
2 Threat perception – the conscious or unconscious estimation that something or someone is dangerous – is a basic mental faculty. Political science has long acknowledged that perceived danger can motivate politically relevant behaviour and attitudes. However, existing theories only partially integrate findings from biology and cognitive science regarding the processing of danger in the mind and brain. The result is an incomplete, and sometimes misleading, picture of the relationship between threat perception and political behaviour. http://www. marikalandau-wells.com/threat-perception (Accessed on 28th May 2020).
3 Jessica A.J. Rich. May 4, 2020. 'While Brazil's president fights social distancing, its public health system is fighting the pandemic'. The Washington Post.

https://www.washingtonpost.com/politics/2020/05/04/while-brazils-president-fights-social-distancing-its-public-health-system-is-fighting-pandemic/ (Accessed on 14th July 2020).

4 July 13, 2020. 'Jair Bolsonaro seen outside the Presidential palace wearing mask, maintaining social distancing'.

5 Laila Kearney. April 21, 2020. 'What is a negative crude future and does it mean anything for consumers?' Reuters. https://in.reuters.com/article/global-oil-crash-explainer/what-is-a-negative-crude-future-and-does-it-mean-anything-for-consumers-idINKBN2230A4 (Accessed on 14th July 2020).

6 S&P 500® https://www.spglobal.com/spdji/en/indices/equity/sp-500/#overview (Accessed on 14th July 2020).

7 Christopher Condon, Rich Miller, and Craig Torres. April 9, 2020. 'Fed to Buy Junk Bonds, Lend to States in Fresh Virus Support'. Bloomberg. https://www.bloomberg.com/news/articles/2020-04-09/fed-unleashes-fresh-steps-for-as-much-as-2-3-trillion-in-aid (Accessed on 14th July 2020).

6

THE DEADLY APRIL

'Blame Game and Search for
a Coronavirus Vaccine'

30 April 2020: Is the 'News Sentiment Impact' on Markets Back in Business?

27 April 2020: Oil, Again

22 April 2020: Oil's Historic Fall: Precipitated by Quickly Worsened Sentiment?

21 April 2020: Crude and Coronavirus: Oil Futures in Negative for the First Time in History and Its Key Implications

20 April 2020: Markets and Coronavirus Sentiment: The Battle between Optimism and Pessimism

17 April 2020: News Sentiment on Donald Trump Does Not Matter for Markets? No, It Does Not - Not Really?

15 April 2020: Is Trump Losing the Perception Battle in Media and Why Does this Matter for Markets?

9 April 2020: Is the Fed Making Data on Fundamentals Irrelevant for Markets?

8 April 2020: Why Does Local News-Based Sentiment Analysis Matter?

6 April 2020: Coronavirus: Darkest Before the Dawn or No Light at the End of the Tunnel?

1 April 2020: Coronavirus Sentiment versus Aggregate Market Sentiment and the Base Rate

30 April 2020: Is the 'news sentiment impact' on markets back in business?

Over the last few weeks, the debate on the dichotomy between the fundamentals of economy and the direction of financial markets has been at its peak. In a related discussion in our 9 April write up, 'Is the Fed Making Data On Fundamentals Irrelevant For Markets?', we also had spoken about how the signals from the fundamentals of economy – such as jobless claims – and what the Fed is doing are pulling the financial markets in the United States in opposite directions.

In this context, the impact of Jobless Claims News Flow on markets is interesting. In the morning of the United States of America time on 30 April, it was reported that another 3.8 million Americans filed for unemployment benefits last week – sending the six-week total above 30 million since the coronavirus pandemic started to impact United States economy. The news that initial jobless claims were 3.84 million in the week ended on 25 April following 4.44 million in the prior week. This 3.84 million figure was almost 10% more than expected.[1]

While a 1.5% decline in S&P 500 is not much, it is still against the trend of the week as well as the month. For a while, the arguement was that the coronavirus' impact was on prices, and it was the Fed's action that was much bigger than anticipated and was the driving force behind market's movement. Is the reaction of S&P 500 to jobless claims an indication that this arguement is reversing? Is this the Fed action on prices already while the coronavirus impact could be worse, and will that matter for markets?

It is too early to claim that. However, the next few weeks will be interesting. Will the United States economy's fundamentals get worse? Will this impact the markets negatively? Will the Fed start doing more to address that? There are many questions and little clarity, but news sentiment will be interesting to watch for sure.

27 April 2020: Oil, again

Monday, 20 April was a historic day for crude oil industry, but, not in a good way. The May United States oil futures contract went into negative territory for the first time in history. The reserves are full and there is simply no place to store more crude oil, and almost everyone is avoiding accepting delivery of physical crude. Eventually, the contract crashed to an unimaginable –US$37.63 a barrel – a decline of US$55.90 a barrel! Prices also set a historic low of –US$40.32 during the day.

However, it is not just about a storage problem. While that may be an issue for the May contract, the bigger and more fundamental and structural concern is regarding demand. The global oil demand is down by more than 30% due to the coronavirus pandemic, and the lockdowns in several countries. The June contract also ended down 16% to US$20.43 a barrel. While this is in positive territory, a 16% decline is huge, and the prices are low in absolute terms as well.

This is visible on the EMAlpha Oil News Sentiment tracker as well. While the market movements like 20 April's are related to specific reasons like storage issues, the general sentiment on the demand side is extremely negative. As you can notice from our oil sentiment chart (Fig. 6.1), this is at the lowest levels after the impact on sentiment seen during the dip in March because of supply glut expected as a result of the price war between Russia and Saudi Arabia.

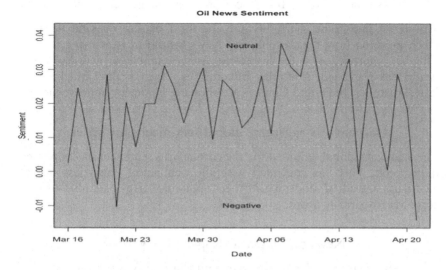

Figure 6.1 EMAlpha Oil Sentiment Hit All Time Low on 20 April.
Source: Courtesy of EMAlpha.

Should we equate this with what could happen in the global economy and other financial markets worldwide? No, we should not, not really – at least not immediately. The first reason is that the May futures contract – contracts to buy or sell a quantity at a designated price and time (i.e. contracts for assets, especially commodities or shares, bought at agreed prices but delivered and paid for later) – in negative territory was more related to a specific challenge associated with how to accept delivery when there is no storage. Second, the impact on oil demand is already factored in to some extent, and markets are not pricing in a big recovery in the short term. Third, for some countries that are net importers – like India and China – it will be a mixed impact with some positives along with some negatives.

There are two more data points which will support what we are saying. The first is Saudi Aramco's stock price or the stock price between SAR 25 to SAR 30 during March and April 2020. The biggest and most profitable oil company in the world is under stress, either because of very low liquidity or less market focus on what happens in the next few months, but the stock price is largely doing fine. The other is S&P 500. It fell following the oil crash, but, considering whatever has been happening in the markets in terms of volatility over the last few months, the fall was by no means exceptional. This implies that markets are less worried, and the concern is limited to oil only. However, it is surely interesting and we need to keep an eye on this.

Coronavirus country-by-country sentiment time series

This is an important chart, because the local market reaction depends much more on how the Coronavirus News Sentiment is evolving locally. This has improved over the last week, as the number of new cases and deaths has plateaued. A number of countries – such as the United States, Italy, Australia, India and China – are showing sentiment improvement.

Coronavirus aggregate global sentiment time series

The aggregate global sentiment on the coronavirus sentiment has improved quite a bit. This has coincided with the number of countries starting to discuss a gradual reopening of their economies, as the number of new coronavirus patients drops.

News sentiment for topical keywords

Because markets are influenced by the sentiment for news flow around some very important and immensely popular keywords, the results are important for market direction. The news sentiment is in the deep negative territory for the United States President Donald Trump. His recent coronavirus briefings fiasco[2] most certainly has been a big contributor to this negative

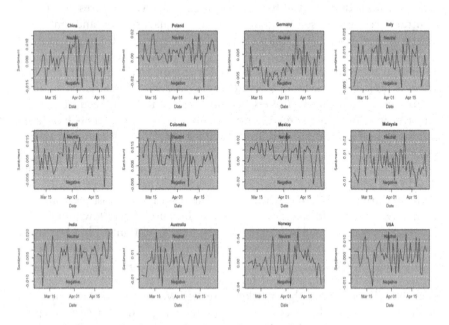

Figure 6.2 Country-By-Country Sentiment Score for Select Countries Focusing on Coronavirus-Related News.

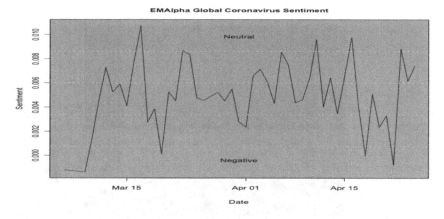

Figure 6.3 Aggregate Coronavirus Global Sentiment.

sentiment. The United States Economy Sentiment has also been quite negative, notwithstanding the fact that the United States stock market did not really take much of a beating as oil fell.

Crude oil news sentiment

As we discussed above, the EMAlpha Oil News Sentiment hit an all time low on 20 April. It has, however, recovered quite a bit since last Monday, as the oil price quickly rebounded back to its Monday morning level. A high level of oil price volatility should be expected in the coming weeks.

Aggregate india equity market sentiment

Even though there were a few positive movements in the Indian equity market and Facebook decided to invest US$5.7 billion in Reliance Jio last week, the overall sentiment is still low.[3] The EMAlpha Sentiment Score for the Indian Market continues to struggle.

22 April 2020: Oil's historic fall: Precipitated by quickly worsened sentiment?

As we highlighted in our previous write-up on crude oil and its link with the coronavirus pandemic, 'Crude and Coronavirus: Oil Futures in Negative for the First Time in History and Key Implications', the most bizarre price movement was oil futures this week. As May WTI futures traded in negative, the historic fall in crude oil prices prompted us to investigate this issue further – in particular, with how Oil News Sentiment fared around that time. However before that, here is a little bit of background.

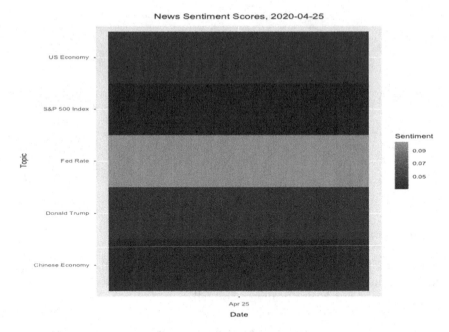

Figure 6.4 News Sentiment for Select Topical Search Terms.

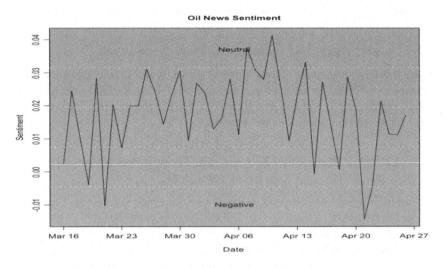

Figure 6.5 Daily Oil-Related News Sentiment (March and April 2020).

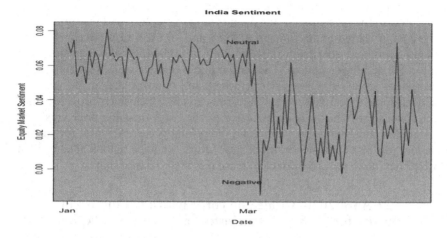

Figure 6.6 India Equity Market Sentiment Signal.

In our 2 March 2020 update, we had discussed the sudden fall in Indian Equity Markets. In the last hour and a half on that day, the NIFTY 50 Index lost more than 3% – admittedly, this currently does not look significant after 3–4% intraday moves have become normal in last few weeks. However remember, this was the first of March, before the exceptional market volatility had taken over the markets. The markets were in green and going strong, but this move was completely unexpected and very quick.

However, how did that happen on 2 March in the India Market? The fall was caused by news that two fresh cases of the coronavirus were detected in India. There was absolutely nothing else which could have explained such a drastic fall in the NIFTY 50 Index other than the news on the coronavirus. As we have seen, after the coronavirus had become a global issue, the market performance in several countries became strongly linked with local news flow and underlying sentiment on the coronavirus-related developments. This is what we have been tracking in our newsletters too. The latest one is 'Markets and Coronavirus Sentiment: The Battle between Optimism and Pessimism' on 20 April 2020.

Now look at this in the context of the fall of crude oil. The Oil News Sentiment plot for 20 April shows how the oil sentiment has fallen to a level lower than what it was in mid-March or when the Saudi-Russia talks broke down, and oil prices and the stock market fell. It is possible that the sentiment might also have sharply fallen before the oil crash. To see if that may have been the case, we looked at the change in daily oil sentiment from positive to negative. The point is that, due to the oil crash, the EMAlpha Daily Oil Sentiment went from positive to negative. To make it easier, we have rescaled these three things: (a) sentiment, (b) trends search result and (c) price.

For the ease of comparison, we multiplied the oil sentiment by a factor of 2000, so the oil sentiment for the morning of the 20th and the morning of the 21st in United States time are 0.0185 and –0.0143 respectively. The Oil News Sentiment goes from 0.0185*2000 to –0.0143*2000. Therefore, we have rescaled the sentiment. The bottomline is that we see a clear collapse in sentiment around the time prices crashed, and this was also linked with the sudden spike in searches for 'oil'. It is too early to conclusively prove whether the spike in searches was an indicator of the crash or if the price crash led to sudden surge. However, this is an interesting occurrence and, for sure, it cannot just be a coincidence. In the near future, we hope to look at some high frequency news sentiment data to tease out these relationships.

21 April 2020: Crude and coronavirus: Oil futures in negative for the first time in history and its key implications

There is limited visibility as of now when the oil demand will recover, and this is putting a huge pressure on producers who are still bickering on proposed production cuts. For many of them, oil exports are a significant part of their revenues, and they cannot seem to easily agree on who needs to cut production to bring back some stability in prices. The low demand and low crude prices actually made some of them more desperate in their attempts to increase production and gain market share.

This is visible on the EMAlpha Oil News Sentiment tracker as well. While the market movements like Monday's are related to specific reasons like storage issues, the general sentiment on the demand side is extremely negative. As you would probably notice from the chart, this is at the lowest levels after the impact on sentiment seen during the dip in March because of supply glut expected as a result of price war between Russia and Saudi Arabia.

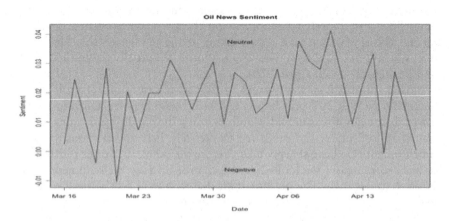

Figure 6.7 EMAlpha Oil News Sentiment.

Should we equate this with what could happen in global economy and other financial markets worldwide? No, we should not, not really – at least not immediately. The first reason is that the May futures in negative was more related to a specific challenge associated with how to accept delivery when there is no storage. Second, the impact on oil demand is already factored in, to some extent, and markets are not pricing in a big recovery in the short term. Third, for some countries which are net importers – like the United States, China and India – it will be a mixed impact with some positives along with some negatives.

20 April 2020: Markets and the coronavirus sentiment: The battle between optimism and pessimism

Just like everyone else, we are also struggling to figure out until when the divergence between sentiment on coronavirus-related parametres and market performance may continue. This week was also very good for S&P 500 – because it has now gained more than 25% in less than a month – and more or less, this is the situation elsewhere too. Most markets are up by at least 15–20%, and we are now far away from the lows of March.

However, this is only half of the story. The on-ground situation on the coronavirus seems to be telling something very different. On Global Coronavirus News Sentiment and Country-By-Country Coronavirus Sentiment, things continue to deteriorate. Except for a few exceptions like the United States of America and China, most countries are struggling to contain infections, and the statistics are plummeting. Similarly, the Global Coronavirus Sentiment has deteriorated sharply this week.

Why does the market seem to not be perturbed? There could be multiple reasons including (a) it had corrected much more than it should have; (b) the Fed is injecting so much liquidity in the system, and that is driving the markets; (c) the coronavirus news are already priced in, and things have actually improved in worst affected countries – such as China, Spain and Italy. Whatever it may be, the deteriorating news sentiment on the coronavirus has not made much impact on markets.

The details and inferences from the coronavirus and news sentiment

The discussion on the six parametres is as follows: (a) Coronavirus Country-by-Country Sentiment Time Series, (b) Coronavirus Aggregate Global Sentiment Time Series, (c) Daily Coronavirus Sentiment Heat Map for Countries, (d) News Topic Sentiment for Keywords, (e) Crude Oil News Sentiment and, (f) Aggregate India Equity Markets Sentiment.

Coronavirus country-by-country sentiment time series

This is one of the most important charts, because market reaction locally depends much more on how the Coronavirus News Sentiment is evolving locally. This has deteriorated a bit versus last week, and this week with 9 out of 12 countries reflecting deterioration versus 8 out of 12 countries last week. The good news is that both the United States of America and China – the most important affected countries - show considerable improvement.

Coronavirus aggregate global sentiment time series

The aggregate global sentiment on coronavirus sentiment has deteriorated sharply as there are talks about a 'W-shaped' infection trajectory[4] and possibilities of the next coronavirus wave. This deterioration is at odds with the improvement in the United States of America and China. The more important takeaway is that the deterioration is rather sharp, and Global Coronavirus Sentiment is at the lowest level seen in more than a month. This is not good news.

Daily coronavirus sentiment heat map for countries

The sentiment has gotten better in Canada, China and Sweden, but things do not look that good in India, Iran, Korea and Poland. There is a dichotomy here as the heat map on an aggregate basis looks better in general

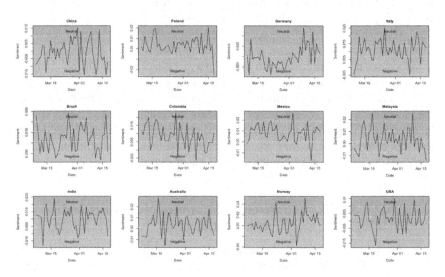

Figure 6.8 Country-By-Country Sentiment Score for Select Countries Focusing on Coronavirus-Related News.

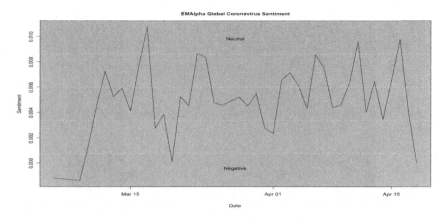

Figure 6.9 Aggregate Coronavirus-Related News Sentiment.

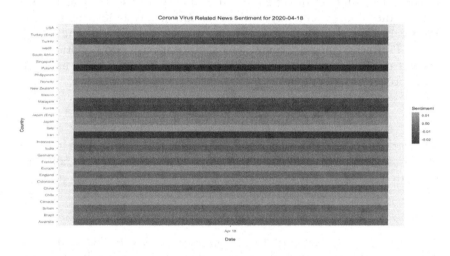

Figure 6.10 Coronavirus-Related News Sentiment Heat Map.

than how it looked last week. While, as we discussed previously, the Global Coronavirus Sentiment has deteriorated sharply and on a country-by-country basis, there has been a worsening of sentiment. We have no idea why this should be the case.

News topic sentiment for keywords

Because markets are influenced by the sentiment for news flow around some very important and immensely popular keywords, the results are

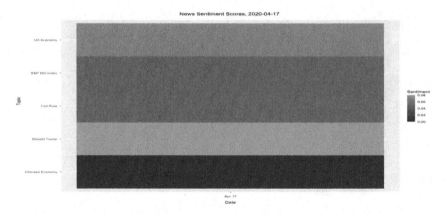

Figure 6.11 News Sentiment for Select Topical Search Terms.

important for market direction. There is a very high level of pessimism around the Chinese economy, and this situation was almost the same as last week. The big swing continues to be on news sentiment around United States President Donald Trump. The sentiment on Trump continues to swing from one extreme to another week after week, and, there has been an improvement this time.

Crude oil news sentiment

The markets are negative on demand environment, as reports from multiple countries continue to realize how consumption and demand have fallen off the cliff.

Aggregate india equity markets sentiment

This is now operating in a narrow band, and, in line with this change, the market has become much less volatile. Overall, we do not think the change in the India Market Sentiment is significant this week.

17 April 2020: News sentiment on donald trump does not matter for markets? no, it does not – not really?

On our previous note, 'Is Trump Losing the Perception Battle in Media and Why Does this Matter for Markets?', we had written that how sentiment from news flow on United States President Donald Trump had quickly worsened and why that may be important for the direction of markets. The perception that Trump has handled the 'corona crisis' poorly has been fairly strong in media, and our point was that this could hurt the markets.

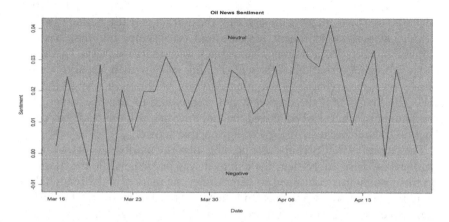

Figure 6.12 Daily Oil-Related News Sentiment.

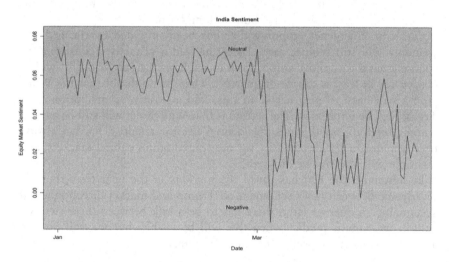

Figure 6.13 Aggregate India Equity Markets Sentiment.

One arguement against this logic was that there is absolutely no link between 'Trump' and 'United States markets'. On the contrary, while Trump may be doing badly on news flow sentiment, the markets have been doing rather well. After the market hit bottom on 23 March, S&P 500 has gained 25% and during this time, (a) the coronavirus crisis has worsened significantly in the United States; (b) the common perception is that the handling of this major health and economic challenge by the United States President has not been optimal. How do we explain that, and why do we say that Trump matters for market?

Yes, there is a dichotomy here. When you look at the broader market (i.e. S&P 500 or Dow), there is no sign that the market is really bothered about Trump. The news sentiment may be bad on Trump, but that has not stopped markets from staging a very quick and smart recovery. Therefore, can we conclude that markets and Trump will go their separate ways. However, there are reasons why that may not be the right way to look at this. The first is that the market is not responding to Trump, rather, it is responding to what the Fed hads done and how the 'risk on' trade has come back in flavour because of the Fed's proactive stance.

The second is that perhaps it is possible that the market has priced in the coronavirus crisis more than the extent it was needed. While the numbers on the coronavirus continued to deteriorate, the market had already fallen more than what was warranted and, hence, started to recover. The third is that, since the market is still more than 15% below its February peak, the impact of the coronavirus has not been ignored by the markets despite the Fed injecting so much of liquidity and buying all kinds of risky assets. However, none of this means that markets can continue to ignore the sentiment on Trump over a medium to long term.

Once the emergency response that has been provided by the Fed, the economy will still require careful steering and a proactive, consistent response from the administration. Even in the best-case scenario, this will be needed for at least a couple of quarters. There is no doubt that the White House will have to play a role in this, and a positive contribution from Trump will be important. The second is that Wall Street will still be eagerly waiting for the United States presidential election results. That has always been a major factor of curiosity for the United States capital markets, and this time will also not be different.

In summary, the Fed has saved the markets in the near term, but the divergence between news sentiment on Trump and market direction is not sustainable. Sooner or later, there has to be a link between these two. Of course, we cannot predict when this will be visible, but we will not bet against this to last for very long, in all certainty.

15 April 2020: Is trump losing the perception battle in media and why does this matter for markets?

Our news sentiment tracker over last 15 days tells us that news flow on United States President Donald Trump had quickly worsened, and it has worsened significantly. On 6 April, we wrote 'Because markets are influenced by the sentiment for news flow around some very important and immensely popular keywords, the results are important for market direction. The biggest positive jump is seen for United States President Donald Trump'. However, things have changed completely on news sentiment for Trump a week later. There was a sharp dip in sentiment in media coverage on Trump and the way he is handling the coronavirus crisis – both in terms of his ability and intent.

This was peculiar for two reasons. The first is that in the past, United States presidents have mostly benefitted from crises, and difficult situations have usually worked for them politically as well as from the media coverage's point of view. It happened with FDR during the Second World War, with JFK during the Cuban Missile Crisis, with Bush Senior during the First Gulf War (although he lost his re-election bid for different reasons, such as poor record on economy which was brilliantly exploited by Bill Clinton) and with Bush Junior during 9/11.[5]

The other is that the coronavirus crisis has helped the majority of global leaders in getting a strong boost in their image. It has helped the President of France – Emmanuel Macron and also Japanese Prime Minister – Shinzo Abe. This is the situation elsewhere too. The crisis has not done anything to dent the image of Justin Trudeau in Canada, Narendra Modi in India or Boris Johnson in UK. Even Angela Merkel from Germany and Vladimir Putin from Russia also have not been doing too badly.

While it is true that we do not know much about the impact on Xi Jinping - the President of China, as it is too early to understand because of the lack of credible data from the country. The only exception could be Jair Bolsonaro of Brazil because of his poor handling and more so because of his irresponsible media statements about the potential negative impact of the coronavirus as a health emergency.[6] Overall, it is safe to say that the coronavirus crisis may have been a health crisis or economic crisis; however, it has not been a political crisis for most global leaders who are at home with these problems so far.

Then, why it is happening with Trump and why is the coronavirus crisis also a media crisis for him? While it is always easy to look at reasons with the benefit of hindsight, the inconsistent approach, underestimation of the crisis and rushing to lift the lockdown could have been the key factorss in making Trump an easy media target and for this thought to resonate with the common people. In short, the sentiment in news on Trump is negative, because the media has been highlighting how Trump has failed to show true leadership and has been by and large evasive in his approach.

Why is this important for markets? There are two reasons: (a) how Trump is in handling the coronavirus crisis is important for the United States markets over next few weeks; (b) though it is too early to talk about this and the core voter base of Trump may still remain unaffected, the negative news sentiment may play a role in the United States presidential elections if it sustains. The race will be close; there is no doubt, and even a small swing could change the end result. Markets have been kind to Trump so far, and if Biden gets elected, then that may be a big negative for the United States markets. It is too early to confirm, but this is an interesting scenario nonetheless.

9 April 2020: Is the fed making data on fundamentals irrelevant for markets?

The Fed is clearly on an overdrive these days, and it is doing 'whatever it takes'. The coronavirus pandemic has clearly made the United States Central Bank extremely active, and it began with an announcement of emergency interest rate cut in the first week of March. Now, interest rates have become almost zero, and the Fed is also doing big-scale asset purchases. Since 2008 when Quantitative Easing (QE) proved effective in averting a huge disaster during Global Financial Crisis (GFC),[7] QE has become a 'tool of choice' for the Fed.

The Fed not only brings down the longer term interest rates on mortgage, keeps other loans remaining low and helps businesses and the purchasing power of customers, but it also indulges in large-scale asset purchases. The interesting part is that the Fed has not fixed a timeline or quantum for these purchases and hence, sent a strong signal to the markets that it will not stop until the time the crisis gets resolved or until the Fed runs out of options. As of now, the market is indicating that it is attaching a much higher probability to the Fed becoming successful in its efforts.

This leads to a dichotomy here. Take a look at the Bloomberg home page at around 1500 hours GMT on 9 April 2020. While anyone focusing on the big jobless claims and not looking at the second news item about the Fed buying Junk and CLOs will clearly miss the big picture on the direction of the markets, how the signals from fundamentals of the economy – such as jobless claims – will be interpreted and how markets will react to what the Fed is doing will pull the markets in opposite directions.

Thereforre, while the jobless claim news report is at the top, the market is saying that it is focusing less on that and more on other news which is that the Fed is delivering on its promise. It is even buying junk and doing everything to provide stimulus wherever it can and wherever it might be effective. Look at the S&P 500 chart for last five days, and it is clear to anyone following all three data points; Fed action, the impact of the coronavirus on fundamentals of the United States economy and the direction of markets.

There will always be questions like: (a) Is the Fed doing more than it should? (b) Will it work this time even though it may have worked in GFC? (c) Is this the most efficient method? (d) Is the Fed ignoring the long-term consequences of its actions? (e) Will the ammunition last during the time the coronavirus keeps impacting the economy? Of course, these will be valid questions, and the views will be subjective on many of these issues. Whether what the Fed is currently doing is right or wrong will be the discussion for some other day. However and at least for the time being, the markets are telling you that what the Fed is doing is working, and it is working really well so far!

8 April 2020: Why does local news-based sentiment analysis matter?

In news flow sentiment analysis, the question often is being asked is, 'In this day and age of global interconnection, does local news still matter anymore?' Let us first look at two samples below:

Pankaj grew up in a small town in India and had access to newspapers in both English and Hindi – the local language. There were small local newspapers that focused solely on news related to the city and its surroundings, and there were bigger national-level newspapers that were published in both English and Hindi. On the surface, the bigger newspapers seemed to be covering the same issues – be it in English or in Hindi. However, he noticed that, while local newspapers were mostly focused on city news, even the national newspapers were very different in English and in Hindi. English language readers did not get to see the same news as the Hindi readers. Why? The reasons may be related to several things, like perceived differences in their interest areas or even socioeconomic indicators, but this was a fact that Pankaj noticed over and over again.

The situation has hardly changed. As readership became viewership - with readers moving from print to television - and later transformed into online consumption of news via digital media, the difference between English and local language media did not go away entirely. In fact, the Netflixes and the Amazons have realised that local content will be the backbone for them in any country. They have had to tweak their programs, as per the audience's taste. As recent trends from the content these companies are developing suggest, the difference in viewers' profile makes a difference in what the viewer will like and what they will not. The content in English will not appeal that much to people who do not understand the language so well, even after it has been dubbed in the local language or subtitles are provided. No wonder, Netflix and Amazon are both investing heavily in Hindi content in India.

Does all this really matter for the markets?

Anyone with experience in watching business news in multiple languages for the same country will confirm that it is possible that the difference might actually matter. Our experience with news collection for different countries in different languages confirms this. English news and translated (from the local language to English) news can be quite different. Issues, discussions and views can look so different between the two that one begins to wonder if one is still really looking at the news flow on the same subject. We have highlighted such divergence for countries like China, Japan and Turkey in our previous newsletters and blogs. When news flow is different, sentiment analysis will not be the same. Therefore, there are situations when the sentiment analysis scores could be different.

Such a difference can become even more pronounced during situations that are not normal, such as situations that display a departure from 'business as usual'. Moreover, indeed, we are observing this with the Coronavirus-Related News Flow. We are noticing that for several countries, including China, the news on the same topic (e.g. the impact of COVID-19 on the economy or the impact on the stock market) are actually very different in different languages. Fig. 6.14 illustrates this for Turkey and Japan. Some topics of discussion appear in local language media but not in English media. Intuitively speaking, and a hunch does get confirmed when one does a careful comparison, the English news media appears more sanitised. This reminds us of a family discussing certain topics only within the four walls of their home – topics that they would prefer not discussing in front of the neighbours.

All of this points to the difference between sentiment analysis, all conclusions drawn, on the basis of English and the local news media. The difference is not always small. It might be that analysis becomes necessary to check what is the more important driver of sentiment: is it the English news sentiment or the local news sentiment?

6 April 2020: Coronavirus: Darkest before the dawn or no light at the end of the tunnel?

This discussion focuses on three important points from our sentiment analysis.

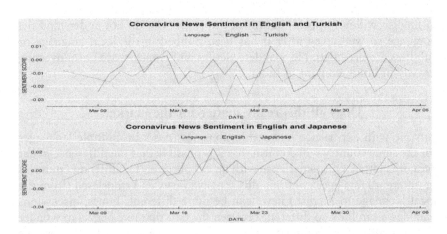

Figure 6.14 Average Coronavirus News Sentiment Lower in English versus Local Languages.
Source: Courtesy of EMAlpha.

- **Coronavirus Country-by-Country Sentiment Time Series** – The 'big news' of this week is 'bad news'. Over the last few days, the Coronavirus News Sentiment has deteriorated in 11 out of the 12 countries in our main panel – the United States of America, China, Germany, Brazil, Italy, India, Mexico, Malaysia, Norway, Colombia, Australia and Poland. This does not inspire much confidence that we are anywhere close to recovery. More importantly, out of the 11 countries in which sentiment has turned negative, more than half – a total of six – see a rather sharp decline.
- **News Topic Sentiment for Keywords** – When we do sentiment analysis for some keywords such as 'Donald Trump', 'Fed Rate', 'Nasdaq Composite', 'Chinese Economy' and 'US Economy', we find that there has been a big turnaround in news sentiment for the United States President Donald Trump after his proactive steps over the last week or so. This matters for its linkage with how quickly and efficiently the biggest economy of the world will respond to the coronavirus threat. The bad news here is that things do not look that great for S&P 500 and the United States Economy Sentiment.
- **Daily Coronavirus Sentiment Heat Map for Countries** – The relative scores matter much more than absolute scores in the case of the Coronavirus News Sentiment in terms of its impact on local markets. When we do a country-by-country time series analysis for the Coronavirus News Sentiment, we find that: (a) the United States is among the worst on a relative scale as compared to other countries, such as Hungary and Norway; (b) the Coronavirus Sentiment for the United Kingdom saw a big change as things have improved considerably in absolute terms and 'as compared to other countries'; (c) Japan and the Philippines also show improvement and are doing better than others.

Coronavirus country-by-country sentiment time series

This is one of the most important charts, because market reaction locally depends much more on how the Coronavirus News Sentiment is evolving locally. The important takeaways are the following:

- Generally, things are looking gloomy when we do the country-by-country analysis for the Coronavirus Sentiment. The Coronavirus Sentiment has deteriorated sharply in several countries including the United States of America, India, Norway, Italy, Mexico and Colombia.
- One of the most noticeable drops after momentary massive improvement is in the Coronavirus Sentiment in China. As the infection cases spiked, the fears of the 'second wave' led to a big decline.
- The only positive news is from Malaysia, where there has been an improvement in sentiment on the coronavirus. However, the fact

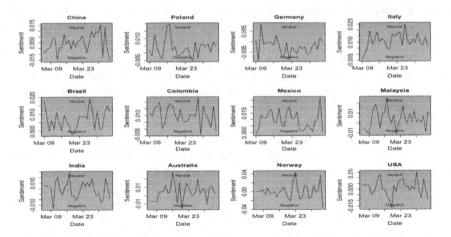

Figure 6.15 Country-By-Country Sentiment Score for Select Countries Focusing on Coronavirus-Related News.

that six out of 12 countries are reflecting sharp deterioration, and 11 out of 12 countries are showing a dip makes this chart very depressing.

Daily coronavirus sentiment heat map for countries

When we do a country-by-country time series analysis for the Coronavirus News Sentiment and look at relative change on two scales: (a) as compared to other countries and (b) versus the immediate past – that influence the market direction locally – we notice the following:

- The United States and China are the prominent countries that have deteriorated over the last few days in relative terms. The others are Norway, Hungary, Colombia and Chile.
- After several weeks, there is some improvement noticeable from Europe and Japan. The United Kingdom, the Philippines, Israel and Indonesia also show improvement.

News topic sentiment for keywords

Because markets are influenced by the sentiment for news flow around some very important and immensely popular keywords, the results are important for market direction.

- There is a very high level of pessimism on whether the Fed's attempts will help the markets and the economy.

74

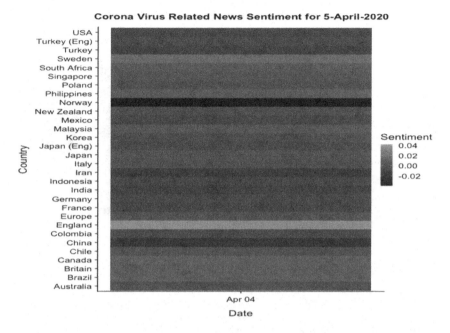

Figure 6.16 Coronavirus-Related News Sentiment Heat Map.

- The sentiment has started to improve in the Chinese economy, but the biggest positive jump is seen for United States President Donald Trump.

Crude oil news sentiment

Crude oil prices are closely linked to markets, and we track this separately.

- Over the last few days, we have seen a small improvement in sentiment after a big fall. This is driven by news reports that there would be a pause in the price war between major players in the market - Russia and Saudi Arabia.
- It will be interesting to see if this will be enough to support markets next week. So far, it has not really helped much.

Aggregate india equity markets sentiment

India is one of the major EMs we track, and it is also interesting for a few reasons: (a) the crude oil price decline helps the economy significantly and is a big plus for the country's economy; (b) the coronavirus is still in its initial phases in India, and the next few weeks will be 'make or break' this.

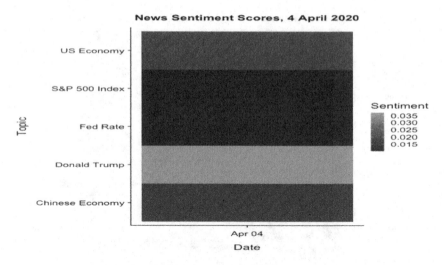

Figure 6.17 News Sentiment for Select Topical Search Terms.

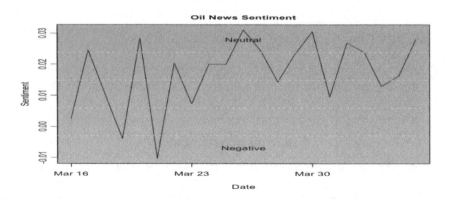

Figure 6.18 Daily Oil-Related News Sentiment.

- This is the big puzzle. The major market indices declined 6–7% for India, though the aggregate market sentiment has improved considerably. While the fall is significant in markets, the spike upwards in sentiment indicates that something is amiss.
- One possible explanation is that the Indian markets are excessively dependent on foreign investors, and they are in no hurry to return to India. Either they were able to find more interesting opportunities in other markets, or they do not have the cash to invest at this point. It is also possible that they may have become more risk-averse under current circumstances and uneager to look at India.

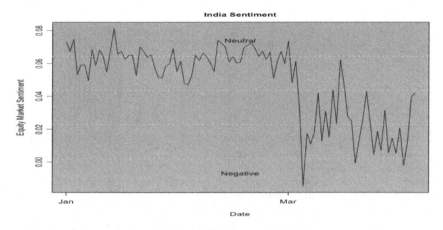

Figure 6.19 India Stock Market Sentiment.

- There is another possibility. Markets may have factored in the spike in the trajectory of coronavirus infections, but there is still uncertainty on its impact on the economy. This week, the market's fall was more consistent and quite unlike what had happened the week before. On the week of 23 March, the big fall on Monday was followed by a consistent recovery which made up for the entire decline by Friday. However, the week of 30 March witnessed more regular and consistent drops.

Coronavirus numbers and statistics

The total number of coronavirus cases continues to increase, having crossed the one million mark globally. The United States has the maximum number of total cases, although, as we mentioned before, the United States is not in the top ten countries when observed through the lens of the number of cases per capita. However, the mood remains downbeat, as we go into the week of 5 April. President Donald Trump has, on multiple occasions, communicated the chances of a 'very painful two weeks'. The EMAlpha Sentiment scores are perhaps just capturing this mood in multiple places.

1 April 2020: Coronavirus sentiment versus aggregate market sentiment and the base rate

In our discussion on the Coronavirus News Sentiment and Indian Markets, we discussed the 'Aggregate Market Sentiment for India' and the 'News Sentiment on Coronavirus Sentiment for Several Countries including India'. Regarding these, the related issues include the following:

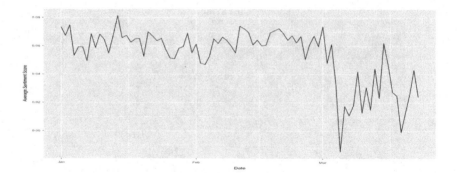

Figure 6.20 India Aggregate Market Sentiment.

1   Why are these two charts showing very different patterns, and how must these be read to take a call on the market?
2   The aggregate chart is showing a sharp drop in March from the levels seen in January and February, while the India graph, along with several countries, shows a fairly stable graph.
3   Why do these charts have different start points (i.e. the aggregate charts begin in January, and the second one in March)?

Therefore, let us explain these differences - what they represent and how they should be used.

1   Chart 23 is speaking about the aggregate market sentiment, and it will be a continuous chart, although we have only shown this since the beginning of January 2020, and, as market sentiment keeps fluctuating, it will keep changing. However, usually, the market gyrations are not that large and you can see that in January and February. The month of March has been very bad for Indian equities, and the Aggregate Market Sentiment Chart shows a significant decline. The other noticeable feature of the Indian markets is that the volatility increased substantially in March.
2   The Coronavirus Sentiment is not a regular chart, and it will not be continuous. Since the coronavirus spread began in India only towards the end of February, the news sentiment started covering this from that time only. The Coronavirus News Sentiment Chart would not be there for January and February for India and for many other countries (except China), unlike the aggregate chart which is continuous.
3   The coronavirus in itself is a negative event, but the change in news flow sentiment would be continuous – sometimes good and sometimes

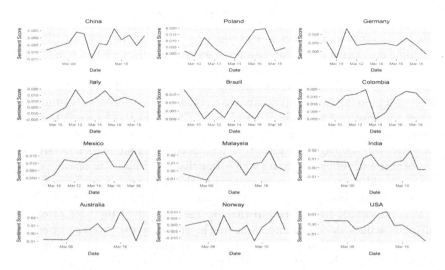

Figure 6.21 Coronavirus News Sentiment for Multiple Countries.

bad. While the sentiment in the news about the coronavirus would keep changing, the overall impact on the market is going to remain negative. Sometimes, the negative impact is less and sometimes it is more. The Coronavirus News Sentiment Chart only talks about this sentiment, which is in a narrow range. It is like watching a very depressing movie or reading a similar type of book. If it has some moments of comic relief, then the sentiment will change for a while, but overall, the movie and the book will still be depressing. The same thing is happening with coronavirus news. Sometimes, there are positive reports like a lesser number of infections and hopes for better control on the spread and that gets captured – making the sentiment positive. However, the overall impact of the coronavirus still remains negative for the markets.

4   Can there be a negative sentiment on the coronavirus and still positive sentiment on markets? Yes, that is possible. For example, if the coronavirus news is very negative, and the market should fall 3% because of it – although it is tough to measure how much impact that should actually be there, but broadly, you can assess by looking at the possible economic impact and how the spread rate compares with other countries etc. – but the market overreacts and falls 5%. In that case, the market experts would start talking about attractive valuation, good buying opportunity, etc. and that will make the aggregate market sentiment positive. Therefore, these could be situations where there is a variance between the sentiment on aggregate market and the coronavirus sentiment.

Why does base rate matter?

We believe that a comment is also needed to explain the base rate. If you examine the aggregate market sentiment more carefully, then you would find that the chart is flatter in January and February, and the sentiment is much above zero. The base rate is somewhere between 0.06 and 0.07. This would look odd to many readers as compared to the Coronavirus News Sentiment - when the base rate is much closer to zero. Why does this happen? It is because the usual market sentiment has a positive bias. Since the absolute values are way above zero, then this would convey that market is always exuberant and would be doing well – but that is wrong. The market sentiment should be measured as compared to the base rate. If the base rate is 0.065, then anything above it is positive, and anything below is negative.

It is important to understand that, in the context of the base rate, the absolute values do not matter that much, and only the distance in either direction from the base rate matters. This can also be understood from the same movie and book example. If a movie is funny, then the overall sentiment will be 'positive' but that does not mean that, at every point, it will be 'positive'. The base rate will be above zero, and the sentiment at any point should be measured versus that base rate. The same things apply to languages.

For example, if Italian is a more expressive language than British English, then the base rate for Italian will be higher than in English. How the sentiment is in a particular article written in either Italian or English should be measured *vis-à-vis* the respective base rates of Italian and English. These are how the typical results would look like:

Article in English (The language base rate is –0.02)

a If the English article scores –0.01, then it has a positive sentiment versus language base rate.
b If the English article scores –0.04, then it has a negative sentiment versus language base rate.

Article in Italian (The language base rate is +0.05)

a If the Italian article scores +0.07, then it has a positive sentiment versus language base rate.
b If the Italian article scores +0.02, then it has a negative sentiment versus language base rate.

Look at the first situation in English versus the second in Italian. The absolute value for the Italian article is higher but still adjusted for the base rate. It is negative versus the article in English. That is about it from us. We hope the different perspectives in the two charts are now easier to understand.

Notes

1 Jeff Cox. April 30, 2020. 'US weekly jobless claims hit 3.84 million, topping 30 million over the last 6 weeks.' CNBC. https://www.cnbc.com/2020/04/30/us-weekly-jobless-claims.html (Accessed on 14th July 2020).

2 German Lopez. May 5, 2020. 'April was another lost month for Trump's coronavirus response.' Vox. https://www.vox.com/2020/5/5/21246327/coronavirus-trump-april-lost-month-jeremy-konyndyk (Accessed on 14th July 2020).

3 Mike Isaac and Vindu Goel. 'Facebook Invests US$5.7 Billion in Indian Internet Giant Jio.' April 21, 2020. The New York Times. https://www.nytimes.com/2020/04/21/technology/facebook-jio-india.html (Accessed on 14th July 2020).

4 Heather Long. 'There's a growing possibility of a W-shaped economic recovery—and it's scary.' April 23, 2020. The Washington Post. https://www.washingtonpost.com/business/2020/04/22/theres-growing-possibility-w-shaped-economic-recovery-its-scary/ (Accessed on 14th July 2020).

5 Peter Baker. 'Presidents Forge Their Legacies in Crises' March 11, 2020. The New York Times. https://www.nytimes.com/2020/03/11/us/politics/president-leadership-crisis.html (Accessed on 14th July 2020).

6 Carlie Porterfield. 'Brazil's Bolsonaro Slights Social Distancing As Coronavirus Deaths Hit 1,000.' April 10, 2020. Forbes. https://www.forbes.com/sites/carlieporterfield/2020/04/10/brazils-bolsonaro-slights-social-distancing-as-coronavirus-deaths-hit-1000/ (Accessed on 14th July 2020).

7 'What Is Quantitative Easing, and How Has It Been Used?' November 27, 2017. The St. Louis Fed On the Economy. https://www.stlouisfed.org/on-the-economy/2017/november/quantitative-easing-how-used (Accessed on 14th July 2020).

7

CORONAVIRUS GOES GLOBAL IN MARCH

'Oops ... It Is Getting Serious'

30 March 2020: The Dichotomy of a Worse Coronavirus Situation and Better Markets
    25 March 2020: For Global Economy and EMs, Better News Sentiment on the United States Helps
    24 March 2020: Coronavirus News Sentiment and Indian Markets on 20 and 23 March
    23 March 2020: Coronavirus, News Sentiment and Investor Behaviour
    18 March 2020: Coronavirus Sentiment: Deteriorating Further and What Did We Learn in India?
    15 March 2020: High-Profile Cases and the Impact on Coronavirus Sentiment
    10 March 2020: EMAlpha News Sentiment: the Markets and Coronavirus
    7 March 2020: Coronavirus, Human Irrationality and Daniel Kahneman
    4 March 2020: Coronavirus Sentiment Watch
    2 March 2020: Coronavirus Impact on Markets: Is Local Sentiment More Important?

30 March 2020: The dichotomy of a worse coronavirus situation and better markets

There have been some key developments and inferences that can be drawn on the Coronavirus News Sentiment and its impact on the global, as well as country-specific, themes. Today's discussion focuses on two very important things:

1   While there is unprecedented coverage of the market impact of Coronavirus COVID-19, the massive volume of this coverage makes it difficult to draw any conclusions.
2   Related market analysis has focused on specific countries, specific asset classes or government and central banks' responses. How do we simplify event analysis and the inferences we can draw?

Coronavirus Country Sentiment

First, the good news is that there has been a marginal improvement in the United States Coronavirus Sentiment. Though still not out of danger, there is some stability in the United States sentiment score. This is mostly due to the US $2.2 trillion stimulus bill signed last week. The other bright spots have been Germany, Norway and Colombia. There is a marginal improvement in the sentiment score for Mexico as well. However, this is where the good news ends. Most of the other countries – such as Australia, Malaysia, India, Brazil, Poland and China – have shown a further decline in news sentiment on the coronavirus. The most depressing news is from Italy. Despite being already the worst affected country, there is absolutely no sign that things are getting better here.

Global Coronavirus Sentiment

The see-saw continues. After the sudden deterioration followed by a bit of recovery, things have started to go downhill once again. Global markets seemed to be in a recovery phase last week, but on Friday, the United States markets reflected the realisation that the coronavirus situation is still not under control.

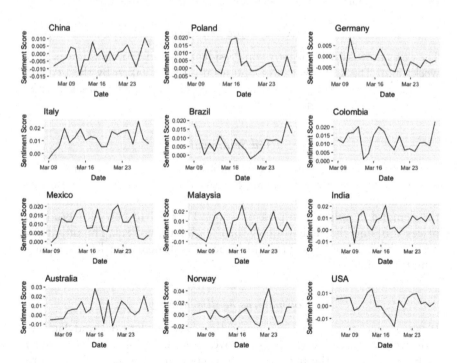

Figure 7.1 Country-By-Country Sentiment Score Focusing on Coronavirus-Related News.

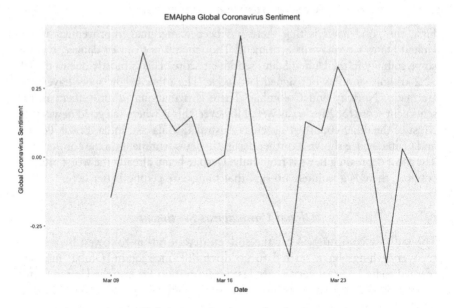

Figure 7.2 Cumulative Global News Sentiment for the Coronavirus.

News Topic Sentiment

The news flow is not as negative on President Donald Trump as it was a few weeks ago. The sentiment is of optimism on steps taken by the Fed too. However, the bad news is from the markets. The sentiment score is negative for the stock market and the economy.

Oil Sentiment

This is an interesting chart. The outlook for oil is concerning on the basis of news flow sentiment. There are concerns on how much production the global markets can absorb and, if we go by this prevailing sentiment, the demand is unlikely to pick up soon. That is bad news for crude oil prices too, and that is bad news for the global markets. The only thing we can hope for is a turnaround in news sentiment, but let us see how long that takes.

Coronavirus Sentiment Map

If you notice, there is a close connection between Fig. 6.2 and Fig. 5.1. However, what is worrisome is the overall darker shade or the more negative score as per the undefined colour code of Fig. 6.2. There are three important things to highlight here:

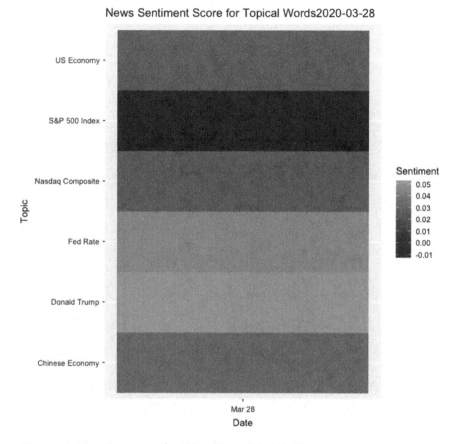

Figure 7.3 News Sentiment for Select Topical Search Terms.

- Japan is still struggling, and news sentiment remains negative on the coronavirus. Europe is also in the same category.
- One of the biggest sentiment declines in recent days is from India, as the number of coronavirus cases increases.
- Overall, the differential in shades across countries has become narrower (i.e. the news coverage indicates that the coronavirus is impacting everyone almost equally now as compared to the previous few weeks).

Coronavirus Numbers and Statistics

The numbers are increasing both for the reported cases and the number of deaths because of COVID-19. While the new China COVID-related cases have decreased, numbers keep increasing in the rest of the world. It is interesting to see these numbers in different normalisations. First, looking at

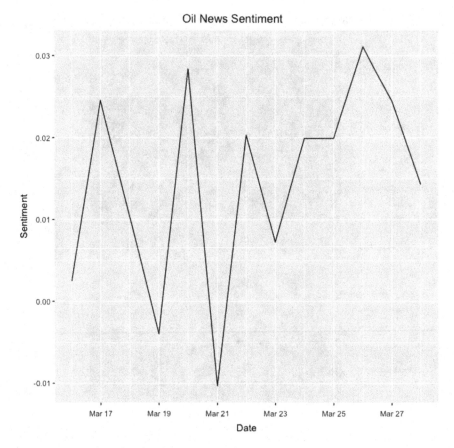

Figure 7.4 Daily Oil-Related News Sentiment.

the top ten countries with the most reported number of cases, the United States is now at the top. There has been a lot of negative news sentiment related to this.

However, averaging the number of cases by the country's population and looking at the top ten countries with coronavirus cases per capita tell a different story. The United States is not in the top ten list. We should point out that, in showing these numbers, we have applied a filter to include only those countries with more than 1,000 reported cases.

25 March 2020: For global economy and EMs, better news sentiment on the United States helps

Over the last ten days, there have been interesting takeaways from sentiment analysis for news flow around some very important and immensely

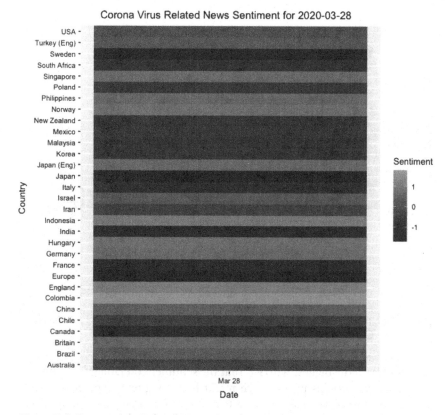

Figure 7.5 Coronavirus-Related News Sentiment Map.

popular keywords – which matter for the United States of America. First, the key positive from this analysis is we find a little bit of improvement in the overall news sentiment on words such as 'Donald Trump', 'Dow Jones Index', 'Fed Rate', 'Nasdaq Composite', 'Chinese Economy' and 'US Economy'.

The key findings as seen in the chart are the following:

1 Though there has been a dip in the last couple of days in sentiment for the Chinese economy, the overall theme is that there has been a massive improvement in the last week.

2 There is some improvement in sentiment for the United States economy too, and that is a good thing which is driven by the hopes that the lockdown will start getting lifted on a case-by-case basis,

3 There is an improvement in sentiment for the Dow Jones Index and Nasdaq Composite – both of which is not a surprise when looking at the United States markets.

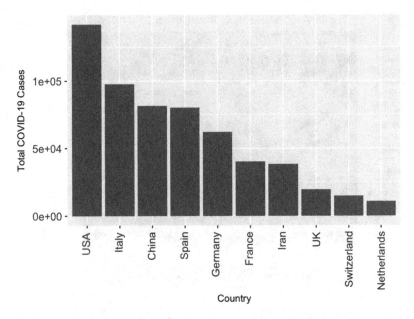

Figure 7.6 Top Ten Countries with the Total Number of Reported Coronavirus COVID-19 Cases.

4   However, the biggest worry is that the sentiment on Donald Trump and Fed Rate remains poor, which might have long term repercussions.
5   On a cumulative basis, the news sentiment for keywords which matter for the United States of America has improved in the last few days, but only by a little.

Overall, the improvement in news sentiment over the United States economy is reflecting in the United States markets as well. However, what is needed now is more confidence in Trump and the Fed in their ability to pull this off.

24 March 2020: Coronavirus news sentiment and Indian markets on 20 and 23 March

From EMAlpha Sentiment scores, the most interesting chart is on India. If we map the aggregate market sentiment for India – not just the Coronavirus News Sentiment for the country, which will be a part of overall sentiment anyway - with the market indices, there is a clear message. The market volatility is not likely to go away until the time when there is some stability in the news sentiment. The smart recovery in market performance on Friday, 20 March when the market was up by about 6%, followed by an

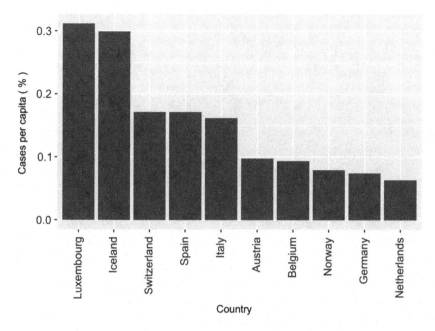

Figure 7.7 Top Ten Countries for Coronavirus Reported Cases per Capita.

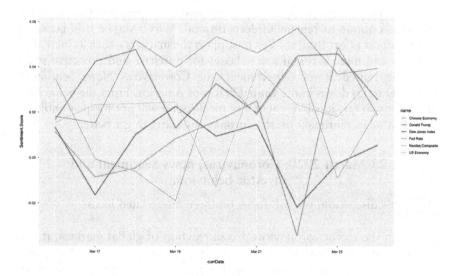

Figure 7.8 News Sentiment for Select Topical Search Terms.

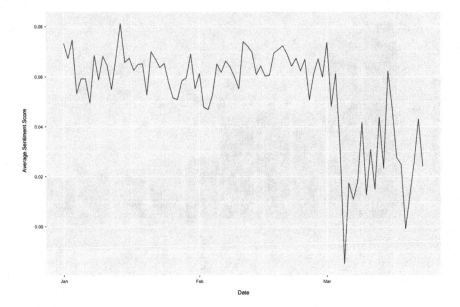

Figure 7.9 India Aggregate Market Sentiment.

even deeper fall on Monday, 23 March when there was a 13%, decline gels very well with the India Coronavirus News Sentiment.

The worst possible news for the global markets is that the United States markets continue to remain in deep turmoil. Why? Maybe it is because, despite all the effort from the Fed to support the markets – such as increased liquidity and more types of asset classes for purchase and proactive steps from the United States Government, the Coronavirus News Sentiment continues to go down in the United States of America. From the behaviour of markets so far, it is likely that any turnaround will not happen until the time that news sentiment on the coronavirus starts to get better.

23 March 2020: Coronavirus, news Sentiment and investor behaviour

In today's discussion, we will focus on three interrelated ideas:

a   From the recent coronavirus-driven reaction of global markets, it has become quite clear that sentiment is a dominant driver of investor behaviour. In an age when the speed of news dissemination is at its peak, market sentiment requires careful consideration by investors.

b   The initial reaction of the markets to global shocks tends to be somewhat broad-based, as all markets react to the same overall

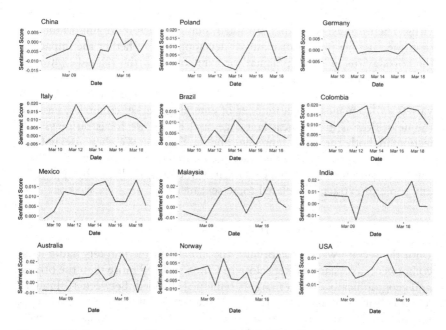

Figure 7.10 Coronavirus News Sentiment for Multiple Countries.

shock. However, as events evolve, local news flow sentiment also starts playing a significant role. High-profile cases lead to further deterioration in sentiment and a more negative market reaction.

c   It is possible to use a systematic approach and use quantitative measures of sentiment to make investment decisions and, more importantly, this can lead to outperformance versus the broader market. The EMAlpha emerging markets model portfolio performance, focusing on India, has delivered significantly better returns versus the market index. More volatility has also meant more divergence.

Coronavirus, Sentiment and Markets

Over the last few weeks, the coronavirus has led to a worldwide scare. As of now, the death toll has already surpassed 10,000, and the number of infections worldwide has already reached 300,000. What makes matters worse is that the total number of confirmed cases may only be a small percentage of actual infections. As expected, this is affecting the global markets as well. There are several important aspects of how markets have reacted to these developments.

The first is that virus attacks are very much like terrorist attacks, they generate more coverage than other events with similar or even higher impact. The second is that the maximum negative impact has been outside of

China because of tough control measures in the country of origin for this virus. The third aspect is that sentiment plays a much more important role than the tangible impact of material developments. Whether the impact of the coronavirus is 'noise', 'signal' or a bit of both, the related sentiment matters much more for markets.

We have been collecting coronavirus-related targeted news flow in a variety of languages. For a number of emerging market countries, most of the news flow is in the local language and, hence, we focus on news collection in both the local language and in English. We then use natural language processing tools to extract the sentiment for each country. While this discussion focuses on the coronavirus, the same tools can be applied to any topic to extract the related topic sentiment.

Phase 1: 10 January to 9 February

Until the second week of February, the impact on the markets had a local component, as Asian markets close to China suffered more than the others, and geographically distant markets remained shielded. Between 10 January and 9 February, as shown by the EMAlpha Sentiment Score, while the most severe coronavirus cases were in its country of origin – China – the maximum market impact was felt in smaller neighbouring countries – like Thailand. During this period, the behaviour of equity markets was related to the number of coronavirus cases.

The EM Alpha Sentiment Score for these countries is observed during the same period - from mid-January until mid-February. The sentiment scores show a clear relationship between sentiment and market performance. For most countries, the sentiment scores went into negative territory, owing to the coronavirus news flow over the last ten days of January. Geographical distance played a role, as illustrated here by Brazil.

Figure 7.11 shows that the Brazilian sentiment was somewhat average compared to Asian countries. On the other hand, the sentiment for Thailand, Indonesia, Malaysia and Hong Kong stayed quite depressed during the 20 January to 31 January period. Out of the countries shown, Thailand saw the most depressing sentiment score during the same period, when its equity market fell sharply. Brazil's sentiment score was more contained and so was its stock index.

Phase 2: 10 February to 2 March

The next phase came from mid-February to the end of February. The market impact became more global as sentiment turned more negative across the globe, as captured in Fig. 7.12 – which shows the EMAlpha Coronavirus Sentiment.

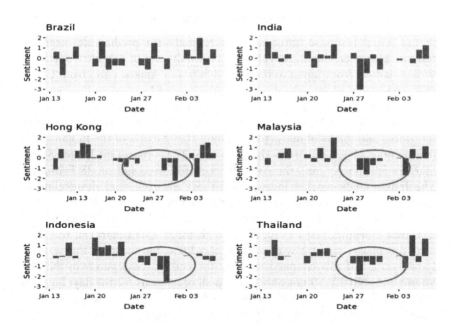

Figure 7.11 Equity Market Sentiment (EMAlpha Sentiment Score) January to February 2020.
Source: Courtesy of EMAlpha.

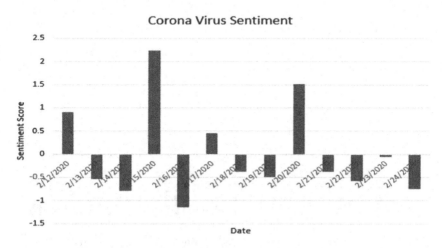

Figure 7.12 Global Coronavirus-Related Sentiment as Measured by EMAlpha.
Source: Courtesy of EMAlpha.

The Importance of Local News

In the initial response, most markets reacted in a predictable, negative fashion. However, this started changing from the end of February onwards. While markets from Japan to the United States of America and from China to Europe were under severe pressure, the role of local news flow and resulting sentiment started playing a more prominent role at this point. There were specific examples of local sentiment leading to a divergence between the global and the local market behaviour. The reaction of the Indian stock market on 2 March illustrates this point. On 27 February, the United States markets fell sharply, and the Asian markets followed suit on 28 February. The Indian stock market index, NIFTY 50, also fell, and the decline in NIFTY 50 was among the 'Top 5 Steepest' over the previous decade, with a fall of more than –3.5%. However, the trend reversed on Monday, the 2 March morning. NIFTY 50, along with other Asian markets, was in a recovery phase, trading with a gain of +2.0% for most of the session. However, all of this changed towards the end of the session. In the last 90 minutes, NIFTY 50 not only gave up all of its gains for the day, but also closed –0.6% down. At one point, the NIFTY 50 was down more than –1.3%. Why did this happen? It turns out that there was a news item that came out at around 2 PM local time about two fresh cases of the coronavirus detected in India (Fig. 7.13).

There was nothing else in the news that could have explained such a drastic fall in NIFTY 50, and it wiped out all of the day's recovery in a matter of an hour. After the coronavirus became a truly global concern, market-to-market performance was much more driven by local news flow

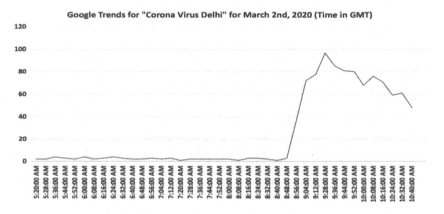

Figure 7.13 As shown by Google Trends Results, news searches related to the coronavirus in India spiked. This led to the Indian stock market's negative performance, while other Asian markets rallied.
Source: Courtesy of EMAlpha.

and underlying sentiment related to local coronavirus-related developments. News flow started strongly impacting smaller emerging markets
compared to developed markets because of the less diversified nature of
local economies.

Phase 3: 3 March to Present

On 9 March, the VIX Index – a widely monitored gauge of market volatility –
shot up to levels not seen since the subprime crisis almost ten years ago. While
the immediate reason was the breakdown of oil negotiations between Russia
and Saudi Arabia, the stage was already set for such a big market move by the
recent developments in the spread of the coronavirus. Fig. 7.14 shows the
Coronavirus-Related News Sentiment on 9 March for a number of countries.

A few interesting observations are in order before we discuss the country-
by-country market impact of news and the underlying news sentiment
shown in Fig. 7.15:

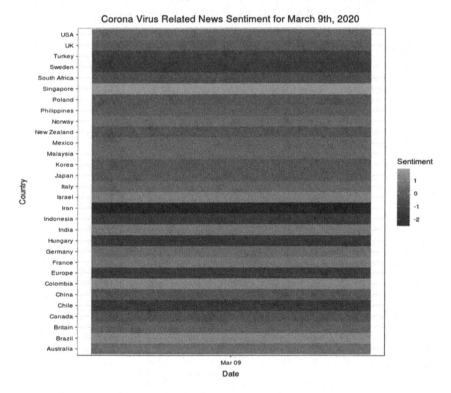

Figure 7.14 EMAlpha Coronavirus Sentiment Scores for 9 March 2020.
Source: Courtesy of EMAlpha.

1   The sentiment score is much more balanced – neither too bad nor too good – if the amount of news captured is reasonably large. This sounds intuitively correct as well. China is a good example of this. The score is not too negative because the news items are large in number.

2   If most of the news is not local, the likelihood of a more negative sentiment score is higher. In the case of Iran, we clearly see this. Most of the news on coronavirus for Iran came from sources that were not local.

3   There are also cases where the news search for a country leads to the capture of news flow which does not directly relate to the country. This influences the final sentiment score. When we do the searches for Turkey, the news flow is mostly about other countries, such as Italy and the United States of America. In fact, the news flow is that, so far, there are no cases of coronavirus in Turkey. Still, the sentiment is negative.

4   Political factors play a role. For example, during this period, the concern in the United States was that President Trump was not dealing with the coronavirus problem earnestly. A large part of the news flow was focused on this trend. It influenced the final sentiment score because negative developments tend to get more coverage.

There are some clear takeaways on how the local country-by-country sentiment on coronavirus news flow has evolved and how it is linked to the performance of local stock markets:

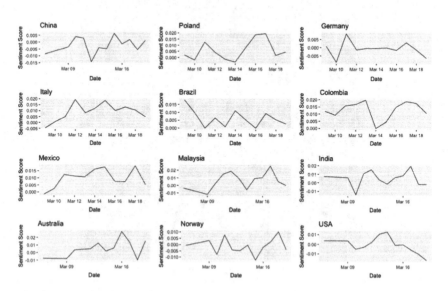

Figure 7.15 Global Coronavirus-Related Sentiment, 18 March 2020.
Source: Courtesy of EMAlpha.

1   On a time-series for individual countries, one observes the significant fluctuations in coronavirus sentiment. In some cases, of which the United States of America is the most prominent, the news flow sentiment deteriorated rapidly.

2   The case is the same with Canada, in which the Coronavirus News Flow Sentiment deteriorated sharply. However, the reasons were perhaps different than the United States'. In Canada, this could be because of a high-profile case of infection (i.e. the Prime Minister's wife).

3   The huge market volatility was linked with the rapid deterioration in Coronavirus-Related Sentiment on one side and the efforts behind policy announcements on the other. If left to the coronavirus alone, things could have been much worse.

4   India is an interesting case, because, after the 'V-shaped' recovery in sentiment, the news flow deteriorated, but at a rate which was not rapid.

5   The variance between countries on a day-to-day basis continues. For example, Japan was the country with the most negative sentiment, while things looked much better for South Korea, Chile and Brazil.

The coronavirus has had a severe impact on global health and the world economy. Are we anywhere close to the bottom? Is the worst over for the markets? For a number of developed and emerging countries, EMAlpha's Coronavirus-Related Sentiment Scores continue to move lower. Assuming that these concerns will continue to be negative for the markets and with a reasonable assumption for the present, the scores seem to indicate that the global markets may not stabilise any time soon (Fig. 7.15).

India's markets continue to swing wildly and, as shown in Fig. 7.16, the important takeaway is that the cumulative market sentiment is still bearish, which may not help in an immediate market recovery.

The news flow sentiment has, as of yet, not hit bottom universally – as indicated by the country-by-country EMAlpha Sentiment Scores. This is the primary reason why we think the time is not ripe yet for market reentry. The world is currently in the 'health emergency response' phase, and only when things stabilise here is an assessment of 'economic damage' even possible. This assessment is going to be a critical input for the extent and the timeline for possible recovery.

18 March 2020: Coronavirus sentiment: Deteriorating further and what did we learn in India?

The latest country-by-country 'coronavirus sentiment' based on news flow continues to show further deterioration in many countries, including the United States of America. However, things have started to look up in China.

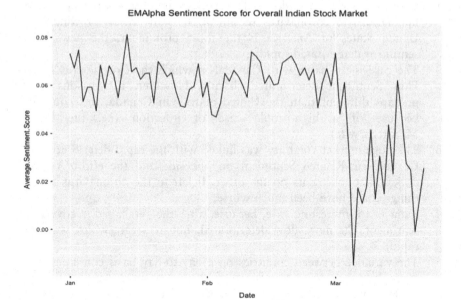

Figure 7.16 EMAlpha Sentiment Score for the Indian Stock Market, 17 March 2020
Source: Courtesy of EMAlpha.

Considering that this is the origin country of COVID-19, it is a good sign. India is seeing a further fall in coronavirus sentiment and that is bearish.

The bigger worry is that the cumulative sentiment (i.e. the sum total of news flow across all countries which we track) continues to plunge, and it is very likely that, unless there is an improvement here, the global markets may not stabilise.

The Indian markets continue to swing wildly, and the other important takeaway is that the cumulative market sentiment is still bearish – which may not help in an immediate market recovery.

15 March 2020: High-Profile cases and the impact on coronavirus sentiment

In continuation with our write up on 10 March 2010, we have some interesting insights on how the local country-by-country sentiment on the coronavirus news flow has evolved and how it is linked to the performance of local stock markets. Some clear takeaways on this include the following:

• On a time-series for the individual countries, one notices huge fluctuations in the coronavirus sentiment. In some cases – in which

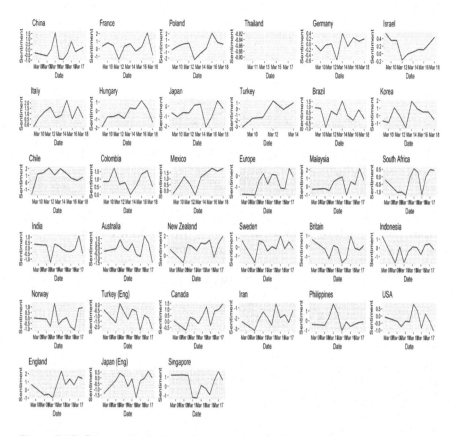

Figure 7.17 Country-By-Country Sentiment on the Coronavirus.

the United States of America is the most prominent – the news flow sentiment has deteriorated rapidly.

- The same is the case with Canada, in which the Coronavirus News Flow Sentiment has deteriorated sharply. However, the reasons are perhaps different than the United States. In Canada, this could be because of a high-profile case of infection (i.e. the Prime Minister's wife).
- The huge volatility noticed in the markets such as the United States is linked with rapid deterioration on one side and the policy announcements on the other. If left to the coronavirus alone, things could have been much worse.
- India is an interesting case because, after the 'V-shaped' recovery in sentiment, the news flow has deteriorated, but at a rate that is not rapid. This reflects in sharp recovery in markets as noticed in Friday's trading session.

The variance between countries on a day-to-day basis continues – for example, Japan is the country with the most negative sentiment on the basis of

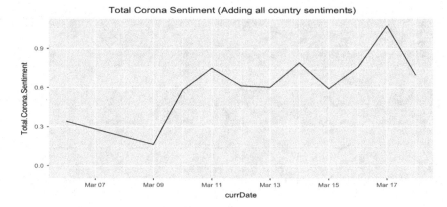

Figure 7.18 Cumulative Coronavirus Sentiment Across All the Countries.

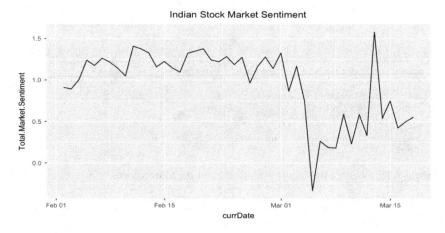

Figure 7.19 Aggregate India Market Sentiment.

news flow for 14 March, while things look much better for Korea, Chile and Brazil.

10 March 2020: EMAlpha news sentiment: The markets and coronavirus

The global markets experience an unprecedented spike in volatility. On 9 March, VIX Index – the widely monitored gauge of market volatility – shot up to levels not seen since the Great Financial Crisis almost ten years ago. While the immediate reason was the breakdown of oil production cut negotiations

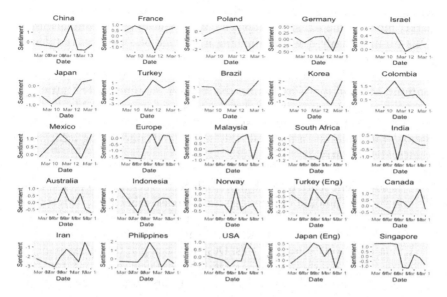

Figure 7.20 Time Series for Daily Sentiment for Countries on Coronavirus.

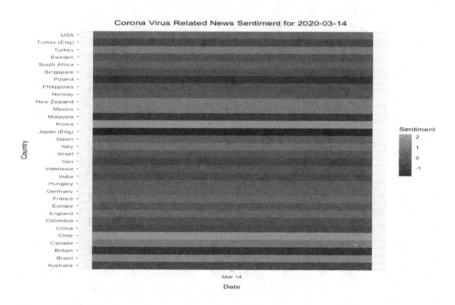

Figure 7.21 Daily Sentiment for Countries on the Coronavirus.

between Russia and Saudi Arabia, the stage was already set for such a big market move by the recent developments in the spread of the coronavirus.

We monitor daily news sentiments in a range of emerging and developed markets. As it has become clear that the Coronavirus-Related News Sentiment could continue to be a driver of market sentiment, we will continue to monitor Coronavirus News and Sentiment. The attached chart shows the Coronavirus-Related News Sentiment on 9 March for a number of countries. There are some interesting observations before we discuss the market impact of the news and underlying sentiment country–by–country.

1   The sentiment score is much more balanced – neither too bad nor too good – if the amount of news captured is reasonably large. This sounds intuitively correct as well because when the sample size is large enough, the influence one particular news will have is going to be rather limited. China is a good example of this. Despite it being at the epicentre of the coronavirus and the coverage of fatalities and new infections, the score is not too negative because the news items are large in number.

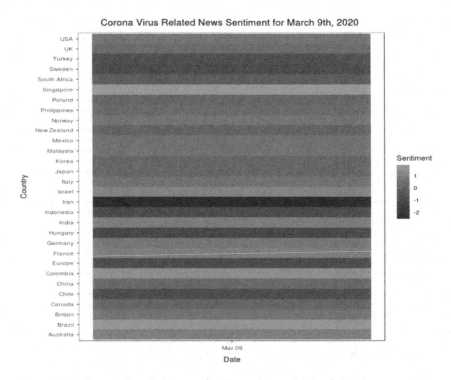

Figure 7.22 Coronavirus Sentiment for Countries on 9 March 2020.

2   If the larger quantity of news is not local, the likelihood of a more negative sentiment score is higher. In the case of Iran, we clearly see this. Most of the news on the coronavirus for Iran has come from sources that are not local. The likelihood or more critical coverage apparently increases with less contribution from local news flow. This will make the sentiment score negative.

3   There are also cases when the search for a country leads to capture of news flow which does not directly relate to the country we are searching the news for. This influences the final sentiment score. Turkey is an interesting case. When we do the searches for 'Coronavirus Turkey', the news flow is mostly about other countries – such as Italy and the United States of America. In fact, the news flow, which is mostly local. talks about how there are no cases of the coronavirus in Turkey so far. Still, the news flow sentiment score is negative.

4   Political factors also play a role. For example, the concern in the United States is that President Trump is not dealing with the coronavirus problem earnestly, and, because of him not taking it seriously, a large part of news flow is focused on this trend. It could influence the final sentiment score, because negative developments will get more coverage when people want to prove this point on Trump.

We look at some of the countries shown in the sentiment chart and summarise the news driving the sentiment.

The United States of America – With S&P 500, Dow and Nasdaq Composite are all down by more than 7%. The impact of the coronavirus continues to torment the biggest and the most important market in the world. When we see the news flow for the United States on the coronavirus, it is dominated by more suspected cases and more confirmations across the country. No surprise, the sentiment is fairly negative. However, there is still a big disconnect on a relative basis (i.e. the sentiment, though negative, is not as bad as many other countries). Still, the United States market performance is among the worst. Purely by looking at the sentiment scores, one would expect the market to go down, but not as much as it did on Monday, 9 March.

The United Kingdom – The United Kingdom is among the most prominent countries where the news flow sentiment has deteriorated sharply over the last few days. From one of the most isolated countries with not much coronavirus coverage as late as a week ago, this has changed drastically, and the news sentiment now looks as bad as most affected countries. The news flow is focused on panic reflecting in the hoarding of items like hand sanitisers and soaps, travel restrictions and the implementation of emergency measures by the government. The FTSE 100 declined by more than 7% on Monday was more severe than many other countries.

Turkey – This is an interesting case. When we do the searches for 'Coronavirus Turkey', the news flow is mostly about other countries - such as Italy and the United States of America. In fact, as per the local news reports, so far there are no cases of the coronavirus in Turkey. However, please note that this was the situation then. As of 14 July 2020, Turkey had the following numbers[1]: Coronavirus Cases: 214,001, Deaths: 5382 and Recovered:195,671.

Still, the news flow sentiment is negative. This mainly captures the sentiment without differentiating which geography the news is talking about. Nevertheless, the net result is still negative for markets with BIST 30, BIST 50 and BIST 50 all correcting by more than 5% on Monday.

Sweden – Sweden's market performance was not very different as OMX Stockholm 30 (OMXS30) was down by more than 5%. The news flow sentiment is very negative, but a large part of news flow is capturing the developments in other countries and not so much in Sweden.

South Africa – The South Africa Top 40 (SA40) was down by more than 6% on Monday. The news sentiment on the coronavirus for South Africa is not as bad as Sweden or Turkey, but it is worse compared to some of the other countries - such as Singapore, Israel, Colombia and Brazil. The interesting thing about the news flow is that many of the news items are not related to the coronavirus. In several other news reports, the discussion is much more about how people are reporting fake coronavirus inflection and illness.[2]

Singapore – The news sentiment in Singapore on coronavirus was much better and, in fact, it was among the most positive in the countries we have covered. The news flow was rather limited and also more routine, and there was nothing in the news that reflected that the coronavirus situation has deteriorated in Singapore. This was also reflected in Singapore in the S68 SGX Index which did not suffer as much on Monday and also recovered the most on Tuesday.

Poland – The news sentiment in Poland is less negative than some of the other countries like Sweden and Turkey. However, the quantum of collected news flow is much more than most of the other countries. The end result is still one of the worst for stock markets in Poland. On Monday, all major indices - including WIG, WIG 20 and WIG 30 - were down by more than 7%.

Philippines – The Philippines stock market (PSEi Composite) corrected by more than 6% on Monday, and it has not shown much recovery on Tuesday. The news flow on the coronavirus does not capture too many news items for the Philippines. This could also be the reason why the news flow sentiment is significantly much more negative than some of the other countries in the neighbourhood.

Norway – On Monday, the OBX was down by more than 8%, and OSEAX was down by more than 9%. The news sentiment is not as bad as some of the other countries, and this makes sense when one looks at the news flow. Though there is a large pool of news flow captured for the coronavirus Norway, most of it is related to other countries. Among the most unrelated topics are news flow from the United States on the coronavirus and reports covering recent developments in Italy.

New Zealand – After a 3% plus fall in NZX 50 on Monday, the stock market in New Zealand has fallen by another 2% on Tuesday. There is not really much coronavirus news flow for New Zealand. The sentiment is somewhere in the middle - neither too positive nor too negative.

Italy – This is one of the worst affected countries. However, the sentiment is not that negative as compared to many other countries, despite a lot of news covering more infections. After a 9% fall on Monday, the FTSE MIB is up by 3% today.

Iran – Iran is the most negative in terms of sentiment, and this is clear from the news flow. The interesting part is that almost all this news has come from other countries - like India and the United States. Virtually nothing came from Iran locally.

India – The Indian markets (NIFTY 50 and Sensex) corrected by 5% on Monday and the markets were closed on Tuesday. The news sentiment has improved compared to the worst sentiment observed over the previous few days. However, this is surely not only because of the lesser number of news items captured, but could also be attributed to news talking more about Prime Minister Dhaka's visit getting cancelled, as well as some of the news items which talked about the spread of rumours. As such, the market reaction on Monday was bad, but not as bad as the carnage in some of the other countries. This is perhaps because India is a net importer of oil and lower oil prices are good for the balance sheet of the country.

China – The news sentiment in China is improving, as there is so much news flow that a clear sentiment score does not emerge in either direction. The news captured is huge, and most of it is local news. Still, because of this massive quantum of news, we see the sentiment score is more balanced as compared to countries - where the number of news items collected is really small.

Brazil – The country has the maximum divergence between the sentiment score on the coronavirus and the stock market reaction. Bovespa was down by 12%, and the news sentiment score is not too bad. The amount of news flow is reasonably large in quantity, and it also covers reports of more infections, and all of this is local news flow.

7 March 2020: Coronavirus, human irrationality and Daniel Kahneman

As reflected in the reaction of global markets to the coronavirus' threat to the global economy, it is easy to see why sentiment is often much more powerful than facts alone. This is not just limited to markets, however.

Events that appeal to human emotions and our primitive instincts always have a disproportionate impact than what objective assessment would warrant. This is true for terrorist threats, fears of recession and how broad-based the impact of negative events will be, in general.

Over the years, many philosophers, psychologists, authors and scientists have spoken about this phenomenon where the impact of news flow of certain events immediately triggers a 'survival reaction' or a 'fight or flight' response – or in market parlance, 'greed or fear' – taking over rational investment decisions. In many of these areas, one of the most elegant explanations and lucid examples backed by years of research and experiments with a large sample size have come from Daniel Kahneman.

In his book *Thinking, Fast and Slow*, Nobel Laureate Kahneman has spoken at length about 'human irrationality' and the way the process of thinking gets influenced by quite unexpected factors. For example, when asked questions such as 'what is the population of Romania?' or 'what is the distance between Mars and Earth?', the answer gets influenced by the numbers one has probably encountered immediately before one replies – whether these were big or small – it does not matter if they were in an altogether different context. Of course, the assumption here is that one does not know the exact answer and is making a guess.[3]

Thinking, Fast and Slow is a very interesting book and, at the same time, it is full of surprises and full of results which one least expects and goes against conventional thinking. One of the biggest lessons from this book is at least an awareness of how much we think we know, but in reality, we do not know. The false sense of confidence we have about many of our ideas and our understanding keeps us away from actually questioning those assumptions.

There are many cognitive biases, and many of them contributing to making markets inherently not rational is the classic efficient market sense. Whether we call it sentiment or something else, it is the underlying basis for overreactions which we usually see in the markets. No doubt, the coronavirus is a serious health issue for the global economy. However, there is hardly any doubt that the fear of the coronavirus and continuous media coverage can lead to fear and panic – a more severe reaction than is actually warranted. Although, who cares for survival rates and transmission rates when the only things everyone is talking about are how many more countries found their first case and how the number of new cases has surfaced in already affected countries.

As of now, news flow and sentiment are more driven by the big picture and less by the actual probability of an individual getting affected. It is hard to tell how long such an overreaction will persist. Let us wait and watch because humans can be more irrational than can be discounted in financial models for the markets and, more importantly, they collectively can remain irrational for a long time.

4 March 2020: Coronavirus Sentiment Watch

As we saw in our recent posts, the markets have reacted strongly to the Coronavirus-Related News Sentiment. While it remains topical, we will try to regularly post a heat map of our country-level sentiment score for coronavirus.

China, Thailand and Iran saw the most negative sentiments among the countries shown above. England saw the least negative sentiment. As the daily sentiment changes for a number of countries, we believe that the sentiment score, which is an input into our systematic trading model, can be valuable in risk managing or creating new signals for any international portfolio.

2 March 2020: Coronavirus impact on markets: Is local sentiment more important?

The sharp downward market movements across the world in the previous week has removed any doubts about the kind of impact the coronavirus would have on the Investor Sentiment. In the initial response, most markets globally reacted in a predictable negative fashion. However, this is slowly changing now. While markets from Japan to the United States of America as well as from China to European markets such as Italy are under severe pressure, the role of local news flow and the resulting sentiment is playing a

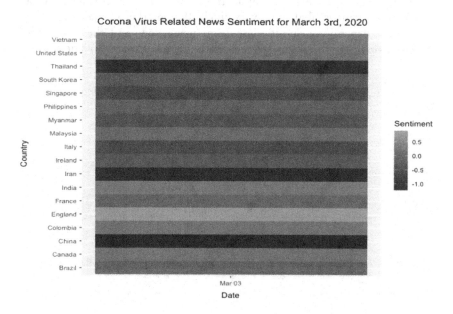

Figure 7.23 Coronavirus Sentiment for Countries on 3 March 2020.

more prominent role now. In this context, the performance of Indian markets is clearly a standout.

Just like the sharp fall in United States markets on Thursday, 27 February followed by a significant decline in major Asian markets on Friday, 28 February, the major Index of Indian markets fell. The decline in NIFTY 50 was among the 'Top 5 Steepest' in the last more than ten years with a fall of more than 3.5%, but the trend reversed today – Monday, 2 March morning.[4] Just like recovery in major Asian markets, NIFTY 50 was also trading with a gain of 1.5–2.0% for most of the session today. There were different explanations offered such as: (a) dead cat bounce, (b) recovery in stocks with more global linkages such as commodity companies and, (c) plain and simple, recovery aligned with other markets in the region.

However, all of this changed towards the end of the session. In the last one and a half hours, the NIFTY 50 not only gave all of its gains for the day, but also closed 0.6% down. This was not the worse though. At one point, the NIFTY 50 was down more than 1.3%. The other important and broader market index in India is the BSE Sensex, and the performance of this was also similar to NIFTY 50. Thus, the intraday fall of 3% was only marginally better than Friday's Indian market performance – completely unexpected and very quick. However, how did this happen? The news announced that two fresh cases of the coronavirus were detected in India.

There was absolutely nothing else that could have explained such a drastic fall in NIFTY 50 and wiped out all the recovery in a matter of just about an hour. What are the implications? (a) After the coronavirus has now become truly global, it is very likely that market-to-market performance will depend much more on local news flow and the underlying sentiment on the coronavirus-related developments locally; (b) The smaller

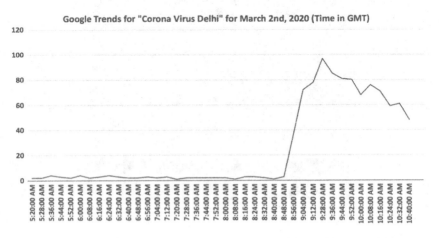

Figure 7.24 Google Trends for 'Coronavirus Delhi' on 2 March 2020.

markets and several emerging markets may perhaps get more impacted in terms of percentage with the news flow compared to developed markets because of less diversified nature of local economies. Honestly, it is not looking very good on sentiment analysis done for virus-related news flow.

Notes

1 https://www.worldometers.info/coronavirus/country/turkey/ (Accessed on 14th July 2020).
2 Shruti Menon. July 01, 2020. 'Coronavirus: The human cost of fake news in India.' BBC. https://www.bbc.com/news/world-asia-india-53165436 (Accessed on 14th July 2020); Katelyn Burns. Apr 15, 2020. 'Survey: 80 percent of Americans said they saw fake coronavirus news in the early days of the pandemic.' Vox. https://www.vox.com/policy-and-politics/2020/4/15/21222458/ study-people-coronavirus-fake-news (Accessed on 14th July 2020); UN News Staff. April 13 2020. 'During this coronavirus pandemic, 'fake news' is putting lives at risk: UNESCO.' UN News. https://news.un.org/en/story/2020/04/ 1061592 (Accessed on 14th July 2020).
3 Kendra Cherry. April 30, 2020. 'How Anchoring Bias Psychology Affects Decision Making.' VeryWellMind. https://www.verywellmind.com/what-is-the-anchoring-bias-2795029 (Accessed on 14th July 2020).
4 NSE. https://www1.nseindia.com/products/content/equities/indices/historical_ index_data.htm (Accessed on 14th July 2020).

8

THE BUILD-UP IN FEBRUARY
'Come on, Do Not Worry Too Much'

27 February 2020: Coronavirus and Markets
9 February 2020: The Coronavirus and How Sentiment Impacts the Market

27 February 2020: Coronavirus and markets

Markets have seen a sharp negative reaction to coronavirus news. The news sentiment has evolved daily, leading to market gyrations. We have tracked the overall market sentiment, specifically in regard to the coronavirus, on a daily basis. As the chart below shows, after a bit of relaxation last week, the sentiment soured again over the weekend. As the markets opened on Monday, this negative sentiment stocked the market nervousness.

The MSCI World Equity Index is also struggling over the last few days. The negative sentiment has directly fed the market capitulation. Emerging and developed markets have fallen. This shows in the performance of a number of emerging market equity indices. The coronavirus has spread in multiple regions beyond Asia by now – Italy, the Middle East and Brazil. It seems likely that the virus-related sentiment will drive the markets for at least some time. How are hedge fund strategies doing with this backdrop? As the Hedge Fund Research HFRX Equity Index shows, these are not doing so well.

9 February 2020: The coronavirus and how sentiment impacts the market

Over the last few weeks, the coronavirus has led to a worldwide scare. As of now, the death toll in China has surpassed 700. According to the official data released by China, more than 3,300 new cases emerged in the last 24 hours alone.[1] What makes matters worse is that the total number of confirmed cases has risen to more than 30,000, and the sceptics fear that this number is only a small percentage of actual infections.

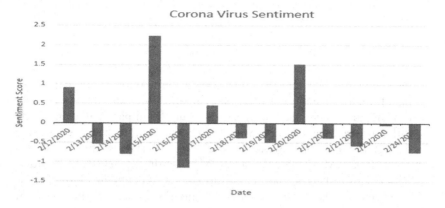

Figure 8.1 Coronavirus Sentiment Day-by-Day.

As expected, this is affecting global markets too. Though it is believed that there is a serious clampdown by Chinese authorities on the type of news flow leaving its borders, the fortunes are fluctuating with each piece of news - good or bad. For example, global markets heaved a sigh of relief when it was reported that Gilead Sciences had offered an experimental drug for coronavirus treatments and testing and that the biotech firm has formalised an agreement with China to conduct a clinical trial of Remdesivir – supposedly an effective drug against the coronavirus.[2]

There are several important aspects of how markets have reacted to these developments:

- The first is that, though this is a global health emergency and there is no proven cure yet in sight, the media coverage is still disproportionate in considering the tangible impact estimated as of now. In the age of rapid information dissemination and the huge role played by social media, this skew is even more prominent. Naturally, financial markets also react more to these events.

- The second interesting aspect is that the maximum negative impact has happened outside of China. One of the worst affected countries from the coronavirus is Thailand. How long it will take before infection rates to stabilise is anyone's guess, but it is quite possible that, due to its size and the diversification in economy, China will be less negatively impacted than some of the other smaller countries in its neighbourhood. More granularly, different markets and companies will react differently to these news developments. The same news can very well be negative for some industries (e.g. airlines and tourism) and good for others (e.g. some specialised pharmaceutical and biotechnology firms, manufacturers of masks, etc.).

- The third aspect is that there will always be some participants in global financial markets who will overreact, and there will be others who will barely flinch. It is difficult to tell *a priori* who is right and who is not, and only time will tell. However, the point is reiterated that sentiment plays a much important role than the tangible impact of material developments. Whether the impact of the coronavirus is 'noise', 'signal' or a little bit of both, the reaction of financial markets proves the age-old dictum 'News may be the same, but the impact could be vastly different because of the varied nature of sentiment'. The tangible impact and news flow matter for the markets but the sentiment matters much more. Moreover, the analysis of sentiment helps one position better with respect to market developments. We will also look at how sentiment evolved over the last one month in some of the worst-hit Asian markets.

After we have spoken about the recent developments related to the coronavirus and related news flow, it is important to mention that the impact on the markets seems to have a local component, as Asian markets close to China have suffered more than others. Geographically distant markets have remained shielded. Let us look at how the EMAlpha Sentiment Score has evolved over the last month for some of these emerging countries as well as the performance of their equity markets.

The first cases were found in China, where the virus has continued to spread. A number of cases have also been found in various other countries. As we mentioned in the prior blog, while the most severe coronavirus cases have been in its country of origin - China - the maximum market impact has been in smaller neighbouring countries, like Thailand.

Fig. 8.2 shows the performance of equity markets in some of China's neighbouring countries which have seen a high number of coronavirus cases. For comparison, we have also included India and Brazil. India borders China, but has seen a relatively small number of coronavirus cases. Brazil has not seen any cases yet. Outside China, the behaviour of equity markets over the last few weeks seems to be related to the number of coronavirus cases. Is there a relation between the coronavirus and market performance? Yes, there is very much a connection.

Fig. 8.3 shows the EMAlpha Sentiment Score for these countries over the last few weeks. The sentiment scores show a clear relationship between sentiment and market performance. For most countries, the sentiment scores went into the negative territory, owing to the coronavirus news flow, in the last ten days of January. Brazil was an exception though. Fig. 5.3 shows that the Brazilian sentiment was somewhat acceptable compared to the Asian countries. On the other hand, the sentiment for Thailand, Indonesia, Malaysia and Hong Kong stayed quite depressed in the 20 January to 31 January period. India also saw a streak of negative sentiment

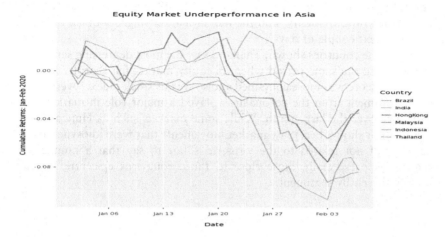

Figure 8.2 Equity Market Performance (Cumulative Returns of Stock Indices) January to February 2020.
Source: Courtesy of EMAlpha

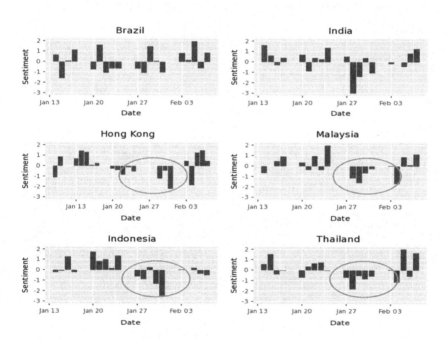

Figure 8.3 Equity Market Sentiment (EMAlpha Sentiment Score) January to February 2020.
Source: Courtesy of EMAlpha

113

around the same period, but it was related to its union budget announcement made on 25 January, and the Indian market staged a quick rebound over the next couple of days.

Out of the countries shown, Thailand saw the most depressing sentiment score during the same period when its equity market fell sharply. Brazil's sentiment score was more contained and so was its stock index. Overall, the news sentiment from the coronavirus played a major role in market performance over the last month. While some markets such as Hungary and Turkey (not shown here) saw market movements that were idiosyncratic in nature and not related to the virus, it is fair to say that a number of economies – especially those close to the coronavirus epicentre – were heavily driven by sentiment.

Notes

1 Associated Press. February 8, 2020. 'Anger and virus cases grow in China with 722 total deaths' India Today. https://www.indiatoday.in/world/story/mainland-china-reports-new-coronavirus-deaths-toll-crosses-700–1644386-2020-02–08 (Accessed on 14th July 2020).
2 Denise Grady. February 06, 2020. 'China Begins Testing an Antiviral Drug in Coronavirus Patients.' The New York Times. https://www.nytimes.com/2020/02/06/health/coronavirus-treatments.html (Accessed on 14th July 2020).

Part III

THE SAMPLES

9

POLITICS, CONSPIRACY THEORIES AND RELIGION

Part III has highlighted some of the more important news flows from across the world, and these news items also include translated news items from foreign languages. It would be important to note at the beginning of this section that these are machine-generated translations in English, and these translations are not done by humans. We also try to assign these news items in different categories in the different chapters of this section.

10 March: Iranian claims dealing with the coronavirus outbreak fell to agencies at the last minute

Machine-generated translation in english:

Iranian claims dealing with the coronavirus outbreak fell to agencies at the last minute. In Iran, which is one of the countries most affected by the coronavirus that emerged in Wuhan, a new unnamed virus has emerged. In the country where the coronavirus outbreak rose to 237, the new virus allegedly released by the United States killed even a 25-year-old nurse.

https://www.sabah.com.tr/dunya/2020/03/09/son-dakika-haberi-iranda-yeni-bir-virus-ortaya-cikti-koronavirus-kadar-tehlikeli-olabilir (Accessed on 11th March 2020)

13 March: American National Security Advisor Accusing China of the pandemic

Machine-generated translation in english:

The world could have wasted two months on the behaviour of the Chinese Government in the fight against a new type of coronavirus infection, because, if Beijing had immediately and accurately informed the data and developments of the outbreak, then the international community could have started on time 'American National Security Advisor' Robert O'Brien said.

https://www.hazipatika.com/eletmod/veszelyben/cikkek/koronavirus_
sokaig_titkolozott_kina/20200312145317?autorefreshed=1   (Accessed
on 14th March 2020)

13 March: China accusing the United States Military of the Coronavirus

Machine-generated translation in english:

A Chinese Foreign Ministry spokesman said on Thursday that the United
States military may have brought the new coronavirus to Wuhan, China.
This has led to a further escalation of the war between the United States and
China. Chinese Foreign Ministry spokesman Zhao Lijian, on his official
Twitter account, said in Chinese and English that the United States lacks
transparency about the epidemic.
  https://www.voachinese.com/a/china-virus-wuhan-milirary-20200312/
5326657.html (Accessed on 14th March 2020)

14 March: Did trump catch COVID-19 from Jair Bolsonaro

Machine-generated translation in english:

United States President Donald Trump and Brazilian President Jair
Bolsonaro met last week. Bolsonaro's handshake with United States
President Trump resonated greatly in the United States. Yesterday,
Brazilian media reported that Bolsonaro had acquired the new type of
coronavirus (COVID-19). According to breaking news today, the coronavirus has been detected in Bolsonaro.
  https://www.sabah.com.tr/dunya/2020/03/13/son-dakika-haberi-dunyanin-
gozu-donald-trumpta-corona-virus-testi-pozitif-cikti
(Accessed on 15th March 2020)

15 March: 'Coronavirus holidays' and debate on measures adopted by politicians

Machine-generated translation in english:

Are politicians taking a radical measure in the fight against the coronavirus?
Nationwide coronavirus holidays are under discussion. However, would
they really be useful? The coronavirus* is spreading in Germany. In order
to slow down the chains of infection, 'coronavirus holidays' for pupils are
at a debate.

https://www.merkur.de/welt/coronavirus-deutschland-schulen-kitas-ferien-kindergaerten-schulferien-corona-frei-schueler-covid-19-sars-cov-19-zr-13595894.html (Accessed on 16th March 2020)

16 March: Muslims returning to Turkey from Pilgrimage in Saudi Arabia are taken into quarantine

Thousands of Muslims returning to Turkey from a pilgrimage in Saudi Arabia were being taken into quarantine on Sunday due to concerns about the spread of the coronavirus, Turkish officials said. Television pictures showed buses transporting pilgrims along the highway from Ankara's airport to the city as part of an operation to place those returning into student dormitories.

https://globalnews.ca/news/6679316/coronavirus-saudi-arabia-turkey-quarantine/ (Accessed on 17th March 2020)

16 March: Trump Administration Offered the German Pharmaceutical Company a 'Large Sum of Money' for exclusivity on vaccination against the coronavirus

Machine-generated translation in english:

The Trump administration offered the German pharmaceutical company a 'large sum of money' for exclusivity on vaccination against the coronavirus (COVID-19), reported in the media in Germany. The German government is trying to struggle with what it considers an aggressive takeover proposal by the United States, the newspaper 'Day Walt' was reported by sources in the German government.

https://www.themarker.com/wallstreet/1.8677274 (Accessed on 17th March 2020)

19 March: New coronavirus infection is not produced in the laboratory

Machine-generated translation in english:

Studies have shown that the virus that causes the new coronavirus infection is not produced in the laboratory, but rather originated from natural causes. According to Health Day, the United States Scripts Institute conducted research with researchers from the University of Columbia, the University of Tulane and the University of Sydney and reveals no evidence that the new coronavirus has been artificially manipulated.

http://kormedi.com/1313636/ (Accessed on 20th March 2020)

20 March: Trump accuses China of failing to share information on the epidemic

Machine-generated translation in english:

United States President Donald Trump accused China of failing to share information on the epidemic (CNBC) in time. Meanwhile, the number of infected has exceeded 10,000, and the state department has warned United States citizens not to travel abroad and not to return if they are across borders (The Washington Post).

https://www.internazionale.it/notizie/2020/03/20/coronavirus-italia-mondo-20-marzo (Accessed on 21st March 2020)

21 March: 700 cases linked to a mass religious gathering held at a mosque

Malaysia's health ministry reported 153 new coronavirus cases on Saturday, taking the total to 1,183 - one of the highest in Asia. More than 700 of the cases are linked to a mass religious gathering held at a mosque late last month.

https://www.reuters.com/article/us-health-coronavirus-malaysia/malaysia-coronavirus-cases-jump-to-1183-many-cases-linked-to-mosque-idUSKBN2180BW (Accessed on 22nd March 2020)

22 March: Filipinos who attended a religious event in Malaysia linked to a Spike in COVID-19

Manila, Philippines - Authorities are scrambling to trace the Filipinos who attended a religious event in Malaysia – which has been linked to a spike in COVID-19 cases in several countries across Southeast Asia. The *Tablighi Jamaat* congregation held from 27 February to 1 March at Kuala Lumpur's Jamek Sri Petaling Mosque drew an estimated number of 16,000 devotees from about 30 countries.

https://www.aljazeera.com/news/2020/03/coronavirus-philippines-seeks-215-attended-islamic-event-200321143247350.html (Accessed on 23rd March 2020)

25 March: Response of politicians to the coronavirus

The world, as we knew it, changed dramatically in the last few weeks due to the unexpected spread of the deadly coronavirus. Several autocratic heads of states were slow to react to the virus, denying that it was a serious problem in their countries.

https://armenianweekly.com/2020/03/24/erdogans-denial-of-coronavirus-crisis-risks-the-lives-of-80-million-turks/ (Accessed on 26th March 2020)

26 March: Activists launch 'Digital Protest' to end United States Sanctions on Iran

The campaign has been launched to pressure the United States Congress to lift sanctions on Iran as it struggles to deal with COVID-19. Activists have started an online campaign to pressure United States Treasury Secretary Steven Mnuchin to lift sanctions on Iran to help it contain the spread of the coronavirus.

https://www.middleeasteye.net/news/coronavirus-iran-activists-digital-protest-us-sanctions (Accessed on 27th March 2020)

27 March: Coronavirus – where it came from for humans

Machine-generated translation in english:

One of the open questions about the coronavirus is where it came from for humans. Analysis of the family trees of the virus suggests that it originated in bats – a well-known and familiar repository of coronaviruses. However, according to the analysis, the virus from the epidemic pathogen – another kind of animal – and jumped from this to man.

https://www.haaretz.co.il/health/corona/.premium.highlight-1.8714531 (Accessed on 28th March 2020)

28 March: The Verbal War between Iran and the United States

Iran is capable of helping the American people fight the Chinese coronavirus pandemic, but the Islamic Republic does not require any assistance from the United States, according to statements by Major General Hossein Salami - head of Iran's Islamic Revolutionary Guards Corps (IRGC) on Thursday.

https://www.breitbart.com/politics/2020/03/27/irans-irgc-terrorists-can-help-americans-fight-coronavirus/ (Accessed on 29th March 2020)

29 March: Brazil and coronavirus cases in Italy, Germany and Spain

English translation:

Brazil presented a slower evolution of coronavirus cases than Italy, Germany and Spain, according to the Ministry of Health. After 15 days from case number 100, the evolution in Brazil is the slowest among the three European countries.

https://www.gazetadopovo.com.br/republica/breves/coronavirus-evolucao-italia-brasil/ (Accessed on 30th March 2020)

4 April: A cluster of coronavirus cases can be traced back to a single mosque, and now 200 million muslims are being vilified

Six COVID-19 deaths have been linked to a religious gathering in March. This has led to a huge spike in anti-Muslim narratives and misinformation. Indian authorities fear that many thousands of people may have been exposed to the virus as a result of the congregation of the *Tablighi Jamaat* group at a mosque in New Delhi last month.

https://www.buzzfeednews.com/article/nishitajha/coronavirus-india-muslims-tablighi-jamaat (Accessed on 11th May 2020)

5 April: Canada's Health Minister's credulity plays right into China's hands

It is quite likely the case that China has not been completely open and transparent about the extent of its COVID-19 outbreak. It is also the case that such matters are not necessarily relevant in the immediacy of Canada's efforts to contain its own outbreak.

https://globalnews.ca/news/6777529/coronavirus-canada-health-minister-china/ (Accessed on 11th May 2020)

11 April: Churches in Singapore took good friday services online

Churches in Singapore took Good Friday services online yesterday while offering prayers for healing in this time of the coronavirus. More than 100 churches signed up for one-hour slots of prayer from 10 AM to 10 PM, asking God for mercy and intervention. Some churches privately convened online to pray via Zoom or Google Hangouts

https://www.straitstimes.com/singapore/singapore-churches-join-in-praying-for-healing (Accessed on 11th May 2020)

16 April: Chinese foreign ministry spokesperson quotes WHO and said to support that there is no evidence that the coronavirus was released from a laboratory

Machine-generated translation in english:

The Chinese Foreign Ministry spokesman said that, according to the World Health Organisation (WHO), there is no evidence that the coronavirus that has infected more than 2 million people worldwide came from a laboratory. The Chinese Foreign Ministry spokesperson said that the WHO said that there is no evidence that the coronavirus could have been released from a laboratory.

https://www.portfolio.hu/gazdasag/20200416/kina-szerint-nincs-bizonyitek-arra-hogy-a-koronavirus-egy-laborbol-szabadult-el-426412   (Accessed   on 11th May 2020)

16 April: Trump said his government is trying to determine if the coronavirus came from a laboratory

United States President Donald Trump said on Wednesday that his government is trying to determine whether the coronavirus emanated from a lab in Wuhan, China, and the Secretary of State Mike Pompeo said Beijing 'needs to come clean' on what they know. The United States President Trump said that his government is trying to determine whether the coronavirus emanated from a laboratory in Wuhan, China.

https://business.financialpost.com/pmn/business-pmn/reuters-news-schedule-at-6-a-m-gmt-2-p-m-sgt-60 (Accessed on 11th May 2020)

18 April: France said no evidence so far of a link between the new coronavirus and the P4 research laboratory in Wuhan

France said on Friday there was no evidence so far of a link between the new coronavirus and the work of the P4 research laboratory in the Chinese city of Wuhan, where the current pandemic started. The broad scientific consensus holds that SARS-COV-2, the official name of the coronavirus, originated from bats.

https://www.reuters.com/article/us-health-coronavirus-france-lab/france-says-no-evidence-covid-19-linked-to-wuhan-research-lab-idUSKBN21Z2ME (Accessed on 11th May 2020)

19 April: Heavy criticism of the work of the undersecretary of health in Mexico

Machine-generated translation in english:

The President of Mexico, Andrés Manuel López Obrador, came to pass on Saturday with criticism of the work of the Undersecretary of Health in the evening during the news at the second-largest television network in the country and asked the population to heed the advice of Hugo López Gatell.

https://www.sandiegouniontribune.com/en-espanol/noticias/story/2020-04-18/presidente-de-mexico-defiende-al-subsecretario-de-salud (Accessed on 11th May 2020)

20 April: Tension between France and China

Machine-generated translation in english:

There is currently tension between France and China. Recently, the head of French diplomacy, Jean-Yves Le Drian summoned the Chinese ambassador. The head of French diplomacy contemplates that the staff of French retirement homes had been 'slandered' on the Embassy's website in the context of the pandemic

https://www.tunisienumerique.com/coronavirus-france-lambassadeur-de-chine-convoque/ (Accessed on 11th May 2020)

21 April: Political crisis in Brazil and president Jair Bolsonaro

Machine-generated translation in english:

In the midst of a political crisis forged by President Jair Bolsonaro (without party), who participated this weekend in acts that called for the closing of congress and the supreme court and advocated a military intervention, Brazil shows signs of walking in the dark in relation to the real progress of cases and deaths by the coronavirus.

https://brasil.elpais.com/brasil/2020-04-21/drenado-por-crise-politica-forjada-por-bolsonaro-brasil-fica-no-escuro-quanto-a-avanco-real-do-coronavirus.html (Accessed on 12th May 2020)

23 April: Washington not letting up on its 'Maximum Pressure' against Iran

Washington has said that it is not letting up on its 'maximum pressure' campaign against Iran despite the coronavirus, continuing to use sanctions to try to limit Tehran's ballistic missile programme and influence across the Middle East.

https://www.nytimes.com/reuters/2020/04/22/world/middleeast/22reuters-health-coronavirus-iran-eu.html (Accessed on 12th May 2020)

24 April: States face legal hurdles in coronavirus lawsuits against China

Amidst devastating human and economic losses from the coronavirus, two United States states are demanding that China be held accountable for the global pandemic. Mississippi and Missouri can expect significant legal hurdles, but their complaints appear as a growing number of countries are looking to impose costs on China for its initial handling of the crisis.

https://abcnews4.com/news/nation-world/states-face-legal-hurdles-in-coronavirus-lawsuits-against-china (Accessed on 12th May 2020)

26 April: Chinese government official slams Australia's push for an investigation into the coronavirus outbreak

Chinese Government official slams Australia's push for an investigation into the coronavirus outbreak. China has criticised Australia's push for an independent international probe of the coronavirus pandemic, describing the move as 'political manoeuvring.' Australia wants an investigation of China's handling of the coronavirus outbreak.

https://www.abc.net.au/news/2020-04-26/coronavirus-china-slams-australia-over-independent-inquiry/12185988 (Accessed on 12th May 2020)

27 April: Chinese diplomats seem to have tried to influence german officials

Machine-generated translation in english:

Coronavirus in Germany: Chinese diplomats seem to have tried to influence German officials. This was about China's coronavirus management. Because of the coronavirus pandemic, people continue to die worldwide. Researchers are working at high pressure on the development of a vaccine.

https://www.merkur.de/welt/coronavirus-deutschland-news-drosten-nrw-berlin-kurve-zahlen-tote-merkel-statistik-rki-massnahmen-trump-uebersterblichkeit-zr-13697852.html (Accessed on 12th May 2020)

28 April: Iran pushes back against the United States' plan for snapback sanctions

Iran's foreign minister said the United States is dreaming if it thinks it can claim that it is still a participant in the nuclear deal in order to trigger snapback sanctions. Iran's foreign minister has rejected the idea that the United States can claim that it remains a participant in the Iranian nuclear deal.

https://www.al-monitor.com/pulse/originals/2020/04/iran-zarif-us-sanctions-nuclear-deal-coronavirus.html (Accessed on 12th May 2020)

1 May: United States' top intelligence agency, said that the COVID-19 virus is not artificially created or genetically modified

Machine-generated translation in english:

The State Intelligence Agency - the United States' top intelligence agency - said that the COVID-19 virus is not artificially created or genetically modified. China's artificial virus outflow conspiracy theory is denied. The National Intelligence Agency – the chief intelligence agency in the United States – stated in a statement that the 'COVID-19 virus is not artificially created or genetically engineered'.

http://news.jtbc.joins.com/html/245/NB11948245.html (Accessed on 12th May 2020)

2 May: The United States has slapped new sanctions on Iran

The United States has slapped new sanctions on Iran despite claims of its readiness to help the Islamic Republic in its fight against the novel coronavirus (COVID-19) pandemic. In a statement released on Friday, the United States Treasury Department blacklisted dual Iranian and Iraqi national, Amir Dianat, and his company Taif Mining Services LLC.

https://english.almanar.com.lb/1019559 (Accessed on 12th May 2020)

10

THE CORONAVIRUS PANDEMIC'S ECONOMIC IMPACT

11 March: Oil tumbled after a dispute between Russia and Saudi Arabia over production cuts

Panic erupted across Europe yesterday as the price of oil tumbled in response to a dispute between Russia and Saudi Arabia over production cuts, and Italian officials announced that the whole country was to be placed under lockdown to help curb the spread of coronavirus, formally known as COVID-19. Stock markets plummeted across Asia and Europe.

https://www.express.co.uk/news/world/1253308/coronavirus-news-germany-europe-euro-stock-market-angela-merkel-covid-19-eu-news (Accessed on 12th May 2020)

17 March: The United States passed a multibillion aid package to limit the economic damage from the pandemic

The United States House of Representatives passed a multibillion-dollar aid package early on Saturday that aims to limit the economic damage from the coronavirus pandemic. The Republican-controlled Senate is expected to take it up this week. The bill would provide free coronavirus testing for those who need it.

https://www.reuters.com/article/us-health-coronavirus-usa-congress-expla/explainer-whats-in-the-u-s-coronavirus-aid-bill-idUSKBN2132YH (Accessed on 12th May 2020)

21 March: The norwegian central bank may cut rates again

The Norwegian Central Bank may cut rates again to address the 'severe setback' sustained by the Norwegian economy, Governor Oeystein Olsen reiterated on Friday. 'We do not rule out cutting rates again,' Oeystein Olsen told public broadcaster NRK. Norges Bank cut its key policy rate to a record-low 0.25% from 1.0% on Friday.

https://www.reuters.com/article/health-coronavirus-norway-norgesbank/
norways-central-bank-chief-repeats-could-cut-rates-again-idUSO9N28E00V
(Accessed on 12th May 2020)

25 March: Coronavirus pandemic's impact on the Brazilian economy

Machine-generated translation in english:

The Brazilian economy is heading towards a recession this year. With the impact of the coronavirus, banks and consultancies again reviewed the projections for the performance of the Gross Domestic Product (GDP), and part of the analysts give for certain a retraction of activity, which has not occurred since 2016.

https://g1.globo.com/economia/noticia/2020/03/25/com-impacto-do-coronavirus-brasil-deve-voltar-a-ter-recessao-neste-ano.ghtml (Accessed on 13th May 2020)

30 March: A decline in oil prices

Machine-generated translation in english:

Oil prices, completed by a fifth weekly consecutive decline last week, continue to plummet in the shadow of a fall in global demand for energy due to the epidemic of the global coronavirus. The price of crude oil in New York fell below US$20 and the price of oil in London was traded at a low of 17 years.

https://www.themarker.com/wallstreet/LIVE-1.8721579 (Accessed on 13th May 2020)

30 March: One in five people in Britain fear an economic depression

One in five people in Britain fear an economic depression because of the impact of the coronavirus, and a further 52% expect the country's economy to be in recession within a year, a poll by YouGov showed on Monday. 'Almost three quarters expect that Britain's economy will be in depression (19%) or recession (52%) within a year,' YouGov said.

https://www.nytimes.com/reuters/2020/03/30/world/europe/30reuters-health-coronavirus-britain-confidence.html (Accessed on 13th May 2020)

31 March: According to the UNDP, income losses are expected to exceed US$220 billion in developing countries and nearly half of jobs lost in Africa

Machine-generated translation in english:

According to the UNDP, income losses are expected to exceed US$220 billion in developing countries and nearly half of the jobs lost in Africa. It is estimated that 55% of the global population does not have access to social security, and these losses will affect all levels of society.

https://news.un.org/zh/story/2020/03/1053812 (Accessed on 13th May 2020)

31 March: The impact of the coronavirus on small businesses

Everyone is taking a hit, but small independents are feeling the impact of the coronavirus pandemic the most. As a small-scale independent designer, Lejambe is one of the many individuals in the Canadian fashion industry who have lost their entire livelihoods in the span of a few days thanks to the COVID-19 pandemic.

https://www.flare.com/fashion-beauty/fashion-industry-coronavirus-canada/ (Accessed on 13th May 2020)

5 April: Malaysia approves cryptocurrency exchange

Malaysia becomes the next country to approve cryptocurrency exchange amid the COVID-19 crisis. Malaysia's securities commission has given full approval to a cryptocurrency exchange operator to legally operate in the country despite the nationwide lockdown due to the coronavirus pandemic.

https://news.bitcoin.com/malaysia-cryptocurrency-covid-19/ (Accessed on 13th May 2020)

8 April: Coronavirus-induced recession in Germany

Machine-generated translation in english:

The coronavirus crisis triggered a serious recession in Germany from the point of view of leading economic research institutes. Gross Domestic Product is expected to shrink by 4.2% this year, as evidenced by the report submitted to the *Deutsche Presse-Agentur* in advance.

https://www.swp.de/wirtschaft/coronavirus-deutschland-wirtschaftsforscher_-corona-krise-loest-schwere-rezession-aus-45310989.html (Accessed on 13th May 2020)

10 April: Economic rescue package of €500 billion for European Union member states

Machine-generated translation in english:

A significant economic rescue package of more than €500 billion was agreed by finance ministers of the European Union Member States to alleviate the economic crisis caused by the coronavirus epidemic. Charles Michel, the President of the European Council, said that the agreement will serve as a basis for the recovery of Europe.

https://24.hu/kozelet/2020/04/10/koronavirus-540-milliard-euros-a-mentocsomag/ (Accessed on 13th May 2020)

12 April: Rishi Sunak's former goldman sachs boss is to take on treasury post

Rishi Sunak's former Goldman Sachs boss is to take on a key treasury post helping the chancellor as he battles to keep Britain's economy functioning during the coronavirus pandemic. Sky News has learned that Richard Sharp, who spent more than two decades at the Wall Street banking giant, is to become a strategic adviser to Mr Sunak.

https://news.sky.com/story/coronavirus-sunaks-ex-goldman-boss-to-be-adviser-on-crisis-11971965 (Accessed on 13th May 2020)

13 April: Public companies are putting off release of financial statements

An increasing number of publicly traded companies are putting off the release of financial statements for the business year that ended 31 March due to the coronavirus pandemic. They face difficulties in tallying up financial data overseas. Japan's emergency declaration over the virus is also hampering work as many employees work from home.

https://www.japantimes.co.jp/news/2020/04/13/business/corporate-business/coronavirus-japan-accounting/ (Accessed on 13th May 2020)

14 April: Britain Received 1.4 Million New Benefit Claims for Welfare Payments

Britain has received about 1.4 million new benefit claims for welfare payments – about seven times the normal level – since Prime Minister Boris Johnson urged people to stay at home a month ago as the coronavirus outbreak accelerated. 'It is now up to about 1.4 million,' British Work and Pensions Secretary Therese Coffey said.

https://www.nytimes.com/reuters/2020/04/14/world/europe/14reuters-health-coronavirus-britain-benefits.html (Accessed on 14th May 2020)

15 April: The epidemic has disrupted key service sectors, tourism, hospitality and retail

Machine-generated translation in english:

The analysis notes that the epidemic has seriously disrupted key service sectors, particularly tourism, hospitality and retail. This contrasts sharply with the resilience of the services sector during the Great Recession of 2008 and the Eurozone sovereign debt crisis of 2011–2013, particularly in relation to commodity trade.

https://news.un.org/zh/story/2020/04/1054972 (Accessed on 14th May 2020)

20 April: A serious slowdown in the Australian property market

There are alarming signs of a sharp slowdown in the property market thanks to the coronavirus, with the number of residential listings down by nearly 30% for the month before Easter, and sharp drops in searches being conducted on property information group Corelogic's site.

https://www.theguardian.com/world/live/2020/apr/20/australia-coronavirus-live-news-nsw-victoria-qld-contact-tracing-app-schools-exit-strategy-latest-updates (Accessed on 14th May 2020)

21 April: The United Kingdom firms furlough over a million workers due to the coronavirus

British employers have put more than a million staff on temporary leave due to the coronavirus, finance minister Rishi Sunak said, reporting a flood of applications since the government's costliest programme to support the economy opened. The scheme will pay for 80% of employers' wage bills until the end of June for staff suspension during the coronavirus lockdown.

https://www.reuters.com/article/us-health-coronavirus-britain-sunak/over-a-million-uk-workers-furloughed-due-to-coronavirus-finance-minister-idUSKBN2222B2 (Accessed on 14th May 2020)

29 April: Companies in the information and communication sector reported a downturn and failing IT investments

Machine-generated translation in english:

The barely reviving corporate digitalisation was also overwhelmed by the epidemic. Companies in the information and communication sector have themselves reported a downturn, and failing IT investments have an impact on potential GDP - better in the short term. In other subsectors of the sector, we see a very mixed picture.

https://www.portfolio.hu/gazdasag/20200429/a-magyar-gazdasag-jovojet-is-derekba-tori-a-koronavirus-jarvany-428820 (Accessed on 14th May 2020)

11

DISEASE, DEVASTATION AND HOPE

10 March: Information and data play a key role in understanding the problem and finding solutions

Machine-generated translation in english:

When the world faces seemingly uncontrollable challenges, information and data play a key role in understanding the problem and finding solutions. Now that the COVID-19 coronavirus has exploded on the planet and has arrived in Mexico, we face a global public health challenge: infection, recovery, quarantine, restrictions and, sadly, deaths.

https://www.eleconomista.com.mx/politica/Rastreador-de-Coronavirus-Mexico-actualizacion-en-tiempo-real-20200309-0089.html (Accessed on 14th May 2020)

11 March: Researchers looking for volunteers willing to become infected with the coronavirus in exchange for payment

Machine-generated translation in english:

Researchers in the United Kingdom and the United States are now looking for volunteers who are willing to become infected with the coronavirus in exchange for payment. The British Hvivo Institute started recruiting 24 people who will be infected with two different strains of the coronavirus which resemble the COVID-19 virus that is now spreading around the world.

https://www.themarker.com/wallstreet/1.8660379 (Accessed on 15th May 2020)

19 March: Coronavirus has spread to 158 countries

Machine-generated translation in english:

The coronavirus balance sheet is getting heavy in the world! Here, the virus has spread to 158 countries - including Turkey - the coronavirus emerging in Wuhan, China. As the world is alarmed against the coronavirus, positive news continues to come from China - where the outbreak has emerged.
https://www.ahaber.com.tr/galeri/gundem/dunyada-koronavirus-bilancosu-agirlasiyor-iste-ulke-ulke-son-durum (Accessed on 15th May 2020)

24 March: Therapies for new coronavirus infectious diseases

Machine-generated translation in english:

Government authority, promoting clinical trials such as antibody therapy drugs and the development of blood device drugs, the authorities accelerate the development of new coronavirus infectious diseases (COVID-19). In addition to antibody therapy, we are also promoting the development of hemodynamic drugs using plasma of patients with antibody formation.
https://news.joins.com/article/23737884 (Accessed on 15th May 2020)

26 March: Capacities in medical institutions are running out

Machine-generated translation in english:

Capacities in medical institutions are running out. It has now been determined with which priority patients should be treated in Germany. In Germany's hospitals, intensive care units are utilised due to the coronavirus. According to the Frankfurter Allgemeine Zeitung, there is a catalogue of recommendations for action.
https://www.op-online.de/deutschland/coronavirus-deutschland-triage-aerzte-krankenhaus-patienten-behandlung-infizierte-zr-13620992.html (Accessed on 15th May 2020)

27 March: Can nivaquine or plasteril help coronavirus patients?

Could these pills help solve the coronavirus crisis? Experts are studying Nivaquine (L), which contains chloroquine, and Plasteril, which contains Hydroxychloroquine Washington (AFP). Could a pair of decades-old, relatively inexpensive drugs be the solution to the novel coronavirus pandemic?

https://www.france24.com/en/20200327-what-is-chloroquine-and-could-it-cure-the-coronavirus (Accessed on 15th May 2020)

28 March: Private hospitals in have stopped accepting coronavirus patients

Private hospitals in the Philippines' capital Manila have stopped accepting coronavirus patients in the face of surging numbers of sufferers and people seeking tests, the hospitals said. The Philippines has reported relatively fewer infections than many other countries in Southeast Asia, but medical experts say a lack of testing has meant that the scale of the epidemic has gone undetected.

https://www.reuters.com/article/us-health-coronavirus-philippines/like-wartime-philippine-doctors-overwhelmed-by-coronavirus-deluge-idUSKBN21E1X8 (Accessed on 15th May 2020)

29 March: Coronavirus and SARS-COV, who triggered a pandemic in 2003/2004

Machine-generated translation in english:

What makes the virus called SARS-COV-2 so extremely 'successful'? Here are possible reasons: (a) it can fly; (b) it undergoes underneath surgery; (3) it is perfectly adapted with us; (4) it is delivered to the customer. Viruses do not have their own metabolism, nor can they move on their own. However, there is evidence that SARS-COV-2 is surprisingly robust.

https://www.n-tv.de/wissen/Warum-dieses-Coronavirus-so-erfolgreich-ist-article21674007.html (Accessed on 15th May 2020)

2 April: Epidemic exposes health system problems in the United States, the number of deaths exceeds 4,000

The United States epidemic exposes health system problems; the number of deaths caused by new coronavirus has exceeded 4,000. The latest estimates suggest that, in the coming weeks to months, the number of deaths due to the epidemic may be as high as 200,000.

https://www.dw.com/zh/ (Accessed on 15th May 2020)

3 April: India's poor live on promises in the wake of COVID-19 Crisis

There is no food, no work and no clue when relief will come. That is life now for millions of informal workers in India, starved of a way to feed themselves or to get the help pledged by the government to survive a three-week coronavirus lockdown. Almost a week after the government announced billions in aid, nothing is yet disbursed.

https://www.deccanherald.com/national/coronavirus-indias-poor-live-on-promises-in-wake-of-covid-19-crisis-820542.html (Accessed on 15th May 2020)

6 April: Boris Johnson Tested Positive and had been Self-Isolating

Johnson tested positive ten days ago and had been self-isolating at his official residence since then. 'This is a precautionary step', said the spokeswoman. She said the 55-year-old prime minister still had a high temperature. Johnson, one of the first world leaders to be diagnosed with COVID-19, had continued to work and lead cabinet meetings via teleconference.

https://www.washingtonpost.com/world/europe/coronavirus-britain-queen-elizabeth-speech-address/2020/04/05/f550ba50–7746-11ea-a311-adb1344719a9_story.html (Accessed on 16th May 2020)

9 April: In New York, more people died from the coronavirus than in the attack on the World Trade Centre on 11 September 2001

Machine-generated translation in english:

In New York, more people died from the coronavirus than in the attack on the World Trade Centre on 11 September 2001. As of Wednesday, the number of outbreak deaths in the city is 4,571 - which does not include people who died at home. 6,268 patients died in the state of New York.

https://tvn24.pl/swiat/koronawirus-w-usa-zmarlo-wiecej-osob-niz-w-hiszpanii-flagi-opuszczone-do-polowy-4549743 (Accessed on 16th May 2020)

10 April: Boris Johnson left intensive care on thursday evening as he continues to recover from COVID-19

Prime Minister Boris Johnson left intensive care on Thursday evening as he continues to recover from COVID-19, but he remains under close observation in the hospital. Johnson, 55, was admitted to St Thomas' Hospital on Sunday evening with a persistent high temperature and cough and was rushed to intensive care on Monday where he spent three nights receiving treatment.

https://www.reuters.com/article/us-health-coronavirus-britain-johnson/uk-pm-johnson-leaves-intensive-care-remains-under-observation-idUSKCN21R34I (Accessed on 16th May 2020)

11 April: Modi's India is not prepared for the coronavirus

Modi's India is not prepared for the coronavirus. The largest lockdown in history arrived with a four-hour notice. At 8 PM on 24 March, Narendra Modi, the prime minister of India, appeared on television for the second time in a week to announce that, starting at midnight, the entire country was going to be curfewed to slow the spread of COVID-19.

https://foreignpolicy.com/2020/04/10/modis-india-isnt-prepared-for-the-coronavirus/ (Accessed on 16th May 2020)

17 April: Brazil passes 30,000 cases of coronavirus this 16 April. In total, the country has 30,425 cases and 1,924 deaths

Brazil exceeded the mark of 30,000 cases of the new coronavirus and reached the number of 1,924 deaths due to COVID-19, which corresponds to 188 In total. There are 30,425 official cases in the country, according to the latest data from the federal government, an increase of 2,105 diagnoses between yesterday and today.

https://catracalivre.com.br/saude-bem-estar/brasil-passa-dos-30-mil-casos-de-coronavirus-neste-16-de-abril/ (Accessed on 16th May 2020)

19 April: 99-Year-Old British war veteran raised more than US$29 million for the health service

Captain Tom Moore, a 99-year-old British war veteran who has raised more than US$29 million for the health service by walking 100 laps of his garden, will be a guest of honour at the opening of a new field hospital next week. The World War Two veteran, who completed his challenge on Thursday, had raised £23.35 million (US$29.21 million).

https://www.reuters.com/article/us-health-coronavirus-britain-veteran/british-veteran-captain-tom-to-be-honoured-at-opening-of-coronavirus-hospital-idUSKBN2200PI (Accessed on 16th May 2020)

23 April: Sweden stayed away from the Lockdown, and its capital stockholm may reach 'Herd Immunity' in weeks

Sweden's decision to go the other way in dealing with the dreaded coronavirus even as the world shut down may have paid off. A controversial strategy to keep public life open as much as possible and develop 'herd immunity' against the virus is reportedly working.

https://www.news18.com/news/world/sweden-stayed-away-from-lockdown-and-its-capital-stockholm-may-reach-herd-immunity-in-weeks-2589685.html (Accessed on 16th May 2020)

25 April: Singapore's exemplary handling of the coronavirus epidemic

Machine-generated translation in english:

Singapore's handling of the coronavirus epidemic is exemplary, and many believe it is one of the most progressive and conscious strategies that utilise modern technologies in this country. However, now the country is referred to as one of the new possible epicentres of the coronavirus.

https://www.portfolio.hu/gazdasag/20200425/a-jarvany-uj-epicentrumava-valhat-a-koronavirus-harc-mintaallama-mert-egyetlen-hatalmas-hibat-kovettek-el-428198 (Accessed on 16th May 2020)

27 April: Healthy again, the British Prime Minister says it is too risky to relax the Lockdown yet

Prime Minister Boris Johnson returned to work on Monday after recovering from COVID-19 with a warning that it was still too dangerous to relax a stringent lockdown hammering Britain's economy for fear of a deadly second outbreak. Johnson compared the disease to an invisible street criminal whom Britons were wrestling to the floor.

https://www.reuters.com/article/us-health-coronavirus-britain/healthy-again-british-pm-says-too-risky-to-relax-lockdown-yet-idUSKCN2290IB (Accessed on 16th May 2020)

29 April: The depressing statistics on the coronavirus

Machine-generated translation in english:

According to the summary of Johns Hopkins University, the number of new coronavirus cases in the world reached 3,117,204 people as of 3 PM JST. If you look at the number of infected people by country, the United States has more than 1 million people; Spain has 232,158 people, 200,105 people in Italy and 169,053 people in France.

https://www3.nhk.or.jp/news/html/20200429/k10012410601000.html (Accessed on 16th May 2020)

30 April: World Health Organisation Lauded Sweden as a 'Model' for battling the coronavirus

The World Health Organisation lauded Sweden as a 'model' for battling the coronavirus as countries lift lockdowns – after the nation controversially refused restrictions. Dr Mike Ryan, the WHO's top emergencies expert, said on Wednesday that there are 'lessons to be learned' from the Scandinavian nation, which has largely relied on citizens to self-regulate.

https://nypost.com/2020/04/29/who-lauds-sweden-as-model-for-resisting-coronavirus-lockdown/ (Accessed on 16th May 2020)

2 May: How it was like to live in Sweden during the coronavirus crisis

With Sweden's unusual coronavirus response, the country did not impose a compulsory lockdown and instead trusted people to socially distance themselves. 11 people living there told us what their daily lives were like – from changing their commutes to still eating in restaurants. They say their lives are not normal, and they are making changes to reduce the spread of the virus.

https://www.businessinsider.com/coronavirus-what-life-is-like-sweden-with-no-lockdown-guidelines-2020-5 (Accessed on 16th May 2020)

12

HUMAN NATURE AND THE IMPACT ON NORMAL LIFE

6 March: Australian paper prints blank pages to help tackle toilet paper shortage

An Australian newspaper has printed an extra eight pages to be used as toilet paper after coronavirus fears prompted customers to bulk buy supplies - leaving some supermarket shelves bare. In a bid to tackle the shortage, The NT News provided a practical – if unconventional – solution.

https://www.cnn.com/2020/03/05/world/coronavirus-australia-toilet-paper-scli-intl/index.html (Accessed on 17th May 2020)

9 March: Cancellation of football matches in Germany

Because of the coronavirus, football matches are threatened to be held in front of empty ranks in the coming days, at least if it is according to the Health Minister of North Rhine-Westphalia, Karl Josef Laumann (CDU). His country will implement the recommendation that events with more than 1,000 participants should be cancelled.

https://www.sueddeutsche.de/panorama/coronavirus-deutschland-bundesliga-dortmund-schalke-koeln-gladbach-1.4828033 (Accessed on 17th May 2020)

15 March: Change in customer behaviour following the COVID-19

Machine-generated translation in english:

The largest supermarket network in the country, Grupo Éxito, announced its measures to prevent toiletries and food products from running out soon due to the change in customer behaviour following the coronavirus COVID-19. In recent hours, there has been talk of a possible increase in the purchase of toilet paper, disinfectants, detergents and other types of hygiene products.

https://www.laopinion.com.co/colombia/grupo-exito-anuncio-medidas-para-evitar-el-desabastecimiento-por-el-coronavirus-193502 (Accessed on 17th May 2020)

18 March: Britain's government set out emergency legislation on tuesday to tackle a growing coronavirus outbreak

Britain's government set out emergency legislation on Tuesday to tackle a growing coronavirus outbreak, with measures including giving powers to police and immigration officers to detain people and put them in isolation to protect public health. The legislation also includes measures to allow recently retired National Health Service staff and social workers to return to work.

https://www.reuters.com/article/us-health-coronavirus-britain-emergency/britain-sets-out-emergency-laws-to-tackle-coronavirus-outbreak-idUSKBN2143MW (Accessed on 17th May 2020)

20 March: Queen Elisabeth II released a statement urging people to follow expert advice

Queen Elisabeth II released a statement on Thursday urging people to follow expert advice 'to change our normal routines and regular patterns of life for the greater good of the communities we live in, and, in particular, to protect the most vulnerable within them'.

https://www.washingtonpost.com/world/2020/03/19/coronavirus-latest-news/ (Accessed on 17th May 2020)

22 March: Traffic on roads and highways in the United States has fallen dramatically

In cities across the United States, traffic on roads and highways has fallen dramatically over the past week, as the coronavirus outbreak forces people to stay at home, and everyday life grinds to a halt. Pollution has dropped. A satellite that detects emissions in the atmosphere linked to cars and trucks shows huge declines in pollution over major metropolitan areas.

https://www.nytimes.com/interactive/2020/03/22/climate/coronavirus-usa-traffic.html (Accessed on 17th May 2020)

23 March: Shinzo Abe said the Tokyo olympics may have to be postponed

Japanese Prime Minister Shinzo Abe has said that the Tokyo Olympics may have to be postponed if the games cannot run in 'complete form' because of the novel coronavirus outbreak, the Japan Times reports. Why does this matter? This is the first time Abe has made such a statement.

https://www.axios.com/coronavirus-japan-abe-tokyo-may-postpone-olympics-b70894cc-30d9–461b-8d02–1014f233a659.html (Accessed on 17th May 2020)

1 April: Several countries in latin America and Europe are extending quarantine

Machine-generated translation in english:

In Latin America and Europe, several countries have taken the decision to extend quarantine as a preventive measure to prevent a further escalation of infections with the new coronavirus. The last to make the announcement was Chile, which recorded four new deaths and more than 2,700 infected.

https://www.eltiempo.com/mundo/mas-regiones/cuales-son-los-paises-que-han-alargado-la-cuarentena-por-el-coronavirus-479226 (Accessed on 17th May 2020)

2 April: Tempers are fraying in supermarkets in Paris

In the country's towns, people are denouncing neighbours to the gendarmerie for breaching confinement and leaving their homes too often. Tempers are fraying in supermarkets, with unsmiling shoppers in the Paris suburbs treating others with suspicion. Angry locals are seething over the 400,000 Parisians who are estimated to have fled the capital to spend the lockdown in their holiday homes.

https://www.powerlineblog.com/archives/2020/04/coronavirus-brings-out-the-worst-in-france.php (Accessed on 17th May 2020)

7 April: Florida Beaches remained packed with partying college students

Florida beaches remained packed with partying college students as the coronavirus crisis gathered force, and the Republican Governor was slow to impose social distancing in a tourist-dependent economy. Surfers ride waves despite a Pinellas County beach closure due to the coronavirus disease (COVID-19) restrictions in Treasure Island, Florida, United States.

https://www.reuters.com/article/us-health-coronavirus-usa-states/florida-nevada-may-be-hit-hardest-by-coronavirus-economic-shock-study-idUSKBN21O1SK (Accessed on 17th May 2020)

8 April: Working hours to be reduced in the Arab States, Europe and Asia-Pacific

Machine-generated translation in english:

Working hours are expected to be reduced by 8.1, 7.8 and 7.2% in the Arab States, Europe and the Asia-Pacific, respectively - which is equivalent to 5 million, 12 million and 125 million full-time workers, respectively. According to the report, significant losses are expected for different income groups, particularly in middle-income and high-income countries.

https://news.un.org/zh/story/2020/04/1054392 (Accessed on 17th May 2020)

13 April: Debate on easing of coronavirus measures in Germany is gaining momentum

Machine-generated translation in english:

The debate on the easing of coronavirus measures in Germany is gaining momentum. A simulation makes hope for an immediate end to the coronavirus isolation. Calls for easing the restrictions become louder. Laschet wants to 'timetable back to normality' – calls for easing are louder.

https://www.giessener-allgemeine.de/panorama/corona-deutschland-experten-legen-konzept-lockerung-corona-massnahmen-zr-13634697.html (Accessed on 17th May 2020)

14 April: Europe is warily easing some restrictions

Spain began easing parts of its coronavirus lockdown on Monday, and other Western European countries - such as Italy and Austria - appeared poised to follow suit with fewer restrictions on public activities. Although, will the easing of constraints, however limited, prove to be a beacon of hope or a cautionary tale?

https://www.latimes.com/world-nation/story/2020-04-13/coronavirus-europe-eases-some-restrictions-fears-new-cases (Accessed on 17th May 2020)

17 April: The United States Federal Government proposes to resume daily life

Machine-generated translation in english:

In stages, the United States federal government proposes to resume daily life, 'announced by United States President Donald Trump at the usual daily press conference'. Trump explained that the measures taken to slow the epidemic have worked, and the worst-case scenario has been prevented.

https://www.portfolio.hu/gazdasag/20200417/koronavirus-az-uj-normalitas-jon-a-vilagban-426576 (Accessed on 18th May 2020)

22 April: The huge increase in food retail sales led to a rise in Prices

Machine-generated translation in english:

Together with the new type of coronavirus COVID-19, which influenced the entire world and our country, there was a huge increase in food retail sales. This increase also led to a rise in prices in some categories. Co-founder of BrandZone, Cem Köz, who examined the price increases before and after the coronavirus, said.

https://www.hurriyet.com.tr/teknoloji/koronavirus-surecinde-akilli-telefon-fiyatlari-dusuyor-mu-41500376 (Accessed on 18th May 2020)

25 April: Protesters demand wisconsin governor to Reopen state

A rally outside Wisconsin's capitol building in Madison on Friday drew hundreds of protesters who demanded Democratic Governor Tony Evers reopen the state, even as it reported its largest single-day jump of new coronavirus cases. The reopening of shuttered businesses in states across the country has become a political hot-button issue.

https://www.reuters.com/article/us-health-coronavirus-usa-wisconsin/protesters-demand-wisconsin-governor-to-reopen-state-as-coronavirus-cases-rise-idUSKCN2263E9 (Accessed on 18th May 2020)

28 April: Life in locked down Britain means fewer shopping trips but bigger bills

Britons made fewer shopping trips but spent more when they did venture out for groceries and bought different products as they adapted to life under the country's coronavirus lockdown, industry data showed on Tuesday. Grocery sales in Britain rose by 5.5% year-on-year in four weeks to 19 April, market researcher Kantar said.

https://www.reuters.com/article/us-health-coronavirus-britain-supermarke/in-lockdown-uk-shoppers-make-fewer-supermarket-trips-but-spend-more-kantar-idUSKCN22A0UR (Accessed on 18th May 2020)

1 May: German chancellor merkel announced the latest easing of coronavirus measures

Machine-generated translation in english:

German Chancellor Angela Merkel announced the latest easing of coronavirus measures. Chancellor Merkel and the country leaders discussed further action on the coronavirus crisis in a video circuit on Thursday, 30 April. Also, there was massive criticism from the economy of the course of action of the federal and state governments in the coronavirus crisis.

https://www.merkur.de/politik/corona-deutschland-merkel-kontaktbeschraenkung-lockerungen-lockdown-regeln-news-rki-zr-13744449.html (Accessed on 18th May 2020)

13

BIZARRE, FUNNY AND
FAKE NEWS

6 March: Pangolin meat and the coronavirus cure

Machine-generated translation in english:

Pangolin meat, if it has any effect, also provokes the disease rather than cures it; it tastes bitter and is considered toxic. Several centuries ago, Tang Dynasty alchemist Sun Siqu wrote the prescription set 'emergency thousand gold recipe' and gave this advice: 'There is a live-in disease. Do not eat carp meat; harm people'.
   https://cn.nytimes.com/opinion/20200306/coronavirus-china-pangolins/ (Accessed on 18th May 2020)

9 March: Facebook, Twitter and Google to deal with false information concerning the coronavirus outbreak

Machine-generated Translation in English:

Facebook, Twitter, Google and Tiktok have enlisted to deal with false information concerning the coronavirus outbreak throughout their networks. Social networks have increased alertness in the past month about the spread of conspiracy theories and misleading information that users upload and are working to remove posts with false information.
   https://www.themarker.com/technation/1.8638991 (Accessed on 19th May 2020)

14 March: 'Flashmobs' in Italy to thanks coronavirus warriors

Machine-generated translation in english:

Throughout Italy, shyly and then more convincingly from the balconies and windows, the applause started. Many, according to testimonies and social

146

media, have been able to join the 'flashmob' promoted for today at noon through word-of-mouth on social media and Whatsapp.

https://tg24.sky.it/cronaca/2020/03/14/coronavirus-italia-contagi-news-diretta (Accessed on 19th May 2020)

17 March: Iran has temporarily freed 85,000 Prisoners to combat the coronavirus

Iran has temporarily freed about 85,000 prisoners in an effort to combat the spread of the coronavirus, a judiciary spokesman in the country has said. Gholamhossein Esmaili added: 'Some 50% of those released are security-related prisoners … also in the jails, we have taken precautionary measures to confront the outbreak'.

https://news.sky.com/story/coronavirus-iran-frees-85-000-prisoners-to-combat-spread-of-covid-19–11958783 (Accessed on 19th May 2020)

18 March: Turkey detains 24 people accused of provocative social media posts

Turkish authorities have detained 24 people accused of baseless and provocative social media posts, as the country steps up its efforts to tackle the coronavirus pandemic. The Interior Ministry said on Tuesday that it was investigating 137 people for their posts, Turkish news site Diken reported, as the country awaits President Recep Tayyip Erdoğan's first public appearance to discuss the coronavirus.

https://ahvalnews.com/turkey-coronavirus/turkey-detains-24-people-over-coronavirus-posts-live-blog (Accessed on 19th May 2020)

23 March: South Africa's plan to erect a fence along the border with Zimbabwe

Officials in Zimbabwe have reacted indifferently to South Africa's announcement that it planned to erect a fence along the border with its neighbour as part of measures to stem irregular migration and contain the spread of the new coronavirus. South Africa has reported 202 cases to date.

https://www.zimeye.net/2020/03/22/zimbabwe-unfazed-by-south-africas-fencing-of-the-border/ (Accessed on 19th May 2020)

1 April: India converting 20,000 railway carriages into isolation wards

India has begun converting 20,000 railway carriages into isolation wards to deal with an expected surge in coronavirus cases. Each of the carriages will be converted into medical facilities containing 16 beds each, meaning a total of 320,000 people can be cared for.

https://www.vice.com/en_us/article/bvgkq5/india-is-converting-20000-railway-cars-into-coronavirus-isolation-wards (Accessed on 19th May 2020)

3 April: Scammers take advantage of the moment of crisis

Scammers take advantage of the moment of crisis. In times of social isolation, criminals use online platforms to reach the population. The main channel of contact with the victims has been WhatsApp. Messages are sent with links to forms that, when filled in, inform criminals of the personal data of the victims.

https://www.correiobraziliense.com.br/app/noticia/brasil/2020/04/03/interna-brasil,842067/cuidado-golpes-virtuais-ganham-forca-durante-a-pandemia-de-coronaviru.shtml (Accessed on 19th May 2020)

4 April: The government of Malaysia apologised after a campaign urging women to keep their husbands happy

The government of Malaysia has apologised after a campaign urging women to keep their husbands happy during the coronavirus lockdown sparked outrage on social media. 'We apologise if some of the tips we shared were inappropriate and touched on the sensitivities of some parties', the ministry said in a statement Tuesday.

https://guardian.ng/life/outrage-as-malaysian-government-tells-women-not-to-nag-husbands-during-lockdown/ (Accessed on 19th May 2020)

6 April: Fake video claiming that COVID-19 test kits are 'Contaminated'

A fake video related to COVID-19 which has emerged, claiming that testing kits are possibly contaminated, has been condemned by the Eastern Cape Department of Health. In the video, which has been widely distributed on social media, a man – whose name is known to News 24 – calls on South Africans to refuse COVID-19 testing.

https://www.news24.com/SouthAfrica/News/fake-news-no-covid-19-testing-kits-are-not-contaminated-20200406 (Accessed on 19th May 2020)

7 April: Turkish government spent more effort trying to curb information

The Turkish government has spent more effort in trying to curb the flow of information on the coronavirus rather than fighting it, journalist Miray Erbey wrote for Deutsche Welle on Monday. 'Without transparency and the freedom of the press, the true scale of the epidemic remains obscured and increases the threat to public health', Erbey said.

https://ahvalnews.com/turkey-coronavirus/turkey-prioritises-curbing-information-coronavirus (Accessed on 19th May 2020)

9 April: Scammers selling coronavirus vaccine and fake COVID-19 test kits

Machine-generated translation in english:

'Invest in a company that invents vaccines' scammers who do not yet have the coronavirus vaccine, who impersonate the WHO's all fake 'nationals' allowance first' fraudulent fraud around the new coronavirus infection disease (COVID-19) in the United States. 'There was a result of coronavirus infection in 15 minutes', said a company that sold home test kits in a false advertisement.

https://news.joins.com/article/23750478 (Accessed on 20th May 2020)

12 April: Colombian homoeopath has become popular on social media for his statements against the coronavirus

Machine-generated translation in English:

Harry Brunal is a Colombian homoeopath who has become popular on social media for his statements against the coronavirus. According to him, this coronavirus is not a disease but is instead the beginning of a war against China, and the vaccine will soon be known.

https://www.futbolred.com/fuera-del-futbol/coronavirus-colombia-hoy-medico-de-monteria-dice-que-el-coronavirus-en-mentira-ultimas-noticias-115658 (Accessed on 20th May 2020)

15 April: European police foiled an attempt to cheat german health authorities out of millions of euros by selling them nonexistent face masks

European police have foiled an attempt to cheat German health authorities out of millions of euros by selling them nonexistent face masks for the coronavirus pandemic, Europol said on Tuesday. The police acted in two countries as Germany moved towards gradually lifting restrictions against COVID-19, which has killed about 3,000 people in the country.

https://www.thenational.ae/world/europe/coronavirus-europe-police-thwart-fake-face-mask-sale-to-germany-1.1006119 (Accessed on 20th May 2020)

18 April: Iran parades 'Coronavirus Radar' that can 'Detect Cases from 100 Yards' which looks similar to a fake 'Bomb detector' device

Iran paraded a device this week which they claim can detect coronavirus cases from 100 yards away, but the contraption looks remarkably similar to a fake bomb detection gadget once flogged by a British fraudster. Iranian Revolutionary Guard Chief Hossein Salami boasted that 'local scientists' had invented the 'state-of-the-art' device to detect virus cases 'remotely'.

https://www.dailymail.co.uk/news/article-8230139/Iran-parades-coronavirus-radar-looks-like-fake-bomb-detector.html (Accessed on 20th May 2020)

22 April: Indonesia punishes coronavirus quarantine violators by locking them in 'Haunted Houses'

A local Indonesian politician found a unique way to punish quarantine violators amidst the coronavirus pandemic. Kusdinar Untung Yuni Sukowati, head of Sragen Regency, has begun locking those who disregard the quarantine inside abandoned houses that are believed to be haunted.

https://www.newsweek.com/indonesia-punishes-coronavirus-quarantine-violators-locking-them-haunted-houses-1499189 (Accessed on 20th May 2020)

24 April: Japan mayor under fire for 'Women Dawdle at Shops' remark

The mayor of Osaka has come under fire for suggesting that men should do grocery shopping during the coronavirus outbreak, because women are indecisive and 'take a long time'. Japan is under a state of emergency, and residents in some areas have been asked to shop less frequently and only send one family member out to get supplies.

https://www.straitstimes.com/asia/east-asia/coronavirus-japan-mayor-under-fire-for-women-dawdle-at-shops-remark (Accessed on 20th May 2020)

26 April: France drastically limits the sale of nicotine products

France severely curtailed the sale of nicotine products on Friday after a study suggested that smokers may be less likely to contract COVID-19. A study by the Pitié-Salpêtrière hospital in Paris flagged 'that current smoking status appears to be a protective factor against the infection by SARS-COV-2'.

https://www.euronews.com/2020/04/25/coronavirus-france-drastically-limits-sale-of-nicotine-products (Accessed on 20th May 2020)

30 April: Misleading information has been spreading in india as the authorities attempt to control the coronavirus pandemic

Misleading information has been spreading in India as the authorities attempt to control the coronavirus with strict restrictions on movement throughout the country. Was a peak in the Alps lit up to thank India? This claim refers to an image of the Matterhorn, one of the highest mountains in the Alps, lit up with an image of the Indian flag.

https://www.bbc.com/news/world-asia-india-52384632 (Accessed on 20th May 2020)

Part IV

THE INFERENCES

14

COUNTRY SENTIMENT FOR CORONAVIRUS NEWS

We have been collecting coronavirus-related news for several countries since February, as the deadly pandemic turned global. The idea was to look at the news for underlying sentiment and see if there are any connections between the on-ground situation and the news sentiment. On the basis of extensive sentiment analysis for more than 30 countries, the results are interesting. We will come back this a little later. However, in summary, the EMAlpha Sentiment Analysis closely mirrors the on-ground situation in several countries.

First, here is a little bit on the methodology: (a) we have chosen these countries on the basis of three important factors which are - their relative size, the impact of the coronavirus and the availability of news flow; (b) EMAlpha machines are collecting the daily news and then compute daily sentiment scores; (c) to avoid getting skewed in daily scores influencing the final output, only the mean of average daily scores has been calculated over 57 data points for each country for the period between 6 March 2020 and 2 May 2020; (d) we are not adjusting and normalising the base rates, so average sentiment scores reflect the base rate effect as well.

We think that a small comment on base rates will help here. There are two important drivers here. One is (a) usual market sentiment has a positive bias. Since the absolute values are way above zero, this would convey that the market is always exuberant and would be doing well, but that is wrong. The market sentiment should be measured as compared to the base rate. If the base rate is '0.065', then anything above it is positive, and anything below is negative. The absolute values do not matter that much, and only the distance in either direction from the base rate matters. The next is (b) the country-specific scores differ for base rates. The absolute values of base rates for different countries are different, and the divergence in final sentiment scores versus respective base rate matters more.

We have also divided the two-month period into three distinct phases to assess if there are differences in sentiment scores.

Phase 1 – 6 March 2020 to 26 March 2020
Phase 2 – 27 March 2020 to 14 April 2020
Phase 3 – 15 April 2020 to 2 May 2020

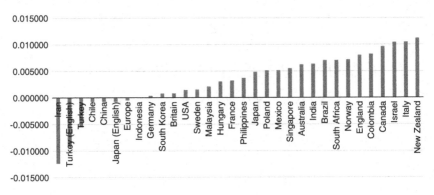

Figure 14.1 Average Coronavirus News Sentiment Between 6 March and 2 May

The primary results

We have learned the following from the EMAlpha Sentiment Analysis:

1. The sentiment scores capture the on-ground sentiment fairly well (e.g. observe where Iran is and where New Zealand stands).
2. The sentiment scores are reflecting not just the impact of the coronavirus pandemic, but also the efforts to contain it (e.g. look at Italy).
3. The sentiment in local news and English news is different, but not by much. For example, observe Turkey (English versus local news) and Japan (English versus local news).
4. Base rates matter and the absolute value of sentiment scores are higher for countries where the base rate is high - in other words, where the usual news sentiment is highly positive (e.g. look at Italy).
5. The severity of the coronavirus crisis is influencing the sentiment scores, but another key factor is what is being discussed by global media about that country.
6. There are other factors. For example, China is blamed that it did not disclose vital information at the right time, and also, there are theories that the coronavirus was born in a lab in Wuhan. All these impact China's score.

Table 14.1 Australia – Daily Coronavirus News Sentiment Scores (From 6 March 2020 to 2 May 2020)

	Consolidated	Phase 1	Phase 2	Phase 3
Mean	0.006204	0.004512	0.004111	0.010200
Median	0.007013	0.00391	0.004064	0.009206
Standard Deviation	0.008794	0.010529	0.007073	0.007643

Source: Courtesy of EMAlpha

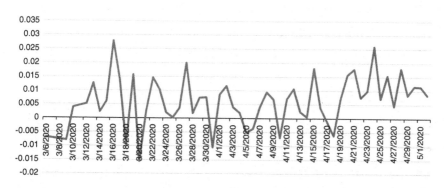

Figure 14.2 Australia – Coronavirus News Sentiment Score (From 6 March 2020 to 2 May 2020)

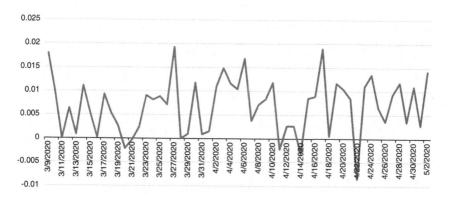

Figure 14.3 Brazil – Coronavirus News Sentiment Score (From 6 March 2020 to 2 May 2020)

7. The smaller countries at extreme ends are usually indicating that, when the quantum of news is smaller, the sentiment scores will get too influenced by a news item.

There are other interesting results in different countries, but it is clear that EMAlpha machines did a great job in capturing relevant news and calculating sentiment scores.

Table 14.2 Brazil – Daily Coronavirus News Sentiment Scores (From 6 March 2020 to 2 May 2020)

	Consolidated	Phase 1	Phase 2	Phase 3
Mean	0.006995	0.006388	0.006618	0.008073
Median	0.008236	0.006384	0.007733	0.009254
Standard Deviation	0.005952	0.005094	0.006445	0.006305

Source: Courtesy of EMAlpha

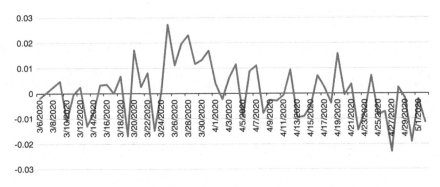

Figure 14.4 Britain – Coronavirus News Sentiment Score (From 6 March 2020 to 2 May 2020)

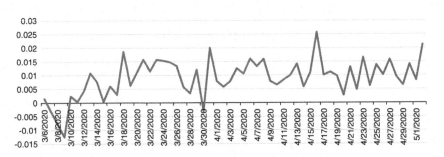

Figure 14.5 Canada – Coronavirus News Sentiment Score (From 6 March 2020 to 2 May 2020)

Table 14.3 Britain – Daily Coronavirus News Sentiment Scores (From 6 March 2020 to 2 May 2020)

	Consolidated	Phase 1	Phase 2	Phase 3
Mean	0.000833	0.001159	0.004780	−0.003679
Median	0.000205	0.002479	0.006063	−0.002268
Standard Deviation	0.010707	0.010989	0.010078	0.009677

Source: Courtesy of EMAlpha

Table 14.4 Canada – Daily Coronavirus News Sentiment Scores (From 6 March 2020 to 2 May 2020)

	Consolidated	Phase 1	Phase 2	Phase 3
Mean	0.009581	0.007702	0.009487	0.011704
Median	0.010013	0.007647	0.008320	0.010133
Standard Deviation	0.006398	0.007720	0.005226	0.005711

Source: Courtesy of EMAlpha

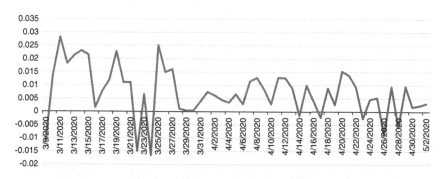

Figure 14.6 Chile – Coronavirus News Sentiment Score (From 6 March 2020 to 2 May 2020)

The sentiment analysis for specific geographies

Australia

The graph for Australia indicates a lot of fluctuation. The mean and median values for all the three phases are positive. The highest value for both mean and median are highest in Phase 3. The standard deviation is also highest at Phase 3. The graph indicates the steepest fall on 20 March 2020.

Brazil

The graph for Brazil indicates its lowest sentiment score on 22 April 2020. The mean and median values are positive, with Phase 3 recording the

Table 14.5 Chile – Daily Coronavirus News Sentiment Scores (From 6 March 2020 to 2 May 2020)

	Consolidated	Phase 1	Phase 2	Phase 3
Mean	0.007225	0.011139	0.002493	0.000405
Median	0.007476	0.013917	0.002493	0.000405
Standard Deviation	0.009343	0.013570	0.005013	0.006591

Source: Courtesy of EMAlpha

Table 14.6 China – Daily Coronavirus News Sentiment Scores (From 6 March 2020 to 2 May 2020)

	Consolidated	Phase 1	Phase 2	Phase 3
Mean	−0.000721	−0.001636	0.001501	−0.004270
Median	−0.001206	−0.001206	0.004299	−0.005111
Standard Deviation	0.008181	0.005541	0.010129	0.006747

Source: Courtesy of EMAlpha

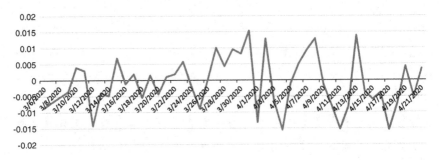

Figure 14.7 China – Coronavirus News Sentiment Score (From 6 March 2020 to 2 May 2020)

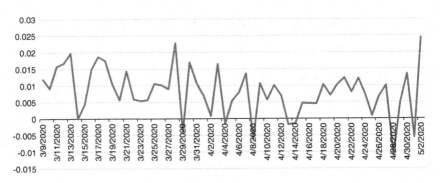

Figure 14.8 Colombia – Coronavirus News Sentiment Score (From 6 March 2020 to 2 May 2020)

highest values for both, but the highest value for standard deviation is indicated in Phase 2.

Britain

The graph for Britain indicates its lowest sentiment score on 27 April 2020. The mean and median values are positive for Phase 1 and Phase 2, with

Table 14.7 Colombia – Daily Coronavirus News Sentiment Scores (From 6 March 2020 to 2 May 2020)

	Consolidated	Phase 1	Phase 2	Phase 3
Mean	0.008181	0.010811	0.006546	0.007068
Median	0.008013	0.010405	0.006847	0.007328
Standard Deviation	0.007206	0.005660	0.007559	0.007796

Source: Courtesy of EMAlpha

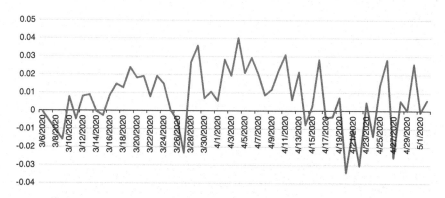

Figure 14.9 England – Coronavirus News Sentiment Score (From 6 March 2020 to 2 May 2020)

Phase 3 recording the lowest values for both in negative, but the highest value for standard deviation is indicated in Phase 1.

Canada

The graph for Canada indicates its lowest sentiment score on 10 March 2020. The mean and median values are positive, with Phase 3 recording the highest values for both, but the highest value for standard deviation is noticed at Phase 1.

Table 14.8 England – Daily Coronavirus News Sentiment Scores (From 6 March 2020 to 2 May 2020)

	Consolidated	Phase 1	Phase 2	Phase 3
Mean	0.008004	0.007090	0.016551	−0.000052
Median	0.007927	0.008038	0.020286	0.001202
Standard Deviation	0.016187	0.010187	0.015742	0.018247

Source: Courtesy of EMAlpha

Table 14.9 Europe – Daily Coronavirus News Sentiment Scores (From 6 March 2020 to 2 May 2020)

	Consolidated	Phase 1	Phase 2	Phase 3
Mean	−0.000476	−0.000030	−0.004164	0.002947
Median	0.000403	0.000867	−0.003616	0.004053
Standard Deviation	0.008946	0.005995	0.008916	0.010301

Source: Courtesy of EMAlpha

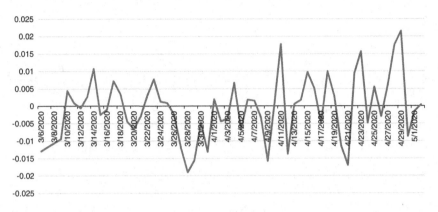

Figure 14.10 Europe – Coronavirus News Sentiment Score (From 6 March 2020 to 2 May 2020)

Chile

The graph of Chile indicates a lot of fluctuations. The mean values for all the three phases are positive. The median, similarly, has positive values for all the three phases. The standard deviation is higher for Phase 1 than the other two values.

China

Only the mean value for Phase 1 is negative, and it is the lowest of all three. The median, similarly, has a negative value for Phase 1, and the other two values are positive. The standard deviation is highest in the second phase.

Colombia

The graph of Colombia indicates a lot of fluctuations. The mean values for all phases - Phase 1, Phase 2 and Phase 3 - are positive. The median, similarly, has got positive values for all the phases. The standard deviation is higher for Phase 3 than the other two values.

Table 14.10 France – Daily Coronavirus News Sentiment Scores (From 6 March 2020 to 2 May 2020)

	Consolidated	Phase 1	Phase 2	Phase 3
Mean	0.003219	0.003325	0.000454	0.006190
Median	0.003112	0.002298	-0.000769	0.006295
Standard Deviation	0.008902	0.008033	0.008047	0.010175

Source: Courtesy of EMAlpha

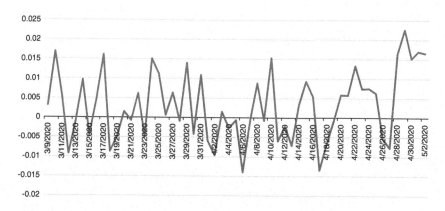

Figure 14.11 France – Coronavirus News Sentiment Score (From 6 March 2020 to 2 May 2020)

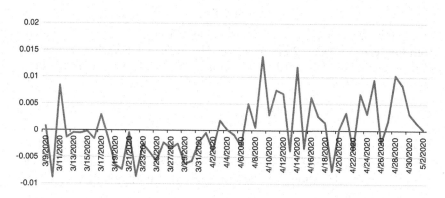

Figure 14.12 Germany – Coronavirus News Sentiment Score (From 6 March 2020 to 2 May 2020)

England

England indicates its steepest fall in sentiment score on 21 April 2020. Only the mean value for Phase 1 is negative. The median values for all three phases are positive, with Phase 2 being the highest.

Table 14.11 Germany – Daily Coronavirus News Sentiment Scores (From 6 March 2020 to 2 May 2020)

	Consolidated	Phase 1	Phase 2	Phase 3
Mean	0.000383	−0.002272	0.000997	0.002664
Median	−0.000419	−0.001605	−0.000466	0.002665
Standard Deviation	0.005239	0.004142	0.005722	0.004707

Source: Courtesy of EMAlpha

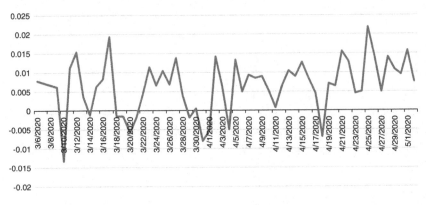

Figure 14.13 India – Coronavirus News Sentiment Score (From 6 March 2020 to 2 May 2020)

Europe

The graph of Europe indicates a lot of fluctuations. The mean values for both Phase 1 and Phase 2 are negative. The median, similarly, has negative value Phase 2. The standard deviation is higher for Phase 3 than the other two phases.

France

The graph of France indicates a lot of fluctuations. The mean values for both Phase 1 and Phase 3 are positive. The median has a negative value for Phase 2. The standard deviation is higher for Phase 3 than the other two values.

Table 14.12 India – Daily Coronavirus News Sentiment Scores (From 6 March 2020 to 2 May 2020)

	Consolidated	Phase 1	Phase 2	Phase 3
Mean	0.006351	0.004843	0.005001	0.009367
Median	0.006711	0.006275	0.006215	0.008915
Standard Deviation	0.007106	0.007718	0.006624	0.006293

Source: Courtesy of EMAlpha

Table 14.13 Indonesia – Daily Coronavirus News Sentiment Scores (From 6 March 2020 to 2 May 2020)

	Consolidated	Phase 1	Phase 2	Phase 3
Mean	−0.000034	0.000648	−0.000079	−0.000707
Median	−0.000614	−0.000724	0.001166	−0.001857
Standard Deviation	0.010886	0.011173	0.006600	0.014286

Source: Courtesy of EMAlpha

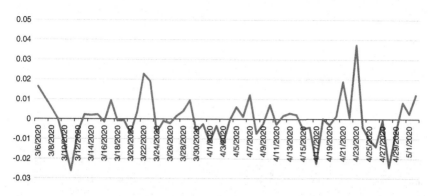

Figure 14.14 Indonesia – Coronavirus News Sentiment Score (From 6 March 2020 to 2 May 2020)

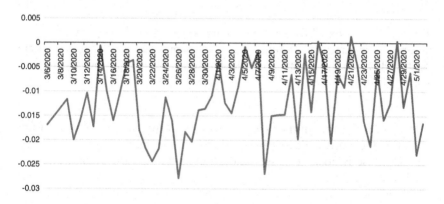

Figure 14.15 Iran – Coronavirus News Sentiment Score (From 6 March 2020 to 2 May 2020)

Germany

The graph of Germany indicates a lot of fluctuations. The mean values for both Phase 1 and Phase 2 are negative. The median, similarly, has got negative values for both Phase 1 and Phase 2. The standard deviation is higher for Phase 2 than the other two values.

Table 14.14 Iran – Daily Coronavirus News Sentiment Scores (From 6 March 2020 to 2 May 2020)

	Consolidated	Phase 1	Phase 2	Phase 3
Mean	−0.012319	−0.014631	−0.011787	−0.010439
Median	−0.013370	−0.015984	−0.013556	−0.010804
Standard Deviation	0.007396	0.007210	0.007096	0.007655

Source: Courtesy of EMAlpha

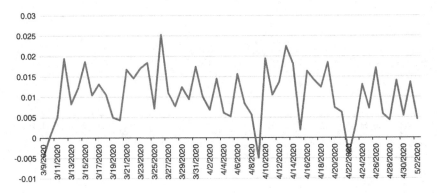

Figure 14.16 Italy – Coronavirus News Sentiment Score (From 6 March 2020 to 2 May 2020)

India

The mean values for all the three phases are positive, with the steepest fall in sentiment score indicated on 10 April 2020. The median values for all three phases are positive. The standard deviation for the second first phase is the lowest.

Indonesia

The mean values for all the three phases are positive, with the steepest fall in sentiment score indicated on 11 April 2020. Only the median for the second phase is positive. The standard deviation for the second phase is the lowest.

Table 14.15 Italy – Daily Coronavirus News Sentiment Scores (From 6 March 2020 to 2 May 2020)

	Consolidated	Phase 1	Phase 2	Phase 3
Mean	0.010430	0.011238	0.010567	0.009374
Median	0.010505	0.011064	0.010034	0.007380
Standard Deviation	0.006656	0.007332	0.006643	0.006117

Source: Courtesy of EMAlpha

Table 14.16 Japan (Local Language) – Daily Coronavirus News Sentiment Scores (6 March 2020 to 2 May 2020)

	Consolidated	Phase 1	Phase 2	Phase 3
Mean	0.004846	0.005358	0.003159	0.006241
Median	0.004373	0.005179	0.002335	0.005237
Standard Deviation	0.008726	0.008639	0.008285	0.009604

Source: Courtesy of EMAlpha

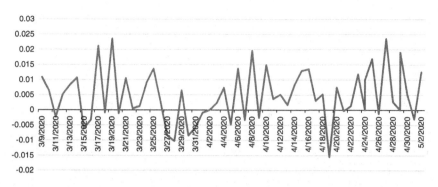

Figure 14.17 Japan (Local Language) – Coronavirus News Sentiment Score (From 6 March 2020 to 2 May 2020)

Iran

The mean values for all the three phases are negative, with the steepest fall in sentiment score indicated on 26 April 2020. The median values for all three phases are negative. The standard deviation for the first phase is the lowest.

Italy

The mean values for all the three phases are positive, with the steepest fall in sentiment score indicated on 9 April 2020. The median values for all the phases are positive. The standard deviation for the third phase is the lowest.

Japan

The mean values for all the three phases are positive, with the steepest fall in sentiment score indicated on 19 April 2020. The median values for all three phases are positive. The standard deviation for the second first phase is the lowest.

The mean values of both Phase 1 and Phase 2 are negative; whereas, the mean for Phase 3 is the highest - with its value in the positive range. The standard deviation is highest in Phase 3.

Table 14.17 Japan (English) – Daily Coronavirus News Sentiment Scores (From 6 March 2020 to 2 May 2020)

	Consolidated	Phase 1	Phase 2	Phase 3
Mean	–0.000721	–0.003898	–0.001284	0.003227
Median	0.000492	–0.009054	0.000416	0.003939
Standard Deviation	0.011154	0.009108	0.012279	0.011265

Source: Courtesy of EMAlpha

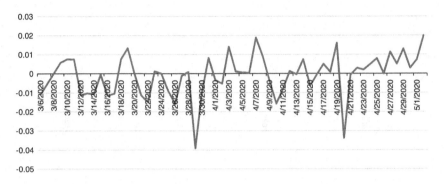

Figure 14.18 Japan (English) – Coronavirus News Sentiment Score (From 6 March 2020 to 2 May 2020)

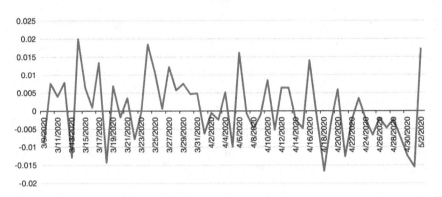

Figure 14.19 Korea – Coronavirus News Sentiment Score (From 6 March 2020 to 2 May 2020)

Korea

The sentiment score fluctuates a lot for the chart of South Korea. The mean for the first phase has a negative value, and the mean value for the third phase is highest. The median value for the third phase is negative. The standard deviation of the first and third phases has a lesser difference compared to the second phase.

Table 14.18 Korea – Daily Coronavirus News Sentiment Scores (From 6 March 2020 to 2 May 2020)

	Consolidated	Phase 1	Phase 2	Phase 3
Mean	0.000812	0.003511	0.001443	–0.002910
Median	–0.000512	0.003995	–0.000512	–0.002357
Standard Deviation	0.008841	0.009690	0.006507	0.009310

Source: Courtesy of EMAlpha

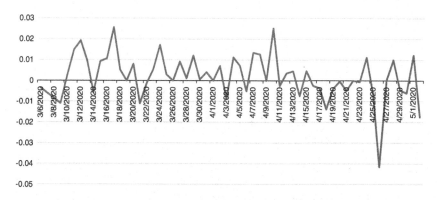

Figure 14.20 Malaysia – Coronavirus News Sentiment Score (From 6 March 2020 to 2 May 2020)

Malaysia

The mean values for all the three phases are negative, and the steepest fall in sentiment score was indicated on 26 April 2020. Only the median for the third phase is negative. The standard deviation for the second phase is the lowest.

Mexico

The mean value was noticeably the lowest in Phase 1 and gradually increased until the third phase. Whereas, the median is highest in the first phase and gradually slows down in the third phase.

Table 14.19 Malaysia – Daily Coronavirus News Sentiment Scores (From 6 March 2020 to 2 May 2020)

	Consolidated	Phase 1	Phase 2	Phase 3
Mean	0.002113	0.005163	0.004633	−0.003766
Median	0.000853	0.005236	0.004117	−0.003065
Standard Deviation	0.010828	0.009872	0.008307	0.012206

Source: Courtesy of EMAlpha

Table 14.20 Mexico – Daily Coronavirus News Sentiment Scores (From 6 March 2020 to 2 May 2020)

	Consolidated	Phase 1	Phase 2	Phase 3
Mean	0.005140	0.009934	0.006181	−0.001382
Median	0.007487	0.010753	0.007746	0.003057
Standard Deviation	0.011179	0.006467	0.009005	0.014483

Source: Courtesy of EMAlpha

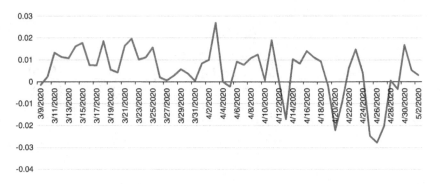

Figure 14.21 Mexico – Coronavirus News Sentiment Score (From 6 March 2020 to 2 May 2020)

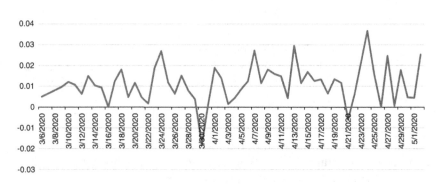

Figure 14.22 New Zealand – Coronavirus News Sentiment Score (From 6 March 2020 to 2 May 2020)

New Zealand

The mean values for both Phase 1 and Phase 2 do not have much difference, but the third phase has a higher mean value. The median gradually increases from Phase 1 to Phase 3. The standard deviation is lowest at Phase 1.

Table 14.21 New Zealand – Daily Coronavirus News Sentiment Scores (From 6 March 2020 to 2 May 2020)

	Consolidated	Phase 1	Phase 2	Phase 3
Mean	0.011156	0.010315	0.010681	0.012547
Median	0.011573	0.010388	0.011518	0.012934
Standard Deviation	0.009181	0.006579	0.010191	0.010504

Source: Courtesy of EMAlpha

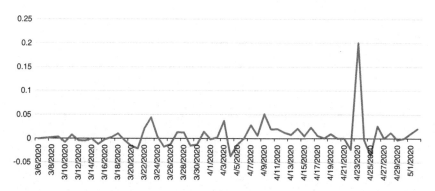

Figure 14.23 Norway – Coronavirus News Sentiment Score (From 6 March 2020 to 2 May 2020)

Norway

The sentiment score for Norway was at its peak on 23 April. The mean and median values are both negative in Phase 1, and the highest mean value was in Phase 3, while the highest median is observed in Phase 2. The standard deviation is highest for the third phase followed by the second phase and is the lowest for Phase 1.

Philippines

The sentiment score for the Philippines has fallen several times throughout the chart. The mean value is highest in Phase 1 and lowest in Phase 3. The standard deviation is higher for the second phase than the other two, which have a lesser difference.

Poland

The standard deviation decreases from Phase 1 to Phase 2, with Phase 3's standard deviation being the highest. The median for Phase 2 is zero, and the median for Phase 3 has the highest value - followed by Phase 2 and then Phase 1. The steepest fall in sentiment score is recorded on 18 April 2020 (i.e. Phase 1).

Table 14.22 Norway – Daily Coronavirus News Sentiment Scores (From 6 March 2020 to 2 May 2020)

	Consolidated	Phase 1	Phase 2	Phase 3
Mean	0.007153	−0.000538	0.008591	0.013751
Median	0.002309	−0.002068	0.012453	0.002773
Standard Deviation	0.031224	0.014841	0.020112	0.048766

Source: Courtesy of EMAlpha

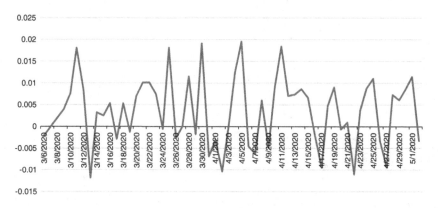

Figure 14.24 Philippines – Coronavirus News Sentiment Score (From 6 March 2020 to 2 May 2020)

Singapore

We can observe the steepest fall in sentiment score for Singapore at around 30 March, with the median positive throughout all the phases. The mean for Phase 1 is higher than the other two phases. The standard deviation for the first and second phase have a lesser difference, but the standard deviation for Phase 3 is higher than the other two phases.

South Africa

We can observe a variation in the values for South Africa. The mean values are reduced for the second phase but gradually increased in the third phase. The country recorded its lowest sentiment score on 8 March 2020. The

Table 14.23 Philippines – Daily Coronavirus News Sentiment Scores (From 6 March 2020 to 2 May 2020)

	Consolidated	Phase 1	Phase 2	Phase 3
Mean	0.003681	0.004516	0.004282	0.002164
Median	0.005018	0.005278	0.005972	0.004207
Standard Deviation	0.007962	0.007283	0.009235	0.007255

Source: Courtesy of EMAlpha

Table 14.24 Poland – Daily Coronavirus News Sentiment Scores (From 6 March 2020 to 2 May 2020)

	Consolidated	Phase 1	Phase 2	Phase 3
Mean	0.005107	0.003536	0.005082	0.006890
Median	0.004583	0.002049	0.005904	0.006073
Standard Deviation	0.008729	0.006998	0.006745	0.012025

Source: Courtesy of EMAlpha

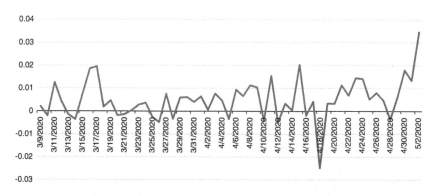

Figure 14.25 Poland – Coronavirus News Sentiment Score (From 6 March 2020 to 2 May 2020)

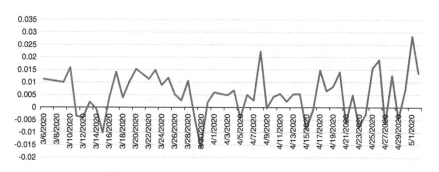

Figure 14.26 Singapore – Coronavirus News Sentiment Score (From 6 March 2020 to 2 May 2020)

same is true for the standard deviation - it decreases in the second phase and again increases in the third phase.

Sweden

The standard deviation gradually increases from Phase 1 to Phase 3, with Phase 3's standard deviation being the highest. The median for Phase 2 is zero. The median for Phase 3 has a negative value, while Phase 1 has a positive value.

Table 14.25 Singapore – Daily Coronavirus News Sentiment Scores (From 6 March 2020 to 2 May 2020)

	Consolidated	Phase 1	Phase 2	Phase 3
Mean	0.005496	0.007040	0.003519	0.005954
Median	0.005339	0.009987	0.004839	0.006632
Standard Deviation	0.008593	0.007489	0.007325	0.010743

Source: Courtesy of EMAlpha

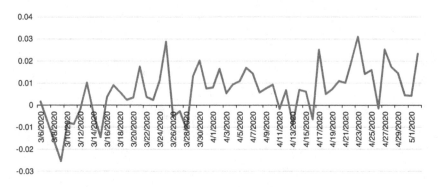

Figure 14.27 South Africa – Coronavirus News Sentiment Score (From 6 March 2020 to 2 May 2020)

Turkey

We can observe the steepest fall in the sentiment score for Turkey on around 26 March, with the median values negative throughout all the phases. The mean values for Phase 1 and Phase 2 are negative, but the mean is higher for the third phase. The standard deviation for The first and second phase have a lesser difference, but the standard deviation for Phase 3 is higher than the other two phases.

Table 14.26 South Africa – Daily Coronavirus News Sentiment Scores (From 6 March 2020 to 2 May 2020)

	Consolidated	Phase 1	Phase 2	Phase 3
Mean	0.007044	0.001683	0.007088	0.012655
Median	0.007110	0.002367	0.007573	0.012525
Standard Deviation	0.010948	0.011859	0.008292	0.010029

Source: Courtesy of EMAlpha

Table 14.27 Sweden – Daily Coronavirus News Sentiment Scores (From 6 March 2020 to 2 May 2020)

	Consolidated	Phase 1	Phase 2	Phase 3
Mean	0.001540	0.002195	–0.002491	0.005104
Median	0.000122	0.000000	–0.002243	0.003559
Standard Deviation	0.014049	0.011692	0.012230	0.017416

Source: Courtesy of EMAlpha

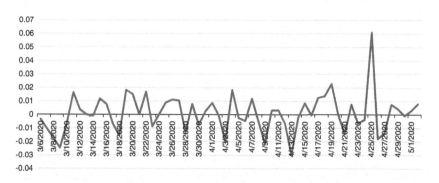

Figure 14.28 Sweden – Coronavirus News Sentiment Score (From 6 March 2020 to 2 May 2020)

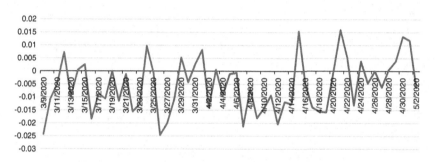

Figure 14.29 Turkey (Local Language) – Coronavirus News Sentiment Score (From 6 March 2020 to 2 May 2020)

We can observe the steepest fall in sentiment score for Turkey on around 20 March, with the median values negative throughout all the phases. The mean values for Phase 1 and Phase 2 are negative, but the mean is higher for the third phase - which has a positive value. The standard deviation for the first and second phase have a lesser difference, but the standard deviation for Phase 3 is higher than the other two phases.

Table 14.28 Turkey (Local Language) – Daily Coronavirus News Sentiment (6 March 2020 to 2 May 2020)

	Consolidated	Phase 1	Phase 2	Phase 3
Mean	−0.005500	−0.008116	−0.006429	−0.001537
Median	−0.006207	−0.009929	−0.009271	−0.000328
Standard Deviation	0.010177	0.010032	0.009992	0.009910

Source: Courtesy of EMAlpha

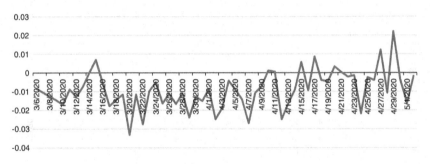

Figure 14.30 Turkey (English) – Coronavirus News Sentiment Score (From 6 March 2020 to 2 May 2020)

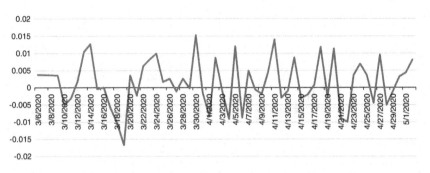

Figure 14.31 United States of America – Coronavirus News Sentiment Score (From 6 March 2020 to 2 May 2020)

Table 14.29 Turkey (English) – Daily Coronavirus News Sentiment Scores (6 March 2020 to 2 May 2020)

	Consolidated	Phase 1	Phase 2	Phase 3
Mean	−0.009094	−0.011915	−0.013326	−0.001649
Median	−0.009285	−0.011610	−0.012820	−0.002255
Standard Deviation	0.010317	0.008894	0.008209	0.010082

Source: Courtesy of EMAlpha

Table 14.30 United States of America – Daily Coronavirus News Sentiment Scores (From 6 March 2020 to 2 May 2020)

	Consolidated	Phase 1	Phase 2	Phase 3
Mean	0.00145272	0.00108473	0.00182172	0.00145166
Median	0.00121971	0.00180963	−0.00057537	0.0019768
Standard Deviation	0.00697181	0.00732713	0.00731205	0.00659512

Source: Courtesy of EMAlpha

United States of America

We can observe the steepest fall in sentiment score for the United States of America at around 18 March, with the median turning negative in Phase 2. The mean values for Phase 1 and Phase 2 are closer, but the mean is higher in Phase 2.

15

COVID-19 HAS TURNED THE WORLD UPSIDE DOWN

Based on what we have noticed in the news and sentiment analysis on the news collection, it is easy to see why this coronavirus crisis has turned the whole world upside down, and it has hit conventional thinking hard. The people from this generation have seen wars. They have seen the collapse of the Union of Soviet Socialist Republics (USSR). They have seen terrorist attacks. They have seen financial bubbles, and they are witnessing climate change, but they have not seen anything like the coronavirus. Anything similar has not been seen for several decades, and, hence, they were not prepared for it, and they also did know how to respond to it. Since it was something that no one really had any prior experience with, the coronavirus pandemic has also led to rethinking some of the things that were always either taken as right or were always taken as wrong.

The best countries in the world are not always the most prepared

The huge crisis, which even the most developed and advanced countries went through, was an eye-opener for the entire world. There have been several news reports on how a country may have a huge stockpile of nuclear warheads, but these are useless when you need nothing more than masks, personal protective equipment (PPE), test kits, medicines and ventilators. As of May 2020, after China, the next hardest-hit countries from the pandemic were Italy, Spain and the United States of America. All of them are advanced, topnotch nations with the best and highest class hospitals and excellent healthcare infrastructures. However, whatever medical facilities they had were woefully inadequate. To be honest, there is no way they could have prepared for this coronavirus crisis, because resources are always limited and whatever is visible at that point gets priority.

No one had anticipated that a virus will spread through the entire world in a matter of a few months, and it would hit the lungs and respiratory systems of its victims. Just like the way the 9/11 incident had exposed the gaps in airport security structures and led to 'from top to down' changes in how the security drills will be carried out at airports and before the passengers enter the airplane, the coronavirus pandemic exposed the gaps in the healthcare apparatus of many countries. A competitive edge in one area does not automatically make a country superior in every field - this was the lesson from the coronavirus crisis for the world. Any crisis leads to re-thinking how to allocate resources and reset in priorities. The news reports on COVID-19 also indicate the same.

Supply chain efficiency was not all that good

The entire mantra of enhanced productivity over the last several decades is based on the improvements in capital and labour practices, which are the two most common factors of production. For any organisation, the idea was to bring down the cost of capital, eliminate expenditure to the maximum possible extent and make labour force more efficient and effective. Moreover, all of this is to make sure that their products and services are available at the most competitive prices for their customers, and they sell only so much in quantity - which will help them maximise profits. There are some generalisations involved here, but this was the template, more or less. An integral part of this entire business cycle was to look at sourcing and supply chains and how to increase efficiency in these.

How are the raw materials with the lowest cost sourced, how are these transported efficiently and in a timely manner to make products available to customers in an optimal manner? However, what was not factored in is that there could be disruptions and the coronavirus crisis brought them to the forefront. When the COVID-19 pandemic hit the plants and factories, workers became unavailable and transport links were broken. The realisation has set in that too much efficiency in supply chains means that the 'margin of error' was really low, and even a very small disruption anywhere in this chain was enough to stop the entire flow. There are several news reports that our machines picked up indicating that this was a serious problem.

Globalisation is not a one-way street

In the last 60–70 years, there have been countless supporting arguments from numerous academicians, business figures and political leaders in why globalisation is the panacea for the ills of local and global economies. The concepts of 'relative competitive advantage', focusing on specialisation along with capitalising on strengths by outsourcing everything which can be done by someone else more efficiently became very popular and these contributed immensely to the growth and expansion of globalisation. There have also been contributing factors like efficient and cheaper air transportation, the advent and supernormal growth in container shipping and cross-cultural influences, but globalisation has been a key driver for the global economy over the last several decades, and it led to exponential growth in international exchanges of goods and services.

The tide has started to turn even before the COVID-19 pandemic as political leaders started to exploit the resentment against globalisation in the local population. However, the coronavirus crisis has added fuel to this fire, and several active participants from major powers - like the United States - have started to strongly highlight this crisis as a strong reason why globalisation requires a clear and logical thought process behind it, and it is not a given that it is only beneficial for everyone. So far, the argument against globalisation was largely emotional as to why it is bad for the local population, but the coronavirus crisis has given a scientific and rational basis to people on why globalisation should be at least stopped if it is not possible to reverse it altogether. This is very clear from the news coverage and sentiment analysis we have done on the coronavirus.

Leadership is not just about power and money alone

There are enough examples in news reports to understand how the government response in different countries was qualitatively different. While there are reports on callousness and irresponsible behaviour of authorities from several countries, there are some encouraging data points as well. There have been many news reports indicating that one of the best countries in terms of handling the coronavirus crisis was Germany. There were articles pointing out how Germany's response was always very data-based and scientific.[1] The usual first response was denial for many countries, but this was not the case with Germany.

Similarly, the policy response from Germany's Chancellor, Angela Merkel, on how to contain the virus in the best possible manner was based on scientific inputs and pragmatic decision-making. There was no official rush to claim that the leaders knew what was unknown to them regarding the different aspects of the disease and, hence, the people were willing to cooperate and support the leadership on their 'plan of action'. The stories about how Germany was dealing with the coronavirus were widely reported in the media. However, there were other examples too, as seen in the news reports which appeared with lesser frequency, from countries where the intensity of the crisis was no less and yet, the handling of the crisis was much better. For example, the reports from Taiwan and Singapore were positive on how these countries handled the coronavirus crisis. This reflects on the quality of leadership, which has got nothing much to do with how powerful a country is and how wealthy it is.

There are stars other than those from sports and movies

The coronavirus has led to the closure of movie theatres and the postponement or cancellation of sports events, with active coverage on how responsible and dedicated healthcare professionals and law enforcement agencies' personnel are helping the people in fighting the battle with coronavirus pandemic. This has led to a 'reset' in how people perceive the relative importance of people in society. While people understand that movies and sports are key sources of entertainment, there are several other sets of people equally important for a society.

There have been many reports on 'coronavirus warriors' which speak about the contributions of doctors, nurses, police, security forces, volunteers among active citizens and other people who have contributed in a positive manner. There is also coverage on how many celebrities, sports and movie stars who did not do enough on their end. There are always possibilities that this is only a temporary realisation, and we will go back to normal, and most likely this will be the case that when the situation normalises – all will be forgotten. However and at least for the time being, the coronavirus pandemic has added a new dimension and a different perspective on many of these relevant issues if we go by the news collection and sentiment analysis.

Rhetoric does not always work in crunch time situations

In the age of 24/7 television, ubiquitous social media and deep penetration of the internet, the environment seemed ideal for people who always had something to do, and these modern advancements knew how to grab their attention. It did not matter that most of it was rhetoric. However, that was before COVID-19 struck. There are news reports that rhetoric from political leaders – like Donald Trump and Jair Bolsonaro – did not exactly help their respective countries in dealing with the pandemic.[2] The non-stop attack on the WHO and China from Trump did not really help the United States of America, and Trump's inconsistent approach led to several faux pas on how the country was seen in dealing with the coronavirus pandemic.[3]

Usually, a crisis is a time when the population gets behind their leader, and the popularity of politician soars. However, that was not the case this time – at least with the United States of America. Our news sentiment analysis was suggesting wild swings on how Trump was doing, and the media coverage was often not positive. It is possible that domestic media could be accused of harbouring a bias against the United States president, but the coverage on Trump from other countries was not different in terms of sentiment. In contrast, there have been stories about people who were leading from the front, but in a more sensible way, despite struggling with

the situation. The New York Governor, Andrew Cuomo had largely positive coverage despite the New York city being in the midst of an
unprecedented crisis because of the coronavirus pandemic.

Nature can strike back when it wants

For several decades now, the countries across the world are bickering at
different forums about who is more responsible for environmental pollution, deforestation and global warming and how should we collectively
fight climate change. There have also been fierce debates on how should we
think about economic growth in the context of the damage suffered by the
environment. Ultimately, the point of contention is who should bear how
much of the cost of protecting the environment and who should address the
issue of climate change. Unfortunately, the story has largely been 'two steps
forward and one step backward', with even the modest goals in progress
remaining unrealistic. However, the lockdowns and discontinuation in the
movement of people and goods to contain the number of infections changed
everything.

While these efforts were intended to control the spread of the coronavirus
pandemic, these also had a positive side effect on air quality and environmental pollution. All of a sudden, news reports started appearing that the
world's most polluted cities in India and China had much more breathable
air; the rivers had cleaner water; the cities were generating less garbage,
and, in general, environmental pollution was much more under control.
This also changed the thinking on how much time nature needs to heal
itself. There have been news reports that, despite the population of the
world being at more than seven billion and after everything we have done to
damage the environment, nature can heal itself rather quickly if it is given
time. There have also been reports that nature knows when and how to take
control back from humans. While the coronavirus crisis may or may not
have been part of such as grand design, there are regular news reports that,
despite all of the scientific progress and medical advancements, we do not
know yet what could strike next.

The coronavirus pandemic has been a great equaliser

There have been several news reports highlighting that it is 'back to basics'
for a large part of the world population, and, hence, the coronavirus pandemic has been a big equaliser. Capitalism has often been blamed for increasing inequality in the world over the last several decades, and the income
gap between the 'haves' and the 'have nots' has been widening. However, the
coronavirus pandemic has led to a situation where vacations in exotic locations are not possible; luxury purchases have been postponed; private jets
are standing idle at the tarmac, and all the money in the world cannot buy

you a vaccine for the coronavirus. Almost everyone is concerned only about the basic necessities and their and their loved ones' safety.

The reports highlight that the percentage spent on categories like entertainment and travel have come down drastically, while the percentage spent on items like groceries and healthcare has gone up substantially. There is extensive coverage on the fact that, no matter what economic background you have, the available options where you can spend your money in are rather limited. Income equality and, much more, even wealth distribution across and also within countries still remain a pipedream, but the coronavirus pandemic has led to more equality in how and where people are spending their money. This was not the best possible way to achieve the goal of equality in the world, but the fact is that this pandemic has done just that. It has not differentiated between the rich and the poor, and the response on how to deal with this pandemic has created equality in several different ways.

Growth is a treadmill that is running faster and faster

There is an interesting trend in some of the news reports that have started to question the basic premise of economic growth. These reports are claiming that modern economic growth is based on more consumption of resources - which supports more production, and, which in turn, requires more customers to consume the output which has been produced in each subsequent period. The measures of economic growth like the Gross Domestic Product (GDP) are like a treadmill where the next financial year will be assessed against the previous one, and you have to run faster to show growth. It does not matter how well you did last year, but if you falter and deliver a lower growth rate this year, then not many people will be happy. It would have been different, and this economic growth would still be acceptable had humans created resources at will.

However, that is not the case. These news reports highlight that yes, we have been able to create wealth – most of which anyway is largely in the paper form. Although, we have not been able to replenish resources, whether these are essential items needed for life – such as air, water and land – or the things which power the engines of the modern economy – such as items like fossil fuels and minerals. This is a dichotomy that more growth does not create more resources, but rather this expedites their consumption. Because of slow economic growth until the 17th and 18th centuries, environmental sustainability was not a challenge then, but this has become a serious problem in the last 100 to 200 years.

The coronavirus news coverage has highlighted these issues in several countries by underlining the fact that the growth model followed by humankind has led to a disbalance, and humanity will fall because of its own weight. This is a challenge that the coronavirus has posed. Such a small event – on the time scale of thousands of years since we have started to live the way we do (e.g. form the time when we started farming 10,000 to 11,000 years ago) – has led to such major chaos in the global economy that we are seeing an unprecedented impact in next few years. Of course, it is not easy to forecast how long this realisation will last, but there have been several reports that talk about the initiation of debate on how to make economic growth more sustainable and adopt a model that is able to withstand shocks better than the one we follow today.

The choice between democracy versus the one-party rule is situational on which works better

There are many news reports comparing the response to the COVID-19 crisis from democratic countries and the countries which have either a one-party rule in theory (China) or in practice (Russia). There is coverage on the good parts and the bad with both systems of government. While countries with the one-party rule are infamous for hiding the true extent of a problem until it is too late, they are also more efficient in containing the crisis. The democratic countries are slower to react, and that hampers their response. There have been reports on how countries like Italy and Spain ignored the early warning signs, how the United States of America did not act until it was too late, and, even after the numbers started to rise, the response was inconsistent.[4]

However, there are also reports that how China did not let the world know about COVID-19 when the infection was in its early stages and was highly localised, and had China shared the information at the right time, then the coronavirus may not have spread to other countries.[5] There have also been reports on how the magnitude of the problem looked bigger in democratic countries, because the information was available freely, and reporting was not artificially and deliberately suppressed by the authorities. While reports are largely one-sided on which system works better in dealing with crises like the coronavirus pandemic, these are also heavily influenced by the source of origin.

However, overall, it is clear from the analysis of these reports that it is difficult to claim which system is better: democracy or one-party rule. The answer depends more on situations and questions like (a) at which stage of the infection spreading is the country at, (b) what is the strategy adopted by the government to handle the coronavirus crisis, (c) which government can work better to stop the infection in other countries. The answer is situational, and specific questions will be better handled than the search for a generic solution.

Conventional thinking changes with new data points

There are several news reports on how some conventional beliefs are changing after the spread of the coronavirus pandemic. For example, there is a widely covered phenomenon that smokers are getting less infected with COVID-19. After many such claims appeared in the media that nicotine could be helpful in preventing the coronavirus from impacting smokers, the World Health Organisation (WHO) had to issue a statement that there are only 'unproven claims that tobacco or nicotine could reduce the risk of COVID-19'.[6] The WHO said in its statement that they are constantly evaluating new research - including research that examines the link between tobacco use, nicotine use and COVID-19.

However, the premier global healthy body added 'There is currently insufficient information to confirm any link between tobacco or nicotine in the prevention or treatment of COVID-19' it said. This claim that nicotine is helpful in fighting the coronavirus first came to light when some researchers from France who were studying the coronavirus linked fatalities published[7] that they have found that the proportion of smokers among COVID-19 deaths was much lower than the proportion in the general population. The claim was based on a theory that if nicotine is already present on human cells, then it may block the coronavirus.

We might say that there is not sufficient data available to prove that is there really a linkage between smoking and possible protection from the coronavirus, but this goes against the conventional view that nicotine is bad for the lungs and that smoking is damaging for the lungs. Nevertheless, here is an interesting situation where news reports were quick to pick this story from France, and the claims began that there is a negative link between smoking and the risk of getting infected from the coronavirus. Similarly, there are other news reports as well that are questioning some of our conventional beliefs that have come under scrutiny because of the coronavirus pandemic.

Reverse migration from cities to villages

There are other important trends as well that are abundantly clear from the news analysis. Migration, so far, only meant that rural people will shift to urban centres, and urbanisation was a key parameter to assess a country's economic progress. Despite housing challenges and a significantly higher cost of living in cities, the move to cities also had aspirational value for rural people. The cities were considered better than villages in terms of options for higher education and the availability of employment opportunities, and both of these factors were important for people who were finding more avenues for growth in careers. Urban centres were also better for lifestyle and entertainment options.

Most of this remains true, but, for the first time, there have been reports of widespread reverse migration from cities to villages. The most interesting part is that there are also reports that real estate prices outside cities have risen faster than the increase in prices in cities. While for many people, pollution in cities has been a reason to consider a shift to villages, this was only a trickle. Can this become a flood as a result of the coronavirus crisis? It is very difficult to say and might also be unlikely, but for sure, the news reports have started to highlight that the COVID-19 pandemic has given a warning to humankind that, just like other major pandemics in the past, cities are always a soft target for viruses.[8]

The reasons are obvious: high population density and people remaining in close physical contact lead to a faster spread of infections. The shift to villages may only be a temporary phenomenon, but this also depends on how long the coronavirus will remain a threat. The longer it takes to control COVID-19, either in the form of an effective treatment or a vaccine, some of these trends will get stronger. There are different versions of this phenomenon, as per news reports, which have been picked up by our machines, and these include a stronger push for social isolation, and cities are a hindrance to this. For sure, horror stories like thousands of people dying from the coronavirus in New York have not been the only reason, but there is a realisation that cities are always the worst affected by any deadly infections and will have more fatalities.

Crude oil prices are in the negative for the first time in history

Monday, 20 April was a historic day for the crude oil industry, but not in a good way. The May United States oil futures contract went into negative territory for the first time in history. The United States reserves were full, and there is simply no place to put the crude oil, and everyone is avoiding accepting the delivery of physical crude. However, this is not just a storage problem. While that may be an issue for the May contract, the bigger and more fundamental and structural concern is on demand. The global oil demand is down by more than 30% due to the coronavirus pandemic and the lockdowns in several countries.

This is putting huge pressure on producers who are still bickering on production cuts. For many of them, oil exports are a significant part of their revenues, and they cannot seem to easily agree on who needs to cut production to bring back some stability in prices. The low demand and low crude prices actually made some of them more desperate in their attempts to increase production and gain market share. While the market movements are related to specific reasons like storage issues, the general sentiment on the demand side was extremely negative.

Now, look at this in the context of the fall in crude oil. The Oil News Sentiment plot showed how the oil sentiment fell to a level lower than what it was in mid-March – when the Saudi-Russia talks broke down and oil price and the stock market fell. We do not have the hourly sentiment data on oil for the entirety of 20 April, but it is possible that the sentiment might also have sharply fallen before the oil crash. The bottom line is that we see a clear collapse in sentiment around the time the price crashed, and this was also linked with the sudden spike in searches for 'oil'. It is too early to conclusively prove whether the spike in searches was an indicator of a crash or the price crash led to a sudden surge, but this is an interesting occurrence and for sure, it cannot be just a coincidence.

Notes

1 Lothar Wieler, Ute Rexroth, and and René Gottschalk. June 30, 2020. 'Emerging COVID-19 success story: Germany's strong enabling environment.' https://ourworldindata.org/covid-exemplar-germany (Accessed on 14th July 2020).

2 Andrew Rosati and Simone Iglesias. July 8, 2020. 'Sick with Covid, Brazil's Bolsonaro defends his virus approach'. The Print. https://theprint.in/world/sick-with-covid-brazils-bolsonaro-defends-his-virus-approach/456593/ (Accessed on 14th July 2020); April 30, 2020. 'President under probe: On Brazil's Jair Bolsonaro.' The Hindu. https://www.thehindu.com/opinion/editorial/president-under-probe-the-hindu-editorial-on-brazils-jair-bolsonaro/article31466623.ece (Accessed on 14th July 2020); May 19, 2020 'Coronavirus: Trump says he is taking unproven drug hydroxychloroquine.' BBC News. https://www.bbc.com/news/world-us-canada-52717161 (Accessed on 14th July 2020); March 23, 2020 "Trump Says Coronavirus Cure Cannot 'Be Worse Than the Problem Itself'." The New York Times. https://www.nytimes.com/2020/03/23/us/politics/trump-coronavirus-restrictions.html (Accessed on 14th July 2020).

3 March 18, 2020. 'Trump Threatens to Leave WHO and Permanently End Funding.' The New York Times. https://www.nytimes.com/2020/05/18/us/coronavirus-updates.html (Accessed on 14th July 2020); Joel Mathis. May 4, 2020. 'Trump was the disaster we should have seen coming.' The Week. https://theweek.com/articles/912493/trump-disaster-should-have-seen-coming (Accessed on 14th July 2020).

4 Angela Giuffrida. March 23, 2020. 'Italy struggled to convince citizens of coronavirus crisis. What can Europe learn.' The Guardian. https://www.theguardian.com/world/2020/mar/23/a-warning-to-europe-italy-struggle-to-convince-citizens-of-coronavirus-crisis (Accessed on 14th July 2020); Austin Williams. March 18, 2020. "We took it lightly': Quarantined Italians record video messages with dire coronavirus warning.' Fox 10 Phoenix. https://www.fox10phoenix.com/news/we-took-it-lightly-quarantined-italians-record-video-messages-with-dire-coronavirus-warning (Accessed on 14th July 2020); Ceri Parker. March 10, 2020. "'Every ventilator becomes like gold' - doctors give emotional warnings from Italy's Coronavirus outbreak." World Economic Forum. https://www.weforum.org/agenda/2020/03/suddenly-the-er-is-collapsing-a-doctors-stark-warning-from-italys-coronavirus-epicentre/ (Accessed on 14th July 2020); April 2, 2020. 'Coronavirus outbreak: Unions allege Spain ignored doctors' warnings.' Global News. https://globalnews.ca/video/6767771/coronavirus-outbreak-medic-unions-say-spain-ignored-doctors-warnings (Accessed on 14th July 2020); April 2, 2020 'Medic unions say Spain ignored doctors' warnings.' Reuters. https://uk.reuters.com/video/watch/idOVC7T0L7V; https://www.kff.org/news-summary/bill-gates-says-u-s-did-not-act-quickly-enough-to-avoid-shutdowns-amid-covid-19-pandemic/ (Accessed on 14th July 2020); Mar 25, 2020. 'Bill Gates Says U.S. Did Not Act Quickly Enough To Avoid Shutdowns Amid COVID-19 Pandemic.'

KFF. https://www.bbc.com/news/world-us-canada-52579200 (Accessed on 14th July 2020).

5 PTI. May 09, 2020. 'China continues to hide, obfuscate COVID-19 data from world: Pompeo.' The Hindu. https://www.thehindu.com/news/international/china-continues-to-hide-obfuscate-covid-19-data-from-world-pompeo/article31540364.ece (Accessed on 14th July 2020); Business Insider. https://www.businessinsider.in/science/news/china-hid-crucial-information-about-the-coronavirus-early-on-hereaposs-what-was-really-happening-while-chinese-authorities-stayed-silent-/authorities-in-wuhan-reported-more-than-40-cases-of-an-unknown-pneumonia-like-illness-to-the-world-health-organization-on-january-3-/photostory/76185695.cms (Accessed on 14th July 2020).

6 May 11, 2020. 'WHO statement: Tobacco use and COVID-19.' WHO. https://www.who.int/news-room/detail/11-05-2020-who-statement-tobacco-use-and-covid-19 (Accessed on 14th July 2020); 'Tobacco and waterpipe use increases the risk of COVID-19.' WHO, Eastern Mediterranean. http://www.emro.who.int/tfi/know-the-truth/tobacco-and-waterpipe-users-are-at-increased-risk-of-covid-19-infection.html (Accessed on 14th July 2020).

7 Ross Cullen. May 07, 2020. 'Nicotine patches trialled to help COVID-19 patients in France.' CGTN. https://newseu.cgtn.com/news/2020-05-07/Nicotine-patches-trialed-to-help-COVID-19-patients-in-France-QiKFRCAzMQ/index.html (Accessed on 14th July 2020); Kabir Firaque. May 5, 2020. 'Does nicotine help fighting COVID-19? The Science behind a Novel Hypothesis.' https://indianexpress.com/article/explained/does-nicotine-help-fight-covid-19-the-science-behind-a-novel-hypothesis-6394013/ (Accessed on 14th July 2020).

8 Somik Lall and Sameh Wahba. April 23, 2020. 'Cities, crowding, and the coronavirus: Predicting contagion risk hotspots.' World Bank Blogs. https://blogs.worldbank.org/sustainablecities/cities-crowding-and-coronavirus-predicting-contagion-risk-hotspots?cid=ECR_FB_worldbank_EN_EXT (Accessed on 14th July 2020); 27 May, 2020. 'Mumbai: How Covid-19 has ravaged India's richest city.' BBC. https://www.bbc.com/news/world-asia-india-52798740 (Accessed on 14th July 2020).

16

WHAT IS SEEN MORE OFTEN IN CORONAVIRUS NEWS?

We have been regularly collecting news across more than 30 countries on the coronavirus to analyse the underlying sentiment, and this has offered us interesting insights on how sentiment has evolved on the coronavirus pandemic along with its disastrous impact. While doing the sentiment analysis, we have also noticed that, when we analyse the news collection on the coronavirus from the end of January onwards, we find that there are some recurring themes in the news flow. While one would expect that the regular tracking of the spread of the coronavirus pandemic will be covered by media – and this includes statistics on new cases, rate of spreading and deaths caused by COVID-19 – there are some other topics which are covered frequently. This leads to some important conclusions about how the news selection and focus of media on what is important in relative importance get influenced by several extraneous factors.

The more common of these items are as follows. Please note that we have listed these recurring themes in alphabetical order, and this does not reflect the relative importance or frequency of occurrence.

The Blame Game Between Countries and Even Non-Government Organisations

This is a recurring theme, and some of the news items that appear more often are: (a) the United States of America is blaming China regularly, and it alleges that China has responded to the pandemic too late and also delayed the news on the spread of this disease and severity of it; this means that it was difficult for other countries to respond, and by the time they did, it was too late,[1] (b) The United States of America has also blamed organisations like the World Health Organisation (WHO) for their inadequate response and also for siding with China;[2] (c) China is defending its response to the coronavirus and is also blaming The United States of America for linking unrelated issues;[3] (d) There is also another side act which is the United States-Iran case, and both these countries have not really found any common ground to postpone their hostilities.[4]

189

The reports when officials from other countries called the 'coronavirus' a 'Chinese virus' and entirely blamed China for its spread and reaching other countries have grabbed much space. There are also reports on a few countries reporting the export of the coronavirus from other countries and this is being blamed for the spread of disease. Overall, there are regular news reports on how even senior officials are participating in mudslinging and blaming other countries for their own problems.[5]

Brazil's Response to the Coronavirus Threat

The response to the coronavirus pandemic from Brazil is an interesting case. While most countries went for 'lockdowns' to contain the virus from spreading, Brazil adopted an entirely different approach. There is regular news coverage not just from Brazil, but also from other countries that Brazilian President Jair Bolsonaro has continued to downplay the COVID-19 situation with his comments and actions.[6] While the pandemic has not been kind to Brazilians, and there is no indication that the curve for the spread of the coronavirus and new inflections is any different for Brazil versus other countries, Bolsonaro has continued to ignore the statistics.

There are reports on how he is mingling with the crowd and taking photos with his supporters. In fact, globally, the criticism of the approach of Brazil's President is so widespread that many news reports have mentioned that the biggest threat to Brazil's COVID-19 response is its President, Jair Bolsonaro. It may or may not be true but there are many news reports with coverage on how Bolsonaro is openly flouting the measures of physical distancing.

Celebrity Connection with the Coronavirus

There is an interesting connection between influential and powerful people getting infected with COVID-19 and news coverage along with the sentiment. An interesting example here is Canada. When Canadian Prime Minister Justin Trudeau's wife was found infected with the coronavirus, and he had to self-quarantine himself for a couple of weeks, this generated a lot of news and also impacted sentiment.[7] The case got more serious with Britain when Prime Minister Boris Johnson had to be hospitalised and spent several days in the intensive care unit (ICU). This almost created a national emergency in the United Kingdom.[8] Not only did news coverage spike, but the sentiment also turned negative as a result.

The illness of Prince Charles may not have generated as much news flow as Boris Johnson,[9] but it was still significant. The same trend was noticed in the United States of America when the White House staff were reported to be infected, and this was a big talking point in media.[10] This was noticed in several countries that, all of a sudden, the news coverage spiked and sentiment got worsened because of celebrity infection news flow. In the end, people reconciled with the fact that the coronavirus does not differentiate between the rich or the poor or powerful or ordinary people.

Conspiracy Theories

This is a recurring theme across countries and across phases. However, when the coronavirus pandemic became more serious and more threatening, the conspiracy theories also peaked. For example, it is very likely that there may still be a significant proportion of people who would believe that this virus did not originate from a wet market in Wuhan, but rather had its source in a carefully devised plan to release the virus from a government laboratory in China.[11] While on the subject, we are not taking sides here, because we do not know for sure. However until that time, this is not conclusively proven, and there is always a 'benefit of the doubt' that the accused should get.

The interesting part is that it is rather disastrous either way. If the virus did originate in a laboratory, the Chinese government machinery convinced the world otherwise. Moreover, if there is no truth in these 'virus from the China Government's laboratory in Wuhan' stories at all, the political use of this crisis is embarrassing for the entire humankind. Nevertheless, this was not the only conspiracy theory. There were reports of other theories too that this was an experiment, that several global powers are involved and many more such speculations and simply, figments of the imagination from fertile minds with vested interests.

Employment Opportunities and the Impact of the Coronavirus on Unemployment

There are several news reports on how the coronavirus pandemic is leading to a severe unemployment crisis. While not all countries report their unemployment figures as regularly as the United States of America does, there are still news reports from almost all countries in how the coronavirus, lockdowns and the rise in unemployment are linked. This has also become a humanitarian crisis in several countries, as a result. The reports of job cuts in different companies across the board, delays in payment of salaries and news coverage on salary cuts are getting picked up very regularly by our machines.[12] There are also reports that small and medium-sized enterprises have been impacted a lot more, and, since they are a source of employment for the majority population, this crisis on unemployment is actually more serious than what we are hearing.

There are fake news on different aspects of the coronavirus crisis- There is more of a 'mischief' element in fake news rather than a 'meticulously planned attempt to misguide and misinform people', as one sees in the conspiracy theories. However, the coronavirus pandemic crisis has become an opportunity for people and, in some cases, even media outlets to spread fake news. In most countries, there is consistent coverage on how this particular news item was fake or how the official sources have denied confirming a piece of particular news. Most of these fake news were related to the impact of the coronavirus, its symptoms, how it spreads and how it can be stopped or can be controlled.

Some of these news reports also highlight how several countries are dealing with this menace. These news reports mention that some of these countries have announced stringent measures like jail terms and heavy fines on people spreading rumours. Some other countries have run an extensive publicity campaign to urge people not to believe in unofficial and unverified news.[13] However, as it happens in most cases when panic ensues, fake news travel faster than genuine news or official information.

A Geopolitical and Business Shift in the Future

This is another very common theme which we find in coronavirus-related news coverage. There are regular news reports on how this crisis will lead to a shift in diplomatic relations, and we are not just talking about the United States of America and China. For example, there are reports on how many European countries are not happy with how China dealt with this crisis, and they have concerns that the Chinese Government did not do enough to control the spread.[14] There are also reports on how China has lost a great opportunity to become a global leader by mismanaging the crisis and not being fully transparent about sharing information and data with other countries.[15] However, this geopolitical shift is just one part.

There are several news items, that consistently and regularly appear across different countries, which talk about how the dependence on China has hurt the economies worldwide. There are also reports that this crisis is leading to a shift of business away from China, as these countries have either already started or will look for alternatives. Countries like Japan are already incentivising their companies to shift manufacturing operations away from China, and this is covered in the news media.[16] There are also reports on how this crisis has created an opportunity for countries like Indonesia, Vietnam, India and others to win in business which is fleeing from China.[17]

Globalisation Paused or Even Reversed

There are news items on how the coronavirus crisis has led to rethinking the entire concept of globalisation. News reports highlight that the severe supply chain disruptions caused by lockdowns and the suspension of transportation links will prompt policymakers in several countries to stop advocating for 'just in time' supply chains and 'outsourcing to the cheapest and most efficient destination'. There were reports on the serious shortage of essential goods such as personal protective equipment (PPE), medicines and ventilators in several countries, and this situation was caused as a result of either 'negligible' or 'insufficient' local manufacturing.

Efficient supply chains were good and saved costs in regular times, but, during the time of crisis, these proved completely ineffective. As per several reports, there were questions in many countries on issues such as if it was a wise strategy to get rid of local manufacturing completely and rely on the outside world even for essential commodities.[18] Interestingly, while there are reports that this crisis will give a further push to online transactions and e-commerce, there were some reports also on the debate around the importance of neighbourhood stores versus dependence on e-commerce giants - these reports highlighting the services rendered by local stores in the times of crisis.

Government response across the countries is also a recurring theme- This is an important recurring theme when reports have been highlighting the debate on the efficiency and effectiveness of the strategy of local governments to fight the coronavirus pandemic crisis. Though some countries like the United States of America (because of their neglect of the coronavirus crisis when it was in its initial phases) and Brazil (because of the approach taken by the Brazilian President, as we have discussed previously too) were more in the news, the government response was a common theme across the world. There were discussions on issues like whether the government reacted too early or too late, whether the response was proper, what went right and what went wrong, if the panic was justified and whether the economic cost was too steep for some segments of the society.

There were usual opposition barbs and potshots taken at the leaders in power, but there was no doubt that scrutiny was deep. In news reports, a few countries stand out. There was a lot of positive coverage on how Germany has handled the coronavirus crisis under the leadership of Chancellor Angela Merkel. Germany's response was highlighted as the most logical and consistent with clear strategy and communication on all levels.[19] There was positive coverage of France's president, Emmanuel Macron, and Japan's Prime Minister, Shinzo Abe, as well.[20]

Hoarding of Essential Commodities such as Food Items

This was another recurring theme in how people start to panic and they react more emotionally and less logically during emergency situations that are less real and more perceived. While the administration and government authorities continue to highlight that there is no shortage of essential goods and basic necessities almost everywhere, the news reports highlight that people have not really paid any attention to them. There are reports from across the world and from almost all countries that the supermarkets have been raided by people and items of daily needs are flying off the shelf so quickly that sections after sections in supermarkets have become empty.

People are excessively hoarding these commodities and buying in large quantities, anticipating that there will be a shortage in supply. There have also been reports from countries like Japan that are known for their civil discipline and impeccable public behaviour that many of their supermarkets have been reporting significant sales increase in the months of March and April, as compared to the same month in the previous year. There have been such reports from several other countries including the United States of America and countries from Europe that the people are indulging in indiscriminate bulk buying of supplies as they have been gripped by fear that there will be serious shortages of goods for daily consumption.[21]

The Impact on Airlines, Travel, Tourism, Prepared Food and Hospitality industries

While the coronavirus pandemic has led to a cancellation of international and domestic travel in many countries, there are several news items covering the impact of the coronavirus pandemic on industries such as airlines, travel, tourism, leisure, prepared food and the hospitality industries. There have been several news articles on how many enterprises from these industries are permanently damaged and will face closure. Survival will remain extremely difficult for others too.[22]

The lockdown's economic impact is generic, but some of the industries which are directly impacted have generated more news coverage. For example, the layoffs at airlines and firms like Airbnb have generated huge media coverage.[23] Amidst all this, it is interesting that some of the news coverage is also about the industries which are benefiting from this crisis. These industries include pharmaceutical and biotechnology firms - the tools and services which help people and organisations in working remotely and providing communication support.

The Oil Demand Slump and Volatility in Crude Prices

There are several news reports on turbulence in oil markets. Oil is a big contributing factor in global financial markets, and commodity prices also affect the other asset classes. While the coronavirus pandemic has impacted the demand in several countries, the crude oil market has turned extremely volatile. There are regular reports on oil supply glut,[24] but there have been three topics where the frequency of news was the highest: (a) the price war and major conflict among some large producers such as Saudi Arabia and Russia, and this also includes the developments on OPEC deliberations, (b) the major price correction and oil price turning negative because there is no storage space and (c) the severe impact on oil-dependent economies such as Saudi Arabia and other countries in the Middle East.

As such, the demand destruction has been directly attributed to the coronavirus pandemic, and there have also been reports on how long this will last and whether this impact is temporary or permanent in nature. Overall, crude oil has been a market where the impact of sentiment is significant, and sentiment has been broadly negative on oil demand which led to the negative sentiment on oil prices as well.

Religion and the Role of Congregations in Spreading the Coronavirus

There have been news reports on how some religious events and congregations played a role in spreading the coronavirus. There have been reports from several countries – including South Korea, India and Malaysia – that several members from the crowds gathered for a religious function were infected with the coronavirus, because some people in those events and congregations were infected. There were cases like thousands of people getting infected from a religious gathering in Delhi and hundreds of people getting affected at a mosque in Malaysia. There have also been several news reports carrying images and stories on how religious gatherings were banned and how the places of worship are empty.[25]

There have also been news reports that how the coronavirus crisis may redefine the role of religion in people's lives and why this crisis is different from the previous pandemics the world has seen - more specifically, in the context of what these unfortunate events did to people's relationship with god and the importance they accorded to religion in their lives. This could include changes like people less willing to travel to religious places and where they find solace in difficult times. It is too early to say if these changes will be permanent, but there are regular stories on how religious practices have altered during the coronavirus crisis.

Sports Events Cancellation and How the Coronavirus May Change Some Sports Forever

The coronavirus crisis has led to the postponement and cancellation of several sports events, including the Olympics in Japan. There are also differences from country-to-country on coverage of sports. For example, in countries like England, there is prominent coverage on how the coronavirus crisis has impacted sports and scheduled events. Similarly, European countries have also covered postponement of football matches in European leagues.[26] Also, before the announcement that the Olympics will not be held as scheduled in July 2020, there were intense speculations on whether the games will be postponed or will be cancelled.[27]

In some countries, the local events also generated news flow, as was the case with the Indian Premier League or IPL - an annual cricket event that is lucrative for both players and the organisers. The IPL is held in April-May every year, and this created intense speculation on the fate of the tournament.[28] Finally, after the event was cancelled, the news reports started appearing if it will be held this year at all or if September-October could be the likely dates for the competition. There have also been stories on how sports figures are raising awareness on precautionary measures in dealing with the coronavirus crisis.

Technology Can Help in Fighting the Coronavirus Pandemic

There have also been news items related to how technologies like Big Data and AI can help in fighting the coronavirus pandemic and how modern technology can help in providing support to medical professionals and research scientists. There have also been reports on how technology can be used to quickly analyse the different strains of this virus and how that can help in developing a vaccine or treatment for the disease. There have also been reports related to how technology has made it possible to support 'work from home' and to achieve higher efficiency and increased effectiveness for organisations and employees.

Our machines collecting the news items for sentiment analysis have picked up numerous stories across countries related to (a) how technology is shaping our response in the fight with the coronavirus, (b) how societies are quickly adapting to changed circumstances with the help of technology and (c) how technology is helping elderly people and the segments of the population that are in distress in dealing with the coronavirus. There are also reports on several new applications that have been specifically developed for handling the coronavirus.

Toilet Paper

This is an interesting entry, and we ourselves are surprised as to why 'toilet paper' appears with such amazing frequency in news reports in the context of the coronavirus. There are several news reports mentioning the rush among people to buy toilet paper and how people have stocked toilet paper, not just for weeks or months to come, but for years. There are also some amusing stories on how a newspaper in Australia published eight pages of toilet paper and how a family ordered ten years of supply for toilet paper.[29] While the rush to buy huge supplies of toilet paper is broadly a part of the general tendency to hoard essential commodities, this has attracted more media coverage compared to other regular items.

While there are stories about how Italians are rushing to buy pasta,[30] and the prices have increased multiple times as a result of how some of the department stores have allocated dedicated time slots for elderly people because they were finding it difficult to shop with huge crowds or how people have been spending hours in billing queues at shops and department stores, the frequency in which the news articles on toilet paper has appeared is noteworthy. This is an interesting, recurring theme in news reports for several countries.

Traditional Medicines and the Efficacy of Treatment for the Coronavirus

In some countries, the coronavirus has created so much panic, and, since there is no conventional cure available, people have started to look for alternatives in their traditional system of medicines. There are news reports, especially from countries which have relatively more developed traditional medicine system because of them being ancient civilisations, on how some of the traditional cures could help coronavirus patients. In places like China and India, there are also reports on how there is official tacit or vocal support for such treatment methods, despite having no conclusive evidence that these are effective.

While it is difficult to argue if a particular line of treatment is effective or not, some of this could also divert attention from following a 'standard operating procedure' for what should be done in COVID-19 cases. It is also important to highlight here that this is not the case with traditional medicines alone, but also that there have also been news reports about Hydroxychloroquine (HCQ) for coronavirus patients. After the United States President Donald Trump vigorously defended the use of HCQ to treat patients, there have been several reports on how this treatment could be ineffective,[31] at best, or fatal for patients because of its several side effects, at worst. Similarly, there have been other reports from different sources that have often been conflicting about what works and what does not in the case of coronavirus patients.

Trump and His Handling of the Coronavirus Crisis

United States President Donald Trump has been a regular subject in news reports. There have been several news reports on topics like (a) Trump's casual and inconsistent approach to the coronavirus crisis in the beginning, (b) his continuous targeting of the World Health Organisation (WHO) and China, (c) Trump's focus which was more on sufferings of the economy rather than the health emergency created as a result of the coronavirus, (d) his utter and continuous disdain for journalists who he either did not like or who asked uncomfortable questions to him, and (e) his support for a questionable line of treatment, including his advocacy for HCQ.

The most interesting thing about the sentiment in news flow related to Donald Trump is that it is widely fluctuating, and the swing is more towards a negative sentiment on how he handled the crisis. Of course, the United States of America is the engine of the global economy and what the United States president says is always important, but from the coronavirus coverage on Donald Trump, it is absolutely clear that his often unexpected and irrational statements generate more media coverage. Mostly, the media coverage on him is in a negative shade, but Trump is never really far away from the news reports on how he has handled the coronavirus crisis, but it is more often because of his statements.

What is the Sentiment We See in This News?

It is interesting to note that the media coverage on the coronavirus pandemic – the news and messages on the crisis – has been made more interesting despite it being one of the biggest and most impactful pandemics we have seen in almost a century. This is not to say that the coverage is more positive than negative on average. However, it only means that news reports have given enough space to other related developments that have impacted the sentiment.

Notes

1 Trump accuses China of failing to share information on the epidemic https://www.internazionale.it/notizie/2020/03/20/coronavirus-italia-mondo-20-marzo (Accessed on 21st March 2020), The verbal war between Iran and United States https://www.breitbart.com/politics/2020/03/27/irans-irgc-terrorists-can-help-americans-fight-coronavirus/ (Accessed on 29th March 2020), States face legal hurdles in coronavirus lawsuits against China https://abcnews4.com/news/nation-world/states-face-legal-hurdles-in-coronavirus-lawsuits-against-china (Accessed on 12th May 2020).
2 Trump said his government is trying to determine if coronavirus came from a lab https://business.financialpost.com/pmn/business-pmn/reuters-news-schedule-at-6-a-m-gmt-2-p-m-sgt-60 (Accessed on 11th May 2020), https://www.statnews.com/2020/05/29/trump-us-terminate-who-relationship/ (Accessed on 15th July 2020).
3 China accusing US Military for the Coronavirus https://www.voachinese.com/a/china-virus-wuhan-milirary-20200312/5326657.html (Accessed on 14th March 2020), Chinese Foreign Ministry spokesperson quotes WHO said to support that no evidence that coronavirus was released from a laboratory https://www.portfolio.hu/gazdasag/20200416/kina-szerint-nincs-bizonyitek-arra-hogy-a-koronavirus-egy-laborbol-szabadult-el-426412 (Accessed on 11th May 2020), Chinese Government official slams Australia's push for an investigation into the coronavirus outbreak https://www.abc.net.au/news/2020-04-26/coronavirus-china-slams-australia-over-independent-inquiry/12185988 (Accessed on 12th May 2020).
4 Iranian claims dealing with the coronavirus outbreak fell to agencies at last minute https://www.sabah.com.tr/dunya/2020/03/09/son-dakika-haberi-iranda-yeni-bir-virus-ortaya-cikti-koronavirus-kadar-tehlikeli-olabilir (Accessed on 11th March 2020), Activists launch 'digital protest' to end US sanctions on Iran

https://www.middleeasteye.net/news/coronavirus-iran-activists-digital-protest-us-sanctions (Accessed on 27th March 2020), Washington not letting up on its 'maximum pressure' against Iran, https://www.nytimes.com/reuters/2020/04/22/world/middleeast/22reuters-health-coronavirus-iran-eu.html (Accessed on 12th May 2020), Iran pushes back against US plan for snapback sanctions https://www.al-monitor.com/pulse/originals/2020/04/iran-zarif-us-sanctions-nuclear-deal-coronavirus.html (Accessed on 12th May 2020), United States has slapped new sanctions on Iran https://english.almanar.com.lb/1019559 (Accessed on 12th May 2020).

5 American National Security Advisor accusing China for the Pandemic https://www.hazipatika.com/eletmod/veszelyben/cikkek/koronavirus_sokaig_titkolozott_kina/20200312145317?autorefreshed=1 (Accessed on 14th March 2020), France said no evidence so far of a link between the new coronavirus and P4 research laboratory in Wuhan https://www.reuters.com/article/us-health-coronavirus-france-lab/france-says-no-evidence-covid-19-linked-to-wuhan-research-lab-idUSKBN21Z2ME (Accessed on 11th May 2020), Tension between France and China https://www.tunisienumerique.com/coronavirus-france-lambassadeur-de-chine-convoque/ (Accessed on 11th May 2020), Chinese diplomats seem to have tried to influence German officials https://www.merkur.de/welt/coronavirus-deutschland-news-drosten-nrw-berlin-kurve-zahlen-tote-merkel-statistik-rki-massnahmen-trump-uebersterblichkeit-zr-13697852.html (Accessed on 12th May 2020), United States's top intelligence agency, said that the Corona19 virus is not artificially created or genetically modified http://news.jtbc.joins.com/html/245/NB11948245.html (Accessed on 12th May 2020).

6 Did Trump catch Covid-19 from Jair Bolsonaro https://www.sabah.com.tr/dunya/2020/03/13/son-dakika-haberi-dunyanin-gozu-donald-trumpta-corona-virus-testi-pozitif-cikti (Accessed on 15th March 2020), Response of politicians to Coronavirus https://armenianweekly.com/2020/03/24/erdogans-denial-of-coronavirus-crisis-risks-the-lives-of-80-million-turks/ (Accessed on 26th March 2020), Brazil and coronavirus cases in Italy, Germany and Spain https://www.gazetadopovo.com.br/republica/breves/coronavirus-evolucao-italia-brasil/ (Accessed on 30th March 2020), Political crisis in Brazil and President Jair Bolsonaro https://brasil.elpais.com/brasil/2020-04-21/drenado-por-crise-politica-forjada-por-bolsonaro-brasil-fica-no-escuro-quanto-a-avanco-real-do-coronavirus.html (Accessed on 12th May 2020).

7 March 29, 2020. 'Canadian PM's wife has recovered from coronavirus illness.' The Hindu. https://www.thehindu.com/news/international/canadian-pms-wife-has-recovered-from-coronavirus-illness/article31196932.ece (Accessed on 15th July 2020).

8 April 7, 2020. 'Coronavirus: Boris Johnson moved to intensive care as symptoms worsen.' BBC. https://www.bbc.com/news/uk-52192604 (Accessed on 15th July 2020).

9 March 30, 2020. 'Coronavirus | Prince Charles recovers from COVID-19, out of self-isolation.' The Hindu. https://www.thehindu.com/news/international/coronavirus-prince-charles-recovers-from-covid-19-out-of-self-isolation/article31207701.ece (Accessed on 15th July 2020).

10 May 09, 2020. 'Coronavirus strikes staffers inside the White House.' The Economic Times. https://economictimes.indiatimes.com/news/international/world-news/mike-pence-spokeswoman-married-to-top-trump-adviser-diagnosed-with-coronavirus/articleshow/75639093.cms?from=mdr (Accessed on 15th July 2020).

11 May 11, 2020. 'Coronavirus: Is there any evidence for lab release theory?' BBC. https://www.bbc.com/news/science-environment-52318539 (Accessed on 15th July 2020); May 31, 2020. 'Coronavirus may have been created in a Wuhan lab 'genetic engineering' experiment.' YouTube. https://www.youtube.com/watch?v=_TB9WLxs0cA (Accessed on 15th July 2020).

12 Pascale Davies. July 24 2020. 'Coronavirus job cuts: Which companies in Europe are slashing their workforces because of COVID-19?' EuroNews. https://www.euronews.com/2020/07/06/coronavirus-job-cuts-which-companies-in-europe-are-slashing-their-workforces-because-of-co (Accessed on 15th July 2020); June 16, 2020. 'Coronavirus: Job cuts warning as 600,000 roles go in lockdown.' BBC. https://www.bbc.com/news/business-53060529 (Accessed on 15th July 2020).

13 Megha Mandavia. March 20, 2020. 'Indian government asks social media firms to control Coronavirus fake news.' The Economics Times. https://economictimes.indiatimes.com/tech/internet/indian-government-asks-social-media-firms-to-control-coronavirus-fake-news/articleshow/74734697.cms (Accessed on 15th July 2020); Bright Opoku Ahinkorah, Edward Kwabena Ameyaw, John Elvis Hagan Jr., Abdul-Aziz Seidu4 and Thomas Schack. June 17, 2020. 'Rising Above Misinformation or Fake News in Africa: Another Strategy to Control COVID-19 Spread.' Frontiers in Communication. https://www.frontiersin.org/articles/10.3389/fcomm.2020.00045/full (Accessed on 15th July 2020).

14 Daniel Woker. April 23, 2020. 'Europe hasn't fallen for China – if anything, it's the opposite.' The Interpreter. https://www.lowyinstitute.org/the-interpreter/europe-hasn-t-fallen-china-if-anything-it-s-opposite (Accessed on 15th July 2020); Bruno Macaes. April 09, 2020. How Europe learned to fear China. Politico. https://www.politico.eu/blogs/the-coming-wars/2019/04/how-europe-learned-to-fear-china/ (Accessed on 15th July 2020).

15 Kyle Jaros. April 09, 2020. 'China's Early COVID-19 Missteps Have an All-Too-Mundane Explanation.' The Diplomat. https://thediplomat.com/2020/04/chinas-early-covid-19-struggles-have-an-all-too-mundane-explanation/ (Accessed on 15th July 2020); Laurie Garrett. February 15, 2020. 'How China's Incompetence Endangered the World.' Foreign Policy. https://foreignpolicy.com/2020/02/15/coronavirus-xi-jinping-chinas-incompetence-endangered-the-world/ (Accessed on 15th July 2020).

16 Bloomberg. April 08, 2020. 'Japan to fund firms to shift production out of China.' ET Auto.com. https://auto.economictimes.indiatimes.com/news/industry/japan-to-fund-firms-to-shift-production-out-of-china/75053048 (Accessed on 15th July 2020); June 09, 2020. 'Japan's big push to bring manufacturing back from China.' Al Jazeera. https://www.aljazeera.com/ajimpact/japan-big-push-bring-manufacturing-china-200609021407622.html (Accessed on 15th July 2020).

17 Jeremy Gordon. April 09, 2020. 'Coronavirus: short-term blow, long-term opportunity for Vietnam.' City Wire. https://citywire.co.uk/investment-trust-insider/news/coronavirus-short-term-blow-long-term-opportunity-for-vietnam/a1343375 (Accessed on 15th July 2020); Milan Thakkar. May 08, 2020. 'COVID-19: An Opportunity For India's Manufacturing Sector?' Businessworld. http://www.businessworld.in/article/COVID-19-An-Opportunity-For-India-s-Manufacturing-Sector-/08-05-2020-191609/ (Accessed on 15th July 2020); Nikhil Inamdar. May 18, 2020. 'Coronavirus: Can India replace China as world's factory?' BBC. https://www.bbc.com/news/world-asia-india-52672510 (Accessed on 15th July 2020).

18 'Local production could solve shortages of essential pandemic-fighting equipment.' Technology Bank For The Least Developed Countries. https://www.un.

org/technologybank/content/local_production_could_solve_shortages_pandemic_
fighting_equipment (Accessed on 15th July 2020); Aslaug Magnusdottir. May 13,
2020. 'How Fashion Manufacturing Will Change After The Coronavirus.'
Forbes. https://www.forbes.com/sites/aslaugmagnusdottir/2020/05/13/fashions-
next-normal/ (Accessed on 15th July 2020); Paul Ventura. 'COVID-19 Could
Lead to Growth of Local Manufacturing.' Shoptech. https://www.shoptech.com/
blog/covid-19-could-lead-to-growth-of-local-manufacturing/ (Accessed on 15th
July 2020).

19 Judy Dempsey. May 12, 2020. 'How the Coronavirus Revived Angela Merkel.'
Carnegie Europe. https://carnegieeurope.eu/strategiceurope/81763 (Accessed on
15th July 2020); Thomas Colson. July 9, 2020. 'Merkel says the coronavirus pandemic has exposed leaders who rely on 'fact-denying populism.' Business Insider.
https://www.businessinsider.in/politics/world/news/merkel-says-the-coronavirus-
pandemic-has-exposed-leaders-who-rely-on-fact-denying-populism/articleshow/
76877765.cms (Accessed on 15th July 2020).

20 'Japan model' has beaten coronavirus, Shinzo Abe declares.' Financial Times.
https://www.ft.com/content/c78baffc-79b8-4da4-97f1-8c7caaad25cf (Accessed
on 15th July 2020); Rajaram Panda. April 27, 2020. 'Abe confronts corona.'
The Statesman. https://www.thestatesman.com/opinion/abe-confronts-corona-
1502881300.html (Accessed on 15th July 2020); June 15, 2020. 'France's
Macron declares 'first victory' over coronavirus epidemic.' CGTN. https://news.
cgtn.com/news/2020-06-15/France-s-Macron-declares-first-victory-over-
coronavirus-epidemic-RkL25RCYDu/index.html (Accessed on 15th July 2020);
June 06, 2020. 'France's Macron accelerates lifting of lockdown after 'first
victory' against Covid-19.' France 24. https://www.france24.com/en/20200614-
live-france-s-macron-charts-next-steps-out-of-covid-19-crisis (Accessed on 15th
July 2020).

21 Stephaie Preston. April 02, 2020. 'COVID-19: Why hoarding supplies is
human nature, according to a psychologist.' World Economic Forum. https://
www.weforum.org/agenda/2020/04/evolution-coronavirus-covid19-panic-
buying-supplies-food-essentials/ (Accessed on 15th July 2020); April 12,
2020. 'Coronavirus hoarding: Why you can stop amassing toilet paper.' The
Conversation. https://theconversation.com/coronavirus-hoarding-why-you-
can-stop-amassing-toilet-paper-135659 (Accessed on 15th July 2020);
March 25, 2020. 'Countries are starting to hoard food due to coronavirus
outbreak, threatening global trade.' The Economic Times. https://
economictimes.indiatimes.com/news/international/world-news/countries-are-
starting-to-hoard-food-amid-coronavirus-outbreak-threatening-global-trade/
articleshow/74805865.cms (Accessed on 15th July 2020).

22 Laura Begley Bloom. Jun 27, 2020. 'You Won't Believe How Many Airlines
Haven't Survived Coronavirus. How Does It Affect You?' Forbes. https://www.
forbes.com/sites/laurabegleybloom/2020/06/27/airlines-coronavirus-travel-
bankruptcy/#3522a075f696 (Accessed on 15th July 2020); 'Air Transport &
COVID-19 Coronavirus.' IATA. https://www.iata.org/en/programs/safety/
health/diseases/ (Accessed on 15th July 2020); 'Tourism Policy Responses to
the coronavirus (COVID-19).' OECD. https://www.oecd.org/coronavirus/
policy-responses/tourism-policy-responses-to-the-coronavirus-covid-19-
6466aa20/ (Accessed on 15th July 2020).

23 Olivia Carville. June 26, 2020. 'Airbnb Layoffs Expose Inequities in a Two-Tiered
Workforce.' Bloomberg Businessweek. https://www.bloomberg.com/news/articles/
2020-06-26/airbnb-layoffs-expose-inequality-between-contractors-and-ftes
(Accessed on 15th July 2020); Kyle Arnold. 'American Airlines prepares to send

out layoff notices to workers.' Post Gazette. https://www.post-gazette.com/business/pittsburgh-company-news/2020/07/14/American-Airlines-delta-united-layoffs-furloughs/stories/202007140078 (Accessed on 15th July 2020); David Meyer. June 11, 2020. "Personnel overhang': All the job cuts each airline has announced so far.' Fortune. https://fortune.com/2020/06/11/airline-layoffs-job-cuts-coronavirus-covid-19-lufthansa-british-airways-emirates-american-airlines-sas-norwegian-easyjet-united-virgin-ryanair/ (Accessed on 15th July 2020).

24 Oil tumbled after a dispute between Russia and Saudi Arabia over production cuts https://www.express.co.uk/news/world/1253308/coronavirus-news-germany-europe-euro-stock-market-angela-merkel-covid-19-eu-news (Accessed on 12th May 2020), Decline in Oil Prices https://www.themarker.com/wallstreet/LIVE-1.8721579 (Accessed on 13th May 2020).

25 Muslims returning to Turkey from pilgrimage in Saudi Arabia taken into quarantine https://globalnews.ca/news/6679316/coronavirus-saudi-arabia-turkey-quarantine/ (Accessed on 17th March 2020), 700 cases linked to a mass religious gathering held at a mosque https://www.reuters.com/article/us-health-coronavirus-malaysia/malaysia-coronavirus-cases-jump-to-1183-many-cases-linked-to-mosque-idUSKBN2180BW (Accessed on 22nd March 2020), Filipinos who attended a religious event in Malaysia linked to spike in COVID-19 https://www.aljazeera.com/news/2020/03/coronavirus-philippines-seeks-215-attended-islamic-event-200321143247350.html (Accessed on 23rd March 2020), A Cluster Of Coronavirus Cases Can Be Traced Back To A Single Mosque And Now 200 Million Muslims Are Being Vilified https://www.buzzfeednews.com/article/nishitajha/coronavirus-india-muslims-tablighi-jamaat (Accessed on 11th May 2020), Churches in Singapore took Good Friday services online https://www.straitstimes.com/singapore/singapore-churches-join-in-praying-for-healing (Accessed on 11th May 2020).

26 Cancellation of Football Matches in Germany https://www.sueddeutsche.de/panorama/coronavirus-deutschland-bundesliga-dortmund-schalke-koeln-gladbach-1.4828033 (Accessed on 17th May 2020) http://www.thefa.com/news/2020/mar/13/fa-premier-league-efl-statement-football-suspended-130320 (Accessed on 15th July 2020); June 12, 2020. 'Coronavirus: How the virus has impacted sporting events around the world.' https://www.bbc.com/sport/51605235 (15th July 2020); April 17, 2020. 'Coronavirus in sport: All the events cancelled or postponed including Premier League, Euro 2020, Olympics, The Open, Wimbledon and Anthony Joshua fight.' talkSPORT. https://talksport.com/football/fa-cup/682305/coronavirus-sport-cancelled-postponed-premier-league-euro-2020-olympics-wimbledon-anthony-joshua/ (Accessed on 15th July 2020).

27 Dan Roan. May 20, 2020. 'IOC's Thomas Bach accepts Tokyo Olympics would have to be cancelled if not held in 2021.' BBC Sport. https://www.bbc.com/sport/olympics/52747797 (Accessed on 15th July 2020); Ahiza García-Hodges, Yuliya Talmazan and Arata Yamamoto. March 24, 2020. 'Tokyo 2020 Olympics postponed over coronavirus concerns.' NBC News. https://www.nbcnews.com/news/world/tokyo-2020-olympics-postponed-over-coronavirus-concerns-n1165046 (Accessed on 15th July 2020).

28 April 16, 2020. 'It's official: BCCI suspends IPL 2020 till further notice over coronavirus.' Business Standard. https://www.business-standard.com/article/sports/ipl-2020-postponed-indefinitely-over-coronavirus-bcci-tells-team-owners-120041500339_1.html (Accessed on 15th July 2020); April 12, 2020. 'Coronavirus: IPL 2020 to be postponed or cancelled amid COVID-19 lockdown? BCCI official provides update.' DNA. https://www.dnaindia.com/cricket/

report-coronavirus-ipl-2020-to-be-postponed-or-cancelled-amid-covid-19-lockdown-bcci-official-provides-update-2820645 (Accessed on 15th July 2020); May 13, 2020. 'IPL 2020: BCCI declares loss of $530 million if IPL 2020 gets cancelled.' Inside Sport. https://www.insidesport.co/ipl-2020-bcci-declares-loss-of-530-million-if-ipl-2020-gets-cancelled/ (Accessed on 15th July 2020).

29 Aleesha Khaliq. March 5, 2020. 'Australian paper prints blank pages to help tackle toilet paper shortage.' CNN. https://edition.cnn.com/2020/03/05/world/coronavirus-australia-toilet-paper-scli-intl/index.html (Accessed on 15th July 2020); March 06, 2020. 'Newspaper prints blank pages to resolve loo paper crisis amid coronavirus scare.' HT Times. https://www.hindustantimes.com/it-s-viral/newspaper-prints-blank-pages-to-resolve-loo-paper-crisis-amid-coronavirus-scare/story-xBuUbwDGGAVQu6qkup2PhO.html (Accessed on 15th July 2020); Joshua Bote. March 10, 2020. 'Family says they bought 12-year supply of toilet paper by accident amid coronavirus scare.' USA Today. https://www.usatoday.com/story/news/education/2020/03/10/coronavirus-australia-family-buys-12-year-supply-toilet-paper/4985534002/ (Accessed on 15th July 2020).

30 'How coronavirus is affecting pasta's complex supply chain.' Financial Times. https://www.ft.com/content/5456bc24-6dd4-11ea-9bca-bf503995cd6f (Accessed on 15th July 2020); Bill Conerly. 'Shortages In The Pandemic: Toilet Paper, Detergent And Pasta?' Forbes. https://www.forbes.com/sites/billconerly/2020/04/09/shortages-in-the-pandemic-toilet-paper-detergent-and-pasta/#2277f056e685 (Accessed on 15th July 2020); Alison Fottrell. March 15, 2020. 'Pasta started flying off the shelves of supermarkets in Milan.' Italy's lockdown hasn't had much impact on the rapid spread of coronavirus — yet.' Marketwatch. https://www.marketwatch.com/story/pasta-started-flying-off-supermarket-shelves-in-milan-as-italy-imposes-nationwide-coronavirus-lockdown-italians-struggle-to-adjust-to-the-new-normal-2020-03-09 (Accessed on 15th July 2020).

31 May 29, 2020. 'COVID-19: Trump feeling 'absolutely great' after taking hydroxychloroquine, says White House.' The Hindu. https://www.thehindu.com/news/international/covid-19-trump-feeling-absolutely-great-after-taking-hydroxychloroquine-says-white-house/article31700470.ece (Accessed on 15th July 2020); Sriram Lakshman. May 19, 2020. 'Despite FDA warning, Trump says he is taking hydroxychloroquine.' The Hindu. https://www.thehindu.com/news/international/trump-says-he-is-taking-hydroxychloroquine-despite-fda-warning/article31619017.ece (Accessed on 15th July 2020); Mario Parker. May 25, 2020. 'HCQ has 'tremendous, rave reviews', Trump says after finishing a course of treatment.' The Print. https://theprint.in/world/hcq-has-tremendous-rave-reviews-trump-says-after-finishing-a-course-of-treatment/428708/ (Accessed on 15th July 2020).

17

HOW DO WE USE SENTIMENT ANALYSIS? A CASE STUDY

Timing the virus: market timing possible with sentiment analysis?

Is it possible to position for market volatility in a systematic and timely manner using sentiment analysis? To answer this question, we consider two major emerging equity markets: Brazil and India. We use our sentiment-based signals, constructed using machine translation and sentiment analysis, on news flow in Portuguese, Hindi and English to trade the broad equity indices in these two countries. However, why are we thinking in this direction? The market's struggle, as a result of the coronavirus pandemic over the past few weeks, has made us think carefully about whether our sentiment analysis provides a truly systematic way to navigate this storm and whether the sentiment data is effective in doing so. Another question that came up is the role of discretionary overrides of quantitative models during times such as the present.

It is not unusual for quantitative analysis focused managers to do a discretionary override of their models during times of heightened market volatility. Should a similar override be done on EMAlpha's Sentiment Signals? Our conclusion is that the sentiment-based system has worked well throughout the recent market swings year-to-date. Jumping around and making tweaks to the investment strategy was based purely on one's opinion about the market's direction and could do more harm than good. This is an important result and implies that you can trust sentiment analysis to take investment decisions and in both situations: (a) during 'business as usual' and (b) in times of increased volatility. This works fairly well.

Now, coming back to Brazil and India, we construct our Brazil and India Sentiment Signals every morning at 8 AM of the local time, and we use it to predict the day's market move. More specifically, if the sentiment improved from the previous day, we go long in the market. If it deteriorated from the previous day, we go short in the market. The result, in terms of the cumulative return in excess of the equity benchmark, is shown in Fig. 17.1. Sentiment signals for Brazil and India seem to have navigated the recent unprecedented market volatility quite well.

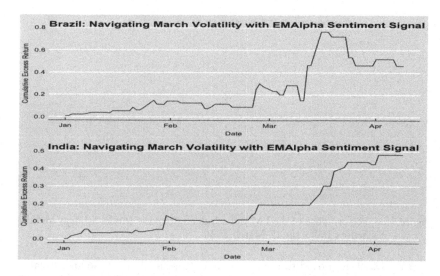

Figure 17.1 Cumulative YTD Returns (Over Respective Country Equity Benchmarks) for Brazil and India. Depending on the morning's equity market sentiment signal, a long or short market position is assumed. Source: Courtesy of EMAlpha.

Figure 17.2 Performance of the EMAlpha India Systematic Model Strategy and Sensex until 27 February 2020.

Indian markets

During the coronavirus pandemic, the negative sentiment directly fed the market capitulation. Both emerging and developed markets fell as the coronavirus spread in multiple regions beyond Asia – from Italy and the Middle

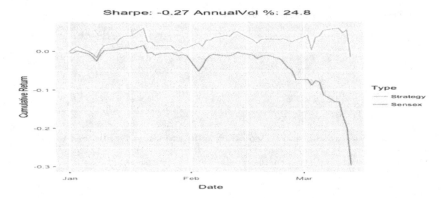

Figure 17.3 Performance of the EMAlpha India Systematic Model Strategy and the Sensex Index on 17 March 2020.

East to Brazil. It started to look more and more likely that the virus-related sentiment will drive markets for some time. Market volatility spiked, and a number of investment fund strategies started performing poorly against this backdrop. However, as EMAlpha monitored the market sentiment and used it as an input to its EM India Strategy, the EMAlpha long/short model systematic equity strategy delivered excess return versus Sensex.

As shown below, the EMAlpha model portfolio incorporating the coronavirus sentiment has done significantly better versus its benchmark BSE Sensex Index.

18

CONCLUSION

The coronavirus pandemic has been a big shock for 'business as usual' and for the entire world. Words like 'pandemic' all of a sudden became central to discussions and the life of people changed completely. Though COVID-19 may not have been the first pandemic the world has seen, it is the first major global disaster humanity has encountered in the 'computer age'. In this book, we have focused on a few specific aspects of the coronavirus including (a) Sentiment Analysis of Coronavirus-Related News Flow, (b) news sentiment versus the real impact on markets and (c) the spread of the coronavirus across countries and the associated news sentiment in these geographies.

The virus attacks generate more coverage than events with a similar or even higher impact, because these are unexpected and, in the age of rapid information dissemination and the huge role played by social media, this is even more prominent. Naturally, financial markets also react more to these events. Whether the impact of the coronavirus is 'noise', 'signal' or a little bit of both, the reaction of financial markets proves the age-old dictum 'News may be the same, but the impact could be vastly different because of the varied nature of sentiment'. The tangible impact and news flow matter for the markets, but the sentiment matters much more.

It has been fascinating to explore the connection of news with a tangible impact on public policy, government response and also on stock markets. There is no consensus on this but arguably, how global financial markets were impacted because of the coronavirus is a far bigger event than even the Global Financial Crisis (GFC) of 2008. The virus hardly did anything significant outside China, not only for weeks, but also for a couple of months. While the beginning was lacklustre for the coronavirus, the crisis continued to aggravate with each passing day. For several months, the numbers have kept on increasing, and the impact kept getting multiplied.

This book is a diary of market analysts and sentiment on the coronavirus. While analysing sentiment, we have tried to remain as objective as possible. We are not trying to inference based on what we want to see and what, in our opinion, is happening in the markets. We get the data, and then we try to see what the data is telling us, and, in the process, we do not add our view nor do we subtract anything which is purely our opinion. We want the readers to see the data and charts and draw their own inferences without our writing clouding their judgement.

Through this book, we try to sensitise the readers to the main drivers of news and market sentiments followed by the assessment of the impact of this sentiment on market direction. In recent times because of the coronavirus, we have seen an unprecedented spike in volatility in the global markets. This big market movement has been driven by the recent developments in the spread of the coronavirus and the news sentiment has continued to be a driver of market sentiment.

This book on Coronavirus-Related News Sentiment and its impact on markets has close linkage with our previous works on Big Data and Artificial Intelligence (AI). The collection of news on a regular and almost real-time basis and the analysis of inherent sentiment is not possible without Big Data and AI tools. After we worked on these texts and explored Big Data and AI applications across diverse fields, we were even more convinced that the implications for financial markets are important - not just because markets react to good or bad news, but also because sentiment would be dynamic and can also be seen differently across different time frames such as 'short term' versus 'long term'.

This is relevant in the context of this book in multiple ways including (a) the daily sentiment on the coronavirus could remain negative, but it might be less negative than yesterday, and that is what the market will focus more on, and (b) the 'base rate' will determine if the sentiment is negative or positive on a relative basis, and absolute levels matter much less; (c) the country-by-country sentiment on the coronavirus will be seen on two parameters – change and status versus others. All of this is dependent on four key factors: (a) one's knowledge of news that one is looking for and its relevance, (b) the most relevant sources for news, (c) the tools one uses for news collection and (d) the sophistication of one's sentiment analysis methods.

Big Data, computing power and cloud computing have all been important in making huge amounts of data, and enormous computing power is available for anyone who is interested. All these developments may seem unconnected at the first instance, but these were not just happening in parallel, but also feeding into one another in some ways. Social media and significantly faster dissemination of data and information are also becoming an important catalyst for news and sentiment analysis. In the last few decades, the way people source information and get their news and updates have changed.

The most important question we are trying to answer in this book is as follows: Is it possible to position for market volatility in a systematic and timely manner using sentiment analysis? In Brazil and India, we use our sentiment-based signals, constructed using machine translation and sentiment analysis on news flow, in Portuguese, Hindi and English to trade the broad equity indices in these two countries. The market's struggle as a result of the coronavirus pandemic over the month of March 2020 has made us think carefully about whether our sentiment analysis provides a truly systematic way to navigate this storm and whether the sentiment data is effective in doing so.

It is not unusual for quantitative-based money managers to do a discretionary override of their models during times of heightened market volatility. Should a similar override be done on EMAlpha's Sentiment Signals? Our conclusion is that the sentiment-based system has worked well throughout the recent market swings year-to-date. Jumping around and making tweaks to the investment strategy based purely on one's opinion about the market's direction could do more harm than good. This is an important result and implies that you can trust sentiment analysis to take investment decisions and in both situations (a) during 'business as usual' and (b) in times of increased volatility. This works fairly well.

Now coming back to Brazil and India, we construct our Brazil and India Sentiment Signals every morning at 8 AM of the local time, and we use it to predict the day's market move. More specifically, if the sentiment improved from the previous day, then we go long in the market. If it deteriorated from the previous day, we go short in the market. The result, in terms of the cumulative return in excess of the equity benchmark, indicates that sentiment signals for Brazil and India seem to have navigated the recent unprecedented market volatility quite well.

During the coronavirus pandemic, the negative sentiment directly fed the market capitulation. Both emerging and developed markets fell as the coronavirus spread in multiple regions beyond Asia – from Italy and the Middle East to Brazil. It started to look more and more likely that the virus-related sentiment will drive markets for some time. Market volatility spiked, and a number of investment fund strategies started performing poorly against this backdrop. However, as EMAlpha monitored the market sentiment and used it as an input to its EM India strategy, the EMAlpha long/short model systematic equity strategy delivered excess return versus BSE Sensex.

INDEX

Printed in the United States
By Bookmasters